Our Mark Twain

Our Mark Twain,

THE MAKING OF HIS PUBLIC PERSONALITY

Louis J. Budd

uℳℳ

University of Pennsylvania Press
Philadelphia • 1983

Design by Carl Gross

Previously unpublished words by Mark Twain are ©1983 by Edward J. Willi and Manufacturers Hanover Trust Company as trustees of the Mark Twain Foundation and are published with the permission of the University of California Press and Robert H. Hirst, general editor of the Mark Twain Project in Berkeley, California. All citations of such material are identified by the following symbol: (†).

Library of Congress Cataloging in Publication Data

Budd, Louis J.
  Our Mark Twain.

  Bibliography: p.
  Includes index.
  1. Twain, Mark, 1835–1910—Biography. 2. Authors,
American—19th century—Biography. 3. Humorists, American
—Biography. I. Title.
PS1331.B9 1983   818'.409 [B]   82–23758
ISBN   0-8122-1204-5
Printed in the United States of America

To
Lorry and Steve,
Gigi and Sylvan, Elżbiecie i Frankowi

Contents

Acknowledgments

A FELLOWSHIP FROM the National Endowment for the Humanities allowed me to devote full time to this study for twelve months. At Duke University the Research Council has unfailingly granted support for travel and other expenses, and the staff of the Perkins Library, particularly Emerson Ford, have helped cheerfully and imaginatively. Robert H. Hirst, Editor of the Mark Twain Papers, has helped me greatly both as first-rate scholar and in his official capacity; to paraphrase James Russell Lowell, undoubtedly God could make a better place to work than Room 480 of the Bancroft Library, but undoubtedly He never has. There and elsewhere I have had the privilege of discussion with fellow Twainians such as John Tuckey, who is always a bonanza of stimulating insights. Collectively they have made my book possible with a body of scholarship and criticism so cogent that I have often forgotten what is borrowed because it seemed so clearly right once they said it. But I do not forget the example of generosity and responsibility they have set. Finally, in more ways than Edwin H. Cady and Bernard I. Duffey suspect, I have benefited over the years from being their colleague, and Dorothy Roberts has always provided the best secretarial support imaginable. Anne Durden patiently typed the final manuscript.

I am grateful to the *South Atlantic Quarterly* and the Duke University Press for permission to reprint my "Mood and Tenses in Interviews with Mark Twain"—essentially the same text as chapter 8 of this book.

I must also especially thank the curators and their staff for help in examining the Mark Twain materials in the Beinecke Library of Yale University, the Clifton Waller Barrett Library at the University of Virginia, and the Henry W. and Albert A. Berg Collection of the New York Public Library.

Introduction

MARK TWAIN IS ALL AROUND US TODAY, almost seventy-five years after his death. A crater on Mercury is named after him; the joke in a strip of *Peanuts* depends on his fame; a cycle of science fiction has transmigrated him, as his glorious earthly self, into an eternal dimension. Any collector of trivia can match these examples. "Mark Twain's words are quoted as often as Anon.'s. They show up in magazine ads, scholarly articles, greeting cards, impromptu insults, even the farewell address to his California countrymen by a President-elect."[1] Not just his words but his images bombard us: Tom whitewashing the fence, Huck and Jim observing the stars, Twain himself waiting for a lecture audience to stop guffawing, the Connecticut Yankee working a "miracle" in Arthurian England, the cub-pilot nervously gripping the wheel, or the king of the banquet circuit brushing cigar ashes off his white suit. For John Barth, Huck floating down the Mississippi belongs to the four greatest images of world literature. Mark Twain is now unquestionably a classic author. Most academics consider him at least "major," and no set of Great Literature, whether bound in tooled leather or plastic, would dare to exclude him. Americans in particular feel not only affection but a bond of proprietorship; they beam over him as they would over a silver flask handed down through the family.

To explain why they do is both too hard and too easy. It is too hard because we cannot diagram the responses to Twain, a mercurial genius loaded with cultural symbols from the start and now magnified by those he invented. Beneath any abstractions, the more instinctively we laugh with a humorist, the more subliminal our reasons for doing so. The "we" turns problematic in itself because reactions to a joke vary stunningly. Surprisingly, I think, Sigmund Freud admired Twain's humor; he especially enjoyed the thin routine about getting a farmer to make good on the green watermelon that Sammy Clemens had swiped. The mysteries of humor aside, the hang-gliding critic who presumes to analyze Twain's appeal to a group, class, and even a nation may dazzle some humanists, but sociologists, particularly those expert in statistics, will punch holes in the underlying method or expose its absence. Likewise, the heyday of psycho-history has ended without convincing many that mass emotion can be charted more objectively than showily. Only the verve and importance of Twain's appeal make it worthwhile to tackle such problems.

Explaining why Twain grew and stays so widely admired is too easy because it slides over the when and the how-come. Impressively early, some flexible, sympathetic minds grasped the enduring Twain. A Dutch critic declared in 1886:

If there is anyone to whom the expression "a man of character" can be applied, it is Mark Twain, "the great humorist, the selfmade man, the brilliant American writer," who holds the pride of place among today's most celebrated authors. He is not only a man of genius, a celebrity, but also a great original, "a moralist *malgré lui* who preaches nature and truth in his works." He is the prophet of truth, dedicated to the task of revealing the truth, of peeling off the layers that hide it.[2]

She went on to cogent details that validate her flourishes and make his triumph sound inevitable. But to get that far he had climbed a tricky road bristling with anxieties and setbacks, and the road ahead held pitfalls. From a less dramatic viewpoint, Twain's eminence kept rising for forty years because he managed to top each success before it died out. For instance—taking him simply as a writer—*The Innocents Abroad* was his flagship for decades, supported by *Roughing It*. But in the mid-1870s he started to weave his still powerful myth of the Mississippi. A later humorist had Jehovah reveal that "Mark's got a river of his own" in Heaven. It's as long as he wants it, and "he has steamboat races on it all the time" while swearing so masterfully that John Milton confesses: "Just to listen to anything as perfect as that makes a better man of me."[3] The next overlap developed the myth of childhood in a sleepy village. *The Adventures of Tom Sawyer* has lasted as his most popular book among general readers, both at home and away, and *Adventures of Huckleberry Finn* came on increasingly strong to where scholarly and freelance critics insist it is a masterpiece. While we may look back at an unshakable ladder, Twain worried about the stability of his fame up until the stagy birthday banquet of 1905, though his first collected edition in 1899 reassured him considerably.

Asking how it all happened leads toward the realization that such eminence as he had achieved (the Dutch critic even called him a celebrity) may not hold up simply through intrinsic merit. Fame compounds itself in a society where publicity has mushroomed into big business. However, the appetite for news about a hero gets catered to so assiduously that overfeeding is possible, followed by sourness and distaste. Americans turned grumpy toward Admiral George Dewey after having deified him for the victory of Manila Bay. But Twain kept on climbing after 1886, at least matching Thomas Alva Edison, J. P. Morgan, and Teddy Roosevelt, who shot up fast through a mixture of Western, military, and political glamor. No formula covers them all. Roosevelt was an exhibitionist but Morgan avoided reporters, unintentionally gilding his awesome financial power with a challenging enigma. Twain combined the strategies of Roosevelt and Edison, demanding the spotlight while convincing the public that it was staring into his private self and finding a spontaneous, smoked-ham individualist.

The following chapters analyze, therefore, not merely Twain's status as a culture-hero but his constant efforts to shape and protect it and to raise it higher. He maneuvered so effectively that it survives among the generations born after his personal touch stopped. Having asked, "Which of all the literary ghosts that people New York would I most covet an hour with?" a leading drama critic decides in 1980 to "cast my vote for Mark Twain." Perhaps Twain worried least about his toughest problem: recognition as a classic author. Instead, while seeing no logic or profit in splitting off his role as public personality from his writings, he made aggressively sure that Mark Twain the man figured large in the newspapers and common talk. Lecturing primarily for the income, he valued the grassroots exposure too; honoring the bonds of sociability with speeches at all kinds of occasions, he realized that his admirers gave him credit for energy and generosity of effort. At home in the briar patch of journalism, he understood and managed the windings of publicity; and if a little slow to catch on that the fresh genre of the interview played into his strengths, he became its master for quality and quantity.

With few mistakes he postured superbly, holding the spotlight and yet not making himself ridiculous or boring. His stardom also took the strength not to crumble under the rebuffs, pratfalls, and careless insults that performing centerstage will bring. The biographers who indict that strength as egomania are implicitly approving the passive tone of most lives. Less accusingly, people charmed by modesty, by the good manners of avoiding bright display and seeming never to brag, may shudder at Twain as an exhibitionist driven by childish instincts he never learned to control. His friendliest admirers can just grin apologetically over his white formal dress suit with silk braid or his delight in parading his crimson Oxford robe. Still they are glad that he insisted on standing out in body as much as spirit.

Twain's campaigning for immediate, lusty fame can, however, trouble anybody who cares about sincerity. His own devotees like to quote him on the sins of pretense. ("The first man was a hypocrite and a coward, qualities which have not yet failed in his line; it is the foundation upon which all the civilizations have been built.") Since Twain's death PR has become a radioactive evil: our elections sink toward a choice between beautifully crafted yet hollow images; the neighborly voice gets warmer with every degree of dishonesty in the commercial "message"; the most rapacious corporations hire the saintliest pitchmen. Reality, physical and ethical, recedes into the cathode-ray tube or floppy disc. But our clutching to recapture it should not deny the fact that we pose constantly—changing from our backstage manner whenever we go on display, wiping the egg off our face and checking all zippers before we open the door. Erving Goffman, who has developed this fact richly, declares on a narrowed point: "deeply incorporated into the nature of talk are the fundamental requirements of theatricality."[4] Within the universal traffic of posturing, Twain's case proves exceptional because of his skill and daring and the innate talent behind them, including his genius as a humorist. So he deserves far better than the defense that "theatricality," as it does for ordinary persons, helped him confront the world and overcome the thousands of tiny shocks that— says Freud—the ego suffers daily. Fortunately for us, he had outstandingly much to contribute to human intercourse. Although I will concentrate on his American career, he justifies my argument in about every country that uses the crafts of printing and binding.[5] My insisting on his success does not mean to concede Twain's dishonesty with or about himself. His moods of self-accusation often plunged to the edge of irrationality, and he regularly warned the public that his character was flawed. He also warned it that he was posturing.

At the risk of sounding like Twain's official biographer, Albert Bigelow Paine, I proceed in the tone of gratitude that his posturing worked and gave us both his writings and his public personality. We would not have those writings as they now stand if he had shaped a substantially different life; biographers once understood that principle better than does their guild today. Within and beyond his books Twain reinforced qualities crucial to the happiness and perhaps survival of humankind: delight in experience, emotional spontaneity, and irreverence toward pomposity, petrified ideas, injustice, and self-pride. The function of a humorist centers in resistance, in a liberating aggression that can spin toward tedious venom or anarchy. But effective naysaying carries over into affirmation. Twain reinforced some old and some modern values: courage in the face of dishonest or carping criticism, candid self-judgment that humbles the delusion of being able to gauge interpersonal reality without error, flexibility of mind and response (when his career is perceived as it happened rather than simplified to suit some theory), respect for the integrity of others, concern for the common welfare, and rapt awareness sweeping from the submicroscopic to the cosmic. While holding no monopoly on those values, Twain embodied them uniquely. My analysis tries to catch that rounded uniqueness, which serves us better than the flattened models that the mass or elitist media keep manufacturing. I hope to make sure that we can enjoy and emulate the quintessential Twain.

CHAPTER 1

"This Shining Mark"

"MARK TWAIN IS DEAD. It would be hard to frame four other words that could carry a message of bereavement to so many Americans," announced the *New York American* on 22 April 1910. Just about every major newspaper in the country ran not only a long story but also an editorial.[1] After all, in the opinion of the *Hartford* (Conn.) *Courant* "no other citizen of the United States, not General Grant nor Theodore Roosevelt, was more universally known." Public concern had mounted since Twain had come back from Bermuda in a wheelchair the week before. Headlines and photographs multiplied up through Sunday the twenty-fourth and tailed off on the twenty-fifth, with reports of his burial in a white suit.

The flood of news was swelled by tributes from the right persons at home and abroad, by at least ten poems, and by old timers' reminiscences in local papers. William Howard Taft issued a statement from the White House, former President Roosevelt added his emphatic wreath, and President-to-be Woodrow Wilson recognized the gravity of the country's loss. By the twenty-third a prominent Brooklynite had suggested that the *New York Herald* start up a fund for a "fine monument" in Central Park. Five hundred boys of Louisville (Ky.) High School, though probably coached by the faculty, paid for a floral spray because Twain had "brightened their lives with innocent laughter and taught them squareness and grit and compassion for the weak." Along with proper adult sorrow, the *Baltimore Sun*—with up and coming H. L. Mencken as the editorialist, probably—delighted in remembering the good times:

MARK TWAIN'S LEGACIES TO AMERICA.

Washington (D.C.) *Evening Star*, 22 April 1910, p. 1

Since far back in the 70s he had been one of our national celebrities, and perhaps the greatest of the clan—beaming, expansive and kindly: a star at all great public feasts; the friend of Presidents and millionaires, of archbishops and actors, welcome everywhere and always in good humor, a fellow of infinite jest. As the years passed his picturesque figure grew more and more familiar and lovable. Every town of any pretensions knew him. He was in ceaseless motion, making a speech here, taking a degree there, and always dripping fun. The news that he was to be present was enough to make a success of anything.

Twain had won more than celebrity, as he well knew. According to his memory of once lounging away a few hours with Robert Louis Stevenson in Washington Square, they discussed the "submerged fame" that "permeates the great crowd of people" who, "deaf to the critics," hold a favorite author in the "home of their heart's affection forever and ever."[2]

New York American, 22 April 1910, p. [19]

In the highly visible range of the public, Thomas A. Edison—one of his few serious competitors for veneration on any count—had inscribed on a dinner menu: "An American loves his family. If he has any love left over for some other person, he generally selects Mark Twain." Recently, Kurt Vonnegut partly explained this emotionalism by observing that Twain, himself the "most enchanting American" in his tales, managed to imply that the reader was "enough like him to be his brother." Eulogies commonly leap to absolutes, but among the many possible points of emphasis, vicarious bonding with the man behind his books stood out. Obviously the *Wilmington* (N.C.) *Morning Star* meant to agree: "How many of us feel that we know Mark Twain? That what he wrote was written for us, with the intimate frankness of a friend talking over a cigar?"

In his talk with Stevenson, Twain contended that the "homage" of the most loyal readers began when they were young. Many whose childhood included *Huckleberry Finn* and, more often, *Tom Sawyer* had grown into their adult niches spread through the levels of literacy. Still, the newspapers reveal the leading images of Twain best. Unlike today, the metropolitan giants took direct notice of the magazines, considering them less as competitors than as allies in expanding the empire of the printed word. Also they showed respect for the leading critics by reprinting them or hiring original essays. At the other end of the scale, the dailies counted on sales to the marginally literate who today have gone over to radio and television. Provincial journals, which imitated big-city standards, had a still more diversified yet faithful audience.

As a compliment, the *Pawtucket* (R.I.) *Times* recognized that Twain's admirers included some "who do not ordinarily read much and may never have enjoyed a book or story." Actually, as many editorials implied, he was a hero to millions of practicing if not formal illiterates who helped his personality to flourish. The *New York Times* guessed he had been "quoted in common conversation oftener, perhaps, than any of his fellow-countrymen, including Benjamin Franklin and Lincoln." A typical headline dubbed him the "most picturesque figure in literature"—not intending to pun on the fact that he had cooperated in becoming possibly the most photographed subject or object since the invention of the camera. In all solemnity it was emphasizing the range and strength of the fame achieved by the "most anecdotalized man in America," according to somebody else's superlative. A certifiable sinner when it came to keeping its clientele agog, the *New York World* sounded the grateful praise that no other writer, native or foreign, had "furnished more news." So many sections of the country took pride in Twain that he could have scrapbooked a mile of columns even before the New York City dailies adopted him in

WHERE THE OLD PILOT WILL ALWAYS HOLD SWAY.

Chicago Daily News, 22 April 1910, p. 1

1900 as a local lion. Because they habitually spoke in terms of the nation, however, they quickly overshadowed the variations of his legend.

Cordially rather than warningly, many obituaries wondered how long his fame would outlive his magnetic presence. Although a natural question, it seldom gets asked so promptly; but the press had never presided over the funeral of such a mixture of panache and substance. Editorials also wondered if his fame owed much more to his charm than his talents. Where celebrity rides on a distinct body of achievement such doubt seldom occurs to contemporaries, who keep underestimating the audacity of debunkers. But that it did come up supplies something of an answer. Twain's era had a consciously vivid picture of him apart from and, in some minds, above the caliber of his writings. He never resented the distinction, never intimated like the Romantic artist that his writings enshrined his personal essence.

As for a reconstruction of that living picture, the obituaries naturally dropped false clues; Twain's burlesque book of etiquette warns that "taffy" is handed out at funerals. Although clubrooms had often rocked from his bawdy moods, President Taft invoked a Victorian bromide: "He never wrote a line that a father could not read to his daughter." But the truth alone could allow a striking diversity of compliments. For many, Twain had to the end stayed the live-wire iconoclast of *The Innocents Abroad* while others imagined him as the nostalgic chum of Tom and Huck. Among those who distinguished the private man from his varied personae yet intuited him through his books, the memory of *Personal Recollections of Joan of Arc* brought tributes to his personal chivalry. Almost each one of his books, including *Is Shakespeare Dead?* found champions for its revealing qualities. While seldom for reasons given today, *Puddn'head Wilson* turned up surprisingly often, praised for its sharpness of eye and ear and its philosophizing. In composite, Twain emerged as more complex than any character his fiction had managed to create.

Far more surprisingly, his faults often made an integrated part of the picture. No doubt a few enemies took revenge while trying to sound bereaved. But many eulogies full of admiration and even taffy rang in some failings. The top writers for William Randolph Hearst got princely salaries because they supposedly had a genius for encapsulating mass opinion. In his flagship *New York American*, the editorial, perhaps by the once renowned Arthur Brisbane, saluted Twain as "curiously and intimately American" and as both democrat and fierce achiever. However, because his irony had often questioned Hearstian jingoism, he was condescended to as the "man of boundless optimism, who has never troubled to understand the great tragedies of nations." Also, bafflingly, he had "no natural acerbity, and consequently no real talent for satire." The mixture of accolades, inconsistencies, criticism, and fuzziness about details typifies the final newspaper image of Twain.

We tend to forget that hardly anybody has read all of Twain's books. As now, readers went to the ones they somehow expected to like, and they remembered best those that surpassed expectations. Likewise, the larger

Chief of American Men of Letters

MARK TWAIN IS DEAD.

It would be hard to frame four other words that could carry a message of personal bereavement to so many Americans.

He was easily the chief of our writers, by the only valid test. He could touch the emotional centre of more lives than any other.

He was curiously and intimately American. No other author has such a tang of the soil—such a flavor of the average national mind.

Europeans who complain that we denied Walt Whitman, misunderstood Emerson and have admired only those who write in old world fashions should be satisfied at least with Mark Twain, and with our unwavering taste for him.

He was our very own, and we gathered him to our hearts.

In ages to come, if historians and archaeologists would know the thoughts, the temper, the characteristic psychology of the American of the latter half of the nineteenth century, he will need only to read "Innocents Abroad," "Tom Sawyer" and "Huckleberry Finn."

Mr. Clemens's books were the transcript of his life. And that life was the kind of life that the average American man of his time has believed in and admired.

He was the man that rose from the ranks without envy or condescension.

The man that hated dogmas and philosophies and loved a flash of intellectual light.

He was the man that cared much to get rich, yet would sweat blood to pay his debts.

The man of boundless optimism, who has never troubled to understand the great tragedies of nations.

The deepening sense of the twentieth century—with its feeling that there are social problems that cannot be resolved by pleasantries—has somehow left our dear prophet, with all his delicate and tender ironies and his merry quips, a little in the rear.

Mark Twain was never fortunate in his polemics. He was not effective as the champion of a cause. What he wrote of the Congo was hardly more creditable or convincing than his crusade against Mrs. Eddy.

He had no natural acerbity, and consequently no real talent for satire.

His genius was full of bravery and brightness and the joy of life.

And in the strength of his serene and laughing spirit generations of Americans will go forth to do deeds that he himself could never have conceived.

New York American, 22 April 1910, p. [20]

THERE IS A TIME TO LAUGH AND THERE IS A TIME TO WEEP

Baltimore American, 23 April 1910 (copy from Mark Twain Project, Bancroft Library, University of California)

public registered selective facets of his personality. Too simplistically and even too kindly, Twain held that "our heroes are the men who do things which we recognize, with regret and sometimes with a secret shame, that we cannot do." A hero's supporters can have reasons that would offend him. Millions idolized Dwight D. Eisenhower as the resolute warrior while others trusted his beaming, fatherly smile; but at least some voted for him as a genial amateur in politics who would let big government suffer from neglect. The writers of editorials that confronted Twain's faults may simply have wanted to break through the clichés or may have decided that honesty was overdue even though debunking ordinarily waits out a decent period of mourning. A heartening possibility is that he had set so high a level of frankness about himself that the truth seemed appropriate. Whatever the motives, acknowledging his faults humanized the portrait and cooled anybody's urge toward a first-hand exposé.

During the last fifty years the critical judgments of Twain have basically polarized at whether or not his genius caved in to materialism or else to his psychic immaturities. At his death the differences spread widely, almost bewilderingly, with the party of hope dominating the most obvious pairing—his optimism and pessimism. Optimism included his bequests to the fund of human cheer and his natural kindness of heart; pessimism ranged from an instinct for derision to attacks on vital institutions to gloom about mankind. Since Freudian concepts had only started to affect lay thinking, nobody named hostility and aggression as motives for Twain's humor, though the elegist for the *New York Times Saturday Review of Books*, perhaps drawing on inside contact, observed that "to the last there was always a keen, avid, sometimes slightly unfeeling love of ridiculing whatsoever and whomever he could make ridiculous." Another, far larger public saw and doubtlessly shared the sorrow of *Collier's Weekly* over the "loss of a great and gracious personality" whom "success could not spoil nor adversity embitter."

It would be easy to sneer at the credit Twain got as a supportive force. The world looks much more dangerous now, and our intelligentsia, aghast at the momentum of the "fun" ethic, particularly resent an entertainer who might have created weightier art. So we may feel downcast at how often Twain was eulogized as a fountain of joy. The *Albuquerque Journal* called him the "Apostle of the Smile" whose motto was, "Cheer up"; the *Grand Forks* (N.D.) *Times*, a "sort of neighborhood settlement of good cheer." Twain would have winced at sounding like somebody deserving a shrug from Huck Finn, who did respect "real bully" entertainment. At the extreme of the positive range, the *Wilmington Morning Star* evidently had in mind not even his mildest reformerism but his "wholesome and uplifting" role as "apostle of the good in that of the everyday." All this might pass as small-town naiveté if the *Saturday Review of Books* had not quoted the *San Francisco Argonaut* for one of the "best appreciations," which declared that the "fresh and clean" humorist had taught the Boston Brahmins how a "wholesome" and "mirthful man might scatter wisdom and goodness."[3] Most imperceptively of all, the *New York Observor*, a religious weekly, regretted that Twain's "great optimism" had blinded him to the "sorrows and fears of the great masses."

The homage to a tower of good cheer is perplexing if interpreted as a response to Twain's books alone. Could even *The Prince and the Pauper* or *Joan of Arc* justify it? The answer must expand to the shifting triangle formed by the effects of his writings, the personae he tried to create in his other activities, and the image of him haphazardly constructed by the public. Along that triangle raced the élan he generated as a comic hero. The *Manila Times* came close to the experiential truth: "He had youth of spirit and youth of humor and played almost to the end." This point was reinforced by the *Boston Post* with a fine example: "Spontaneity, playful extravagance, the ignoring of the conventional and the staid, even at the risk of shocking literal and limited beings were characteristic of Mark Twain. His scrawl on a card to a sick man on whom he called, 'God and I are sorry that you are so ill,' was an expression that came from him without the slightest hesitancy over the incongruity." This side of Twain encouraged confidence in the strength of individuality and fearless autonomy. As the *Philadelphia Press* put it, nothing "could tame him. He was a perpetual lesson . . . that the way to get the most in life's game was to play it to the uttermost, going one's own way in one's own way and no other."

His sober impact likewise elicited praise in worthwhile terms. The *Chautauquan*, a voice for tidy earnestness, declared a loss to "literature, humor, humanitarianism, intellectual and moral progress." Long one of Twain's least amused critics before his anti-imperialistic crusade, the *Springfield* (Mass.) *Republican* proclaimed him the "most absolute moralist of American citizenry." Both his ethical and his social force helped inspire the frequent salute to an unrelenting enemy of "shams," almost a keyword for Twain's cult. Its broader synonyms rang through tributes from persons and journals never considered radical, such as the *Savannah News*: "One particularly strong point about all of Mark Twain's writings is his antagonism toward all cant, hypocrisy and 'flap doodle' wherever he chanced to find it—in society, in the school, in the home, in the church or in the professions." Although the rebels of the 1920s charged that their forbears had flinched at grappling for reality, the rationalists of Twain's day believed they had dared to clear the sacred deadwood of centuries from language as much as from underlying social fact. Sinclair Lewis never realized how seriously the ring of conformity had been damaged before he harassed it.

Still the controlling image presented Twain not as a cynic but as the embodiment of genial reason. It surfaced most sharply in the titles of "sage" and "philosopher" woven into his obituaries like laurel wreaths. Outdoing Theodore Roosevelt's "a great philosopher," the *Jacksonville* (Fla.) *Times-Union* headed its editorial with "The Greatest American Philosopher." Although the public overrates the profundity of its oracles, the word did not mean that Twain's fumblings at ontology had won a following. Since the heyday of Poor Richard and the cracker-barrel sages, the humorists who worked through epigrams had earned honorary degrees by acclamation if they hit the note of homely profundity. In 1873 Twain had solemnly praised Josh Billings, his heavy handed contemporary, as a "philosopher." The title has had a continued newspaper life, still not quite over though feeble since the 1930s and no longer able to command royalties from syndication. Meanwhile posterity has kindly forgotten Twain's dullest tidbits of wisdom which drift close to pomposity.

When explicitly named, his irreverence was sometimes identified with heresy rather than insight or lively clowning. No other newspaper went so far as the *St. Louis Republic*: "He never created a lovable character. His good people are prigs or hopelessly gullible. His heroes are skeptics. . . . The light of truth was for him cold and gray and the coming of its morn meant the forgetting of dreams." There spoke a purer pessimist than Twain. Most guardians of the stabilizing consensus chose, however, to ignore the gloomy, agnostic moods revealed more and more often after the mid 1890s. Typically, his streak of "kindly cynicism" was excused as the weariness of old age beset by the deaths of loved ones, as an understandable letdown from a lifetime of bright courage. The *New York Globe and Commercial Advertiser* found him "shot through with sweetness, struggle as he did to be serious and severe." The curmudgeon with a heart of gold flourished long before Hollywood, and Twain's impersonators today feel it effective to give him a nasalized, much harsher voice than he had.

Easier to spot now than in 1910, another pairing came nearer to balancing Twain's images as a plebeian and as a natural aristocrat who had earned a fortune. The favorite American myths of the success fitted nicely the Samuel Clemens who started from poverty, educated himself in manly skills like piloting, and stuck to his ambitions in the face of setbacks that "would appall the generality." His career was indeed remarkable: an image does not have to be a delusion. The truth turned debatable when obituaries stated that his toils had smelted an unalloyed affection for the "medial line of mortals" and their ways. Even the Socialist *Daily Call* certified his personal warmth; and for the apolitical, George Ade testified that "the housewives loved him for his outspoken devotion to home-cooking." Truth suffered when obituaries, insisting that "no library" had helped him attain his "equality with the most cultivated minds of New England," pumped him up into another anti-intellectual who draws solely on life for a vast learning. The covert encompassing term, then dominant in the system of ethics taught by Departments of Philosophy, was "self-realization," which Twain showed in his "progressive development, a deepening and broadening of forces, a ripening of intellectual and spiritual powers from the beginning to the end of his career."[4] He had proved again how high the common man could rise, not just financially but mentally. Since he had not gone over to the snobs, every cubit of eminence let the plebeians chortle louder about how well one of their own had done.

Twain also commanded the applause of the intensely practical. Many editorials gloated that his books had sold millions of copies for royalties that supported his fine residences. A few highlighted the man of property and business affairs rightfully intimate with tycoons like the now charitable Andrew Carnegie and H. H. Rogers of Standard Oil, perhaps more feared than respected. Seven months after Twain's death the ruling elites headed an audience of five thousand called to Carnegie Hall by the American Academy of Arts and Letters. Any historian recognizes so many names among those listed by the press that he assumes he ought to know the rest—more financiers like J. P. Morgan, judges and other politicians almost as powerful as the Speaker of the House of Representatives, along with socialites from the oldest families and leading portrait painters, writers, and newspaper and magazine editors.

Fully having it both ways, Twain was presented as quintessentially American and yet unique. The patriotic motif, easy to evoke graphically, dominated obituary cartoons ("Columbia in Deepest Grief"), and the captions or labels that named "Uncle Sam" doubtless raised appropriate echoes of his given name, still generally remembered. His Americanism got much of the credit for his world-wide fame, itself often treated gratefully as his greatest achievement—which shed glory on the culture that had shaped him. Why he was so firmly identified as the national soul is harder to pinpoint than what feature of his defensive tactics made it possible such as his avoiding, said the *Philadelphia Bulletin*, the "veneer of semi-cosmopolitanism which has marked not a few American authors." As a matter of fact, while quirkiness had kept him prickly toward the French, he had often tipped toward the veneration for England common among the educated native-born. Luckily, it had not gripped him during the wrong political crisis, and he had always snapped back to enough gusto for the gamier New World to excuse his surprising number of trips across the Atlantic. "Probably no other American could have lived abroad for so many years without being editorially branded as an expatriate."[5] Burnished at crucial moments, his reputation for patriotism had also shielded him in the furnace of anti-imperialism.

Enshrining Mark Twain as Uncle Sam demanded some detail about the nation's character. The *New York American* stopped at the potentially mild praise that "no other author had such a tang of the soil—such a flavor of the average national mind." Although typicality could imply mystic guidance, even a fulfillment of the divine will, most of the patriotic tributes featured Twain as "the buoyant, hopeful and purposeful American" coping in the light of common day. On this level the particulars differed between a mainline, grave strenuosity and a swaggering brashness. Editorials seldom spell out whether "type" refers to the median or "personify" marks the zenith; sure of not being challenged in any case, the larger group preferred to compliment Twain on "stalwart insouciance," a "devil-may-care, generous, frank, kindly spirit," or a passion for "independent thought, fearless criticism, unrestrained humor, democratic feeling, with a certain dash and abandon." The *New York World* had the grace to be humbler: "His virtues were national, his faults were national. Intensely democratic, irreverent often toward traditions, unawed by conventions, with a touch of vulgarity, yet always healthful, never degenerate, hyperbolic in expression, he was a typical American." To complain that this verdict was still mostly self-congratulation expects too much from a mass-circulation newspaper, alert to the feeling that Twain's success heightened the certainty of a collective, laughing triumph over the obstacles of human nature and of history.

The front-page spreads and photographs for which the editorials sounded just a coda featured not typicality but the "Fascinating Life Story of the Greatest Humorist of All Time" (*Boston Post*). The details, both outward and inward, were considered familiar. "Few writers," according to the *Detroit Free Press*, "have taken the public into their confidence in more pleasing and, at times, in more touching manner." In fact the *Kansas City Star* gave him credit for total frankness: "No other man of his time was so well known to the public in all his moods." The longest stories were sure to include his record of good citizenship rounded off by a death-bed check of $6,000 to the local library. The briefest stories, overstating the purity of his heroics, were almost sure to recall his paying off a bankruptcy for which the "courts and the public acquitted him of even a moral responsibility." His home life rated constant mention as "exceptionally beautiful." Subheads like "The World Loves a Lover" honored his devotion to his wife, symbolized by the fervent epitaph which he composed for her gravestone and which the Associated Press "repeats today, the first time in years it has wired a stanza of poetry all over the world." That harmonized with the "Dies of Broken Heart" motif, a favorite for headlines or subheadings while the *Colorado Springs Gazette* listed twenty "ills" that "Beset America's Arch Jester." Beyond the Pagliacci archetype, the broken heart fitted the rigors of having defied fate, with a freewheeling American flair that nevertheless suggested a "chained and harassed" Prometheus. Here virility merged with sentiment. If males dominate Twain's audiences, the weary giants of laissez-faire could find plenty to empathize

UNCLE SAM MOURNS.

Atlanta Journal, 23 April 1910, p. 1

The Vacant Chair at Stormfield

with in the obituaries. Yet he had managed to have his final image acquire the ready emotionality that stereotyped the Victorian woman.

The overarching effect was that he had made his life a public spectacle, indeed a melodrama. An editor who worked with him for decades diagnosed "in Mark Twain's case the evident compulsion, however genially complied with, of the openly dramatized personality."[6] One of his earliest academic admirers would explain how Twain had convinced "his countrymen of his essential fellowship, his temperamental affinity with them": "This miracle he wrought by the frankest and most straightforward revelation of the critical experiences in his own life and the lives of those he had known with perfect intimacy."[7] To our taste he may have brimmed over into bathos, supposedly more marketable then than now. One editorial forgave all his faults because he had written "The Death-Disk"—so tearjerking a story that it melted smoothly into a silent one-reel movie. Yet reporters had never accused him of begging for sympathy. Protected either by his comic twists of phrase or the memory of past slapstick, he had during the 1890s perfected the art of wearing his heart on his sleeve without violating the code for manly reticence except in the eyes of extreme mavericks like Stephen Crane.

His quivers of the upper lip were also made tolerable by his rowdy side when it did not need apology itself. For recalling the 1860s, the West Coast papers had to acknowledge his early bohemian streak, and his enduring vices had paraded too boldly for any coverup. The nicotine stains on his mustache and his much photographed habit of smoking in bed raised mutterings—especially meant for young ears—that the fatal angina came from a "tobacco heart." A sizable minority of editorials called him "intensely human." In context this reminded Twain fanciers of sticky patches like his "querulous and almost crabbed moods" and of sins like his "flamboyant" profanity, which he had not bothered to suppress for Helen Keller—to her delight. Bolder hints celebrated his "racier, ruder speech for more masculine, stalwart ears" that could appreciate his "Rabelaisian joy in the human comedy."[8] To the end Twain's lounging carelessness about clothing and manners had charmed those males who resented the mother's and wife's determination to "comb" them "all to hell" (in Huck Finn's words). A few hearty truthtellers went on to specify Twain's pleasure in good whiskey and the company that social drinking gathers. In starchier words, though his married life showed an "escutcheon 'blameless and white as is a lily flower,'" he was "no anemic mollycoddle, but very much of a man among men." Those who preferred a faintly romantic air could admit "there was plenty of the artistic temperament in him."

This left him far short of satanic or Byronic fumes. Yet he plainly had not masqueraded as a milksop. In the judgment of the *Rutland* (Vt.) *Herald*, "Samuel L. Clemens' weaknesses were definitely known, but were passed over with a smile by everyone, because he was Mark Twain." It did not specify which virtues had earned such tolerance. Or was vicarious pride and pleasure in his willfulness part of the explanation? The *Rochester Democrat and Chronicle* stated that "he never aspired to sainthood, and carefully avoided everything that tended to distinguish him in any way for conventional goodness." If this overstatement handed out more besides taffy, then some kind of resistance to propriety had projected itself through Twain.

To others he directly symbolized a soft nostalgia. In many visible ways he had kept right up to date. Always fascinated by technology, he enjoyed bumping along in the new automobile and posed bravely for snapshots astride it. The obituary cartoons nevertheless preferred to hark back to Tom and Huck, usually rafting on the Mississippi. The cartoonist who showed a motherly figure reading their story to a boy and girl put all three in old-fashioned clothes. To the frequent lament that an "epoch in American life" had ended with Twain, the *Nebraska State Journal* added that the "nation will no more see his like again than it will see another Lincoln." Less portentously, a turning point is announced at the death of many a dignitary, and though not anticipating the debacle of World War I, differing camps agreed on the prospect of sweeping change. The *Call*, using a Marxist forecast, gloomily made Twain the last of the journalists who could get away with defying the business office, itself now falling under the power of the buyers of advertising. But the *Call* joined in the romancing about his adventurous past "when there was a great, wide, free country."

After 1900 Twain liked to joke about his career through the pose of a last battered survivor. Partly he was updating to cover his current situation as he had done for decades. The pose invited the risk of anticlimax intimated in a few obituaries. Still, Tom Sawyer would have envied the "effect" raised by Twain's death. For at least two newspapers he had amounted to an "institution," a concept too impersonal and static, however, to express his long impact as an almost garishly distinct character, as a popular hero who controlled his image more than he obeyed it. Indulgently the *Baltimore Sun* mentioned the "legend" that he took the "pains of a court lady" in teasing his white hair to "just the proper stage of artistic disarray." Another editorial explained that "he posed, if it could be called posing, only in the humorous spirit," and yet another suggested that his "affectations" were "only acted satires." The vital point is that most of Twain's contemporaries found a bedrock of inviolable honesty beneath the shifting surfaces. Helen Keller decided: "He was a playboy sometimes and on occasions liked to show off. He had a natural sense of the dramatic and enjoyed posing as he talked. But in the core of him there was no make-believe."[9]

She did not mean to divorce Twain's open self from a soul held hostage by popularity. Supposedly right after the funeral, the editorial Poet of *American Magazine* (July 1910) argued: "He was a great individual. He was the freest man I ever knew. The hand of public opinion was not heavy on him. . . . He made concessions to it. He treated it as a civilized nation might treat a half-civilized neighboring tribe. But he was never ruled by it." "Never" is heartening but absolute, an invitation to drift into romance rather than to learn from Twain's forty years of sometimes too successful, often difficult, but finally triumphant interaction with the American people, a triumph that proved theirs as much as his.

CHAPTER 2

Live Drama

MARK TWAIN HAD ESTABLISHED a streak of grassroots affection surprisingly early. In 1878 a ne'er-do-well managed to travel free from Cincinnati to Washington, D.C., by charming two railroad conductors and a "boss workman" with a note written to him by Twain. About that time, a book agent let a "dirty, ragged clothed" boy look at her prospectus for peddling *The Adventures of Tom Sawyer*: "'Oh, that's Tom! Isn't it?' And he looked with delight, talking on, 'I've been wantin' dad to buy me one, and he said he would if he had more money than he knowed what to do with. . . . Some boys told me about Tom Sawyer—said he and some other fellers went to their own funerals; gol! musn't that a been fun.'"[1] Such fans admired the author himself. In a still unpublished memoir Twain set down the tribute from a sturdy, cocky adolescent who forgave all his adult ignorance because he had written *Adventures of Huckleberry Finn*. No such boy, we hope, justified the fears of prim librarians about the influence of Twain's novels and grew up into the Bowery bum who shouted, "Hello, Mark!" Of course that book agent found a spread of customers including a black barber who ordered the most expensive binding because "dat Mark Twain's done a heap of good to dese United States."

Contemporaries with inside knowledge of how celebrity works realized, however, that he had gone far beyond depending on the appeal of his books. One obituary called him the "architect of his own reputation," and the *St. Louis Globe-Democrat* observed that he "had a subtle sense of commercialism in his own line, and not even Sarah Bernhardt surpassed him in making himself of continued interest to the public." When a magazine posed him a pious question in 1898 about "books which have most influenced my life," he brassily listed his own, surely creating much more amusement and attention than offense. Among the many later judgments of his showman side, Carl Van Doren's is the most succinct: "He created many characters, but none of them is greater than himself." Robert Frost, his closest modern rival at elevating the man of letters into a popular hero, still counted mainly on the well educated and never approached Twain's ability to snarl traffic on Fifth Avenue.

With varying degrees of reproach, critics have lately deepened a gap between the private Samuel L. Clemens who created masterpieces and a Mark Twain who hungrily sought applause. Although the mind and psyche that guided the working author were just as real as those for the showman—a supportive point for anybody depressed by Frost's biographers—it is time to move on from that gap and appreciate the operative images of Twain, who, incidentally, could sign letters as just Mark and respond to either half of his pseudonym. Actually, while the Clemens within the bosom of family life sometimes regretted his public face, the indecision sprang from differing circuits of mood that in his later years often flowed together. His force and lasting power as an attractive personality would argue that major psychic confluences were pushing forward. During the 1880s, especially, and between 1898 and 1903 he achieved firmer unity of action and feeling than most of us can deliver in far less treacherous contexts. Furthermore, whatever the sufferings of an upstaged Clemens or a harassed Twain, American society has benefited intellectually as much as emotionally from the self presented before and, finally, to it.

That self was much richer than Twain's literary reputation, which of course played its evolving part. While many readers pictured with unusual vividness the author behind the page, these images made spreading circles that thinned out beyond the measurable or overlapped with extra-literary sources. Because of these complexities, analysis had better confine itself for now to the United States, though the implications of his career apply to at least the industrializing democracies and though his charm abroad, if only by correcting notions of New World uniqueness, helps to clarify his cohering image; the mere fact of that charm certainly increased his eminence at home, starting with his triumphs in England during the early 1870s. Analysis of only his American career still incurs four especially challenging yet enlightening problems, which can help to judge the authority of alleged culture-heroes.

First, printed sources seldom reflect opinion passively. Besides the subjectivity of any observer, the spokesmen for the genteel tradition, for example, pulsed with eagerness to elevate taste. Without necessarily aiming to denigrate Twain, their estimates of his current standing carried a strong desire to shape it; their book reviews hid sermonettes on what readers ought to like. Likewise, most editors of magazines and newspapers believed in their mission to inculcate social orthodoxy and proper behavior. Ironically, Twain may have gained more than he lost from their bias, which gave him a firm pattern against which to define himself more vividly. Second, hard analysis of "the public" splinters it into always smaller pieces. By 1899 Twain's case taught a professor at Columbia University that "there are many publics,—as many in fact as there are different kinds of taste." What passes for dominant attitudes often applies solely to that cohort of the populace which feels the right or duty to speak up or merely reacts to a cue from a hired scout. Public opinion as a measurable force was invented late in the nineteenth century with literary polls leading the way during the 1880s. Its reification blurs the fact that Twain was gifted in all varieties of humor, some with vastly different audiences. Third, most people absorb the ruling culture passively if not defensively or at least assume that nobody of consequence cares to know what they think, much less to read their letters to newspapers. Twain's own defense against the elite, "my audience is dumb; it has no voice in print," recognized this pattern. He can demonstrate better how mass adulation works than it can explain him. More specifically, his career encourages friendly suspicion toward those always poised to tell us what our esthetic preferences are.

The fourth problem is unique to Twain among authors because a sizable part of his late constituency had read little if any of his writing, had never heard one of his lectures or the speeches given mostly before select audiences. For millions he functioned primarily as a celebrity, somebody who is unquestionably popular aside from concrete accomplishments. For the leading media of the time his casual doings rated as priority news. This coverage turned his personality into common property that was haphazardly discussed on the horsecar or the front porch among fluid groups, which included members unable or too lazy to read who had formed an opinion by hearsay and so took their part in the bonding conversation. Twain became prime fodder for the "human interest" stories or just the floating paragraphs that filled out the typical newspaper page and served as the broadest level of popular literature before the comic strip. Partly because he lived so long he reached the momentum of a to-be-continued serial. Although high culture may shudder at the quality of the content, the spear carriers for Twain were choosing materials for their frame of values and were absorbing judgments from their peers about what counted in their day-to-day society. Their casual reactions flickered beyond the sensors of any scientific instrument. Still, they mounted up towards tens of millions and deserve the attention of any democratic approach to culture.

The widest circle of admirers that has fair distinctness covered the readers of the lightweight magazines and the newspapers—especially the metropolitan dailies and, above all, those of New York City, which filtered outside their area of revenue and set the tempo for small-town editors wanting to rise above provinciality. It would be fatuous to presume to codify the attitudes among that sea of admirers who responded to Twain as their hero. The values of an articulate layer should not be extrapolated to cover tens of millions, many speaking broken English. The total circulation of the dailies peaked here at one-third of the population. Even the specialists in American Studies have used the term of "culture" loosely, jumping "from the 'literate public' to everyone," although the "imputation of collective beliefs is an extraordinarily complex empirical procedure."[2] Twain's public offered such divergent responses that abandoning analysis might seem wisest except for the fact that his career so undeniably held meaning for it.

Increasingly, different impulses within any extended public can pick clashing heroes, from Albert Schweitzer to Marilyn Monroe, can adulate both an embodiment of the consensus and one of its lively critics, functioning seemingly as a vicarious threat but perhaps in fact as a safety valve. To reach full stature the same hero almost must be claimed by opposing sides. If Twain's freewheeling ways appealed to those who were discontent with modernization and its bureaucracy and the other daily repressions it brought, he could stride forth elsewhere as the champion of official values because of his competitiveness, his thinking in national rather than local terms, his patriotism, his commitment to technology, his gusto for financial speculation, and even his delight in romantic landscape. John G. Cawelti argues that a popular novel (or hero) satisfies a "variety of cultural, artistic, and psychological interests" and, more generally, formulaic attitudes while introducing elements of change and thus achieving a "transition between old and new."[3] Much of the later disagreement about Twain springs from emphasis on either his rebelliousness or his conformities. Furthermore, those who admire his nonconformity refuse to grant that it carried some safe attitudes for ballast and that its acceptance depended on signs that it had limits and, in a basically optimistic culture, did not "oppose everything."

A balanced analysis soon sketches too many on-the-other-hands. That effect brings the temptation to settle for shaped models such as the Trickster, borrowed from cultural anthropology. But Twain's America could not pass for an oral, face-to-face community. Most of his audience engaged his presence through print or even less direct ways. A worse flaw of neat models is that his image changed steadily and, before his career ended, changed qualitatively at least twice. That fact undermines other inviting paradigms based on elemental human nature, though societies large and small do seem to need the privileged jester—Twain liked to claim he was "God's Fool"—who releases collective discontent by offering himself up to ridicule or comically belittling the sacred or personifying freedom through a madcap deviance. On the primitive antisocial level, the id of some admirers wallowed in Twain's joking about bad smells, itches, body noises, and furtive habits that polite discourse wants to ignore. However, he also encouraged more complicated rebellion than that.

Lately, *homo ludens* has aroused a fresh round of theory in which the play instinct is celebrated as not only the escape from routine but the insistence upon emotive and mental willfulness. Twain is a leading exemplar. In composite his career fits the four great archetypes—*homo ludens*, *homo agonistes* enduring pain and competing heartily, *homo aleator* gambling, and *homo fraternalis* advancing the common good.[4] So far, his lasting appeal verifies such universal frames of reference or others. But his works and personality also directly support our sense that shape-shifting reality overruns tidy ideas. That proposition applies in turn to analyses of Twain, who bursts through any pattern that systematizes him. Though he belonged to *homo sapiens* and though his career was rooted in history, any set of abstract terms starts to dull a magnificently particular individual, a homegrown mind that could jeer at "that kind of so-called 'housekeeping' where they have six Bibles to one cork-screw."

Likewise, the universal models distort Twain's relationships with his era. For example, with the sense of community ebbing as industrial capitalism displaced the issues from local to national elections, heroes were needed to revivify the feeling of a concretely shared culture; along with inventing and exploring (in both of which Twain dabbled), literature was a less divisive sphere of activity in which to locate them. Or, from economic history it can be argued that the tenseness of a laissez-faire marketplace created a demand for the frothy entertainer that Twain knew how to be, as when he joked about smoking only one cigar at a time. Much humor depends on the social context, dominated then by a middle class that was dedicated to making good but chafed under the required discipline, that liked to pound itself on the back for individuality but was guiltily aware of its hypocrisies. From religious history it can be argued that the easing of orthodoxy opened a chance for secular entertainment that knew just how far it could dare to go with comedy about the spirit as well as the flesh. Socio-history can show that the urban masses, cut off from the gossip of the small town, were ripe for vicarious intimacy with celebrities, preferably associated with such reminders of the fading pasts as the village or the frontiers. Twain had one of the richest stocks of pasts available, whether by region or occupation. Finally, the undying wish to behold in person the true American, the new man in the New World, called for a fresh supply of candidates. Only a combination of such needs can explain the extent of Twain's triumph. Nevertheless, they cannot tell us why he and not somebody else became their supreme vehicle.

The best way of tying his uniqueness to abstract patterns, of making Twain belong to his times without shrinking him to an effect of them is to trace the evolving impact of his role. The clever hero can serve as a favorite American type who makes a fool of his righteous enemies and thus gratifies the democratic pleasure of seeing pretense leveled down.[5] But his function can grow grittier, more complicated. The revered jester may either relieve pressure damaging to social stability or divert tensions into nonsense. Comic self-assertion can encourage spontaneity in others or simply assure them that the ideal of resistance marches on even while they are knuckling under. On balance, Twain encouraged his public to reach out for autonomy and authenticity. In a subtler message, he achieved by 1900 a heartening degree of frankness about his image-building, a frankness that more than makes up for his moments of fakery. As early as 1863 he openly warned that he had "a sort of talent for posturing."

That posturing operated in and on a relatively new context—the world of commercialized print and the burgeoning industry of publicity. The industry is now so visible that we tend to overestimate its dominance over competing interests. Normally a hero takes up little of an admirer's total life. But we underestimate the self-awareness of both parties in the transaction, at least during Twain's century. The hero was deliberately indulged as an alternative to personal concerns, as the star in a welcomed public drama: a sequence of actions before an audience that participates with some consciousness that "it's only a play." As a writer Twain started from western attitudes based in the newspaper office rather than the book and frankly allied to the trades of publicity and staged entertainment. In his early lectures the deadpan style, punctuated by mock perplexity at the laughter it brings, already proved his skill at establishing a mutual recognition that he was posing. A kindred spirit, P. T. Barnum had risen to fame during the 1850s "not simply because of his enterprise and energy, but because of a special outlook on reality, a peculiar and masterly way of manipulating other people and somehow making them feel grateful for being the subjects of his manipulation." He delighted in telling reporters about his ploys because he not only counted on the "national tolerance for clever imposture" but understood that audiences could cheerfully gather for "something they suspected might be an exaggeration or even a masquerade."[6] Like Barnum, Twain improved on the confidence man by going legitimate and got credit for his shrewdness in managing to do that so openly. For an early fan of "camp," he was parodying the asides that actors shared with the audience of a melodrama; more fundamentally he parodied the Victorians' veneration of sincerity. His posturing increasingly became a shared put-on of a decreasing pool of outsiders. In Twain's late speeches the game of revealing his tactics verged on infinite regression—genially warning that he always lied about himself and so must be doing just that in admitting it. The larger point of that game is that he never wore out his welcome through merely rehashing the old routines. Rather he turned his herohood into a self-feeding process that rose from notoriety to images so vitally attractive that they have swept over the ordinary barrier of taste between generations. Seventy years after his death, admen can use his figure without wasting space to identify it, though a white suit often acts as a cue.

During Twain's forty-year performance the dominant quality was his irreverence, which flashed from *The Innocents Abroad* like an electric storm. Inconsistently, he could support reverential absolutes, particularly about womanhood and the family. But he insisted he had been "born irreverent—like all other people I have ever known or heard of."[7] Confident while in such a mood that he was appealing to a gut instinct he mocked cherished values—Sunday school theology, decorum in dress, parlor wisdoms, electoral politics, or the literalist conscience. Irreverence is always needed to challenge the status quo, which entrenches itself in sacred tradition, and to strip away the clichés that cover up evil or just insensitivity. It had an immediate force for the later nineteenth century. When Twain burlesqued Tennyson's *Idylls of the King* or quipped, "Heaven for climate, and hell for society," he was not merely deriding conventional ideas but striking at the social foundations of the age.

At its best his irreverence worked through comedy and gained privileges of frankness from it. We can only guess at the diagram of his psychic grid, and no theoretician—except perhaps Freud—has tracked humor on a persuasive level of sophistication without paradoxically eroding its base in illogicality or instinct. Whatever the buried sources of Twain's gift its reception by others joined it to a common "mental process, a distinctive feature of the social consciousness." These phrases come from a still respected essay, "The Psychology of Humor," that appeared during his lifetime.[8] It contends that the mainspring within us as audience is the pleasure of liberation from the taut consciousness we need in order to cope with reality. For a tumultuous moment we can transcend the laws of nature.

Humor is the "only objective fact in our experience that dares to defy the world order with impunity, that can violate ruthlessly, without pain and without apology, the manifold human contrivances, social customs and relationships and thereby not only creates the sense of freedom, but also assures us that we may temporarily escape from the uniformities and mechanisms of life." It "bids us look behind the scene where luck, chance, spontaneity and life operate." Without naively assuming that Twain's audience had tenser psyches than ours or resented more the rigidities of economic efficiency, we can feel sure that monotony lurks everywhere and its victims welcome expert resistance to it. Whether just resistant through childlike play or reconstructive through irreverence that constantly threatened to "go too far," Twain's humor operated as a liberating force.

Still, the most important social fact about Twain was not humor but Twain as humorist, a likable personality who expanded into a comic hero. No theory accounting for a class or group can cover his mixture of creating books, lecturing, writing for the newspapers and magazines, public speaking, posing for cameras and interviews, manipulating the press, and expanding his word-of-mouth fame all the way down to passersby who had asked why a crowd was gathering. Hobbes's argument for the "sudden glory" of feeling superior to others can fit only that aspect of Twain which exploited hostility with suspicious ease. Most of the members of most of his publics learned to look to him for a more positive effect and then for personification of the comic spirit.

Usually billeted with drama, the comic hero can win applause at rising levels of cerebration.[9] As a buffoon he leaves us committed to the side of vitality and pleasure, released from intellectuality (as some of Twain's detractors did complain), and hopeful that a happy-go-lucky spirit will beat the odds. When raised to psychiatric significance he can fake paranoia as a screen for releasing energy, celebrating the gross body, and gratifying chaotic fantasies. Or, conceived sociologically, he wages war against rules and systems, delighting the many who would join him if they dared. In his time Twain was particularly admired for his touch for and quickness to radiate mock violence. When most intellectual, the comic hero earns his stature by "courageous perseverance, resourceful intelligence, and a more or less conscious acceptance of the inevitable risks that he chooses to run in his wilfully comic challenge to the deadly seriousness of his world." The personae of Twain's travel books approached this last standard. Some of his later sketches and essays met it; so did his public self after the mid 1890s even if snatches of the buffoon and the sham paranoiac would reappear until his death. It is nevertheless a blunder to peg the finest Twain at any of these levels. His genius stands out in his unsurpassed gift for so many kinds of comedy—from crude, even cruel joking (about the "hare-lip" girl in *Huckleberry Finn*) to irony as chilling as interstellar space.

Twain emerged, however, as not only a comic but also a popular hero. Broadening his constituency that far leads into the heart of a lively debate over terminology. Some would like to divorce "popular" from "mass," which turns pejorative in many contexts or suggests the technicalities of social dynamics. As for "folk" hero, though illiterates enjoyed Twain's image, the backbone of his audience could grasp the articles written about him. On the other hand, it was larger than "midbrow" or "midcult," which could carry the point that the middle class, by 1850 dictating the sanctions of taste, eventually granted Twain a crucial, validating degree of respectability. Likewise—depending on whether the cheap book, the penny newspaper, the entertaining magazine, or the audio-visual complex qualifies as the crucial artifact—different dates can be named as the time when a popular culture reached a density that makes it reasonable to call somebody a genuine national hero with followers in all strata of the society. For Twain's career, anyway, the decisive changes occurred during his boyhood and brought a huge jump in literacy that in turn compounded the kinds of publishing he would exploit. More specifically, his rise as public hero is inseparable from that of the newspapers that sold lively reading, which very much included fillers, columns, and then picture-spreads on interesting personalities. As an insider, Twain understood this linkage better than we have, so far. Furthermore, he expanded it constructively throughout his lifetime. Aside from the gratifications of being a celebrity, he needed and used immediate interaction with his audience to find out how he was going over. This interaction was often mediated by the newspapers, which collectively gave him much better guidance than the scattered reviews in magazines or essays in books.[10]

Well before his birth, intellectuals had begun worrying about the quality of popular culture. As Twain recognized uneasily, he became a focal point in the continuing debate, then centered ordinarily on printed literature. Although a few guardians of quality accepted him as a bridge to the demotic audience, most accused him of bringing down standards. Before rejecting popular culture, its critics still need to distinguish between a moralistic judgment that legislates taste and a psychological approach that empathizes with the human need for release or entertainment. Moreover they will do best to classify esthetic objects and activities not by their content but by the use being made of them. To feel that Renoir's "Boating Party" looks great in an ad for beer hardly equals gusto for the Impressionists. Conversely, many of those who ridicule mass culture consume slabs of it. A devotee of elitist poetry may roar around in one of Detroit's showiest models; users of television and the glossy magazines dip into materials they condemn in principle. In fact too many explications of *Huckleberry Finn* cannot bear to admit its debts to Twain's training as a newspaper humorist.

Popular culture once differed substantially in practice and ideals from that of today, when the youth scene sets the beat while the hucksters follow so well that they lead. For 1870, for example, it is defensible to set up a line between mercilessly exploiting taste and satisfying it in good faith. Although Twain's self-promotion could slide into hokum, a loyalty to his origins and his early experiences saved him from condescending toward popular standards or sneering at the blunders of upward cultural mobility. During the nineteenth century the gap between low and high esthetics did not look so steep or even desirable to as many as it does now. The genteel leadership claimed a mission to recruit the millions in the expanding school system. While elective officials tried to act humble, they also thought it safe to come across as well read because, in turn, the populace had a strong ideal of self-improvement. Twain worried whether his lyceum talks had proved informative and not merely entertaining. During the 1890s, the decade when he mounted into herohood, big-scale entrepreneurs began to envelop popular culture. But for a while much was still oriented toward the realistic world and a social context interwoven with the traditions of its consumers. With Twain's help while also to his benefit it could still offer both worthwhile stimulus and satisfactions.[11]

Romanticizing popular culture would be foolish. Its audience can demand trite patterns, then suddenly stampede after a fad; its ultimate sanction, applied quickly, is salability. But it can pay for vibrant work and seems able to preserve a populist strain that resists corporate deadness, either head-on or through a loyalty to liveliness that turns no wheels but just spins for fun. Twain did his part. Increasingly he also met the more general criterion implied by Richard Hoggart's *Uses of Literacy* (1957). Reared in the British working class, Hoggart neither disowns his roots nor regrets that education along with higher wages has brought the reading habit to the bottom of the social ladder. Yet he is appalled by the "self-indulgence" preached through the mass media and by the "trivial" entertainments that "make it harder for people without an intellectual bent to become wise in their own way." Sometimes a noisy echo, Twain much more often encouraged an earthy self-knowledge.

Still alive in his writings today, this stimulus once flowed at least as strongly from his personality. Skeptics, probing for false legends, brush away his image as a smoke screen and condescend to the public Twain who did fall short of perfect integrity—as any account must that is not a fairy tale. But if heroes on a human scale can happen, Twain qualified as ultimately authentic, deserving of accolades more than an exposé. To imply that he should have acted very differently is to forget that he fashioned one of the prized characters of our culture, that his unique élan overrode any posing. His climb to herohood took shrewdness, courage, toughness, and perseverance. Achieving it loosened the grip of editors anxious to enforce the reigning literary conventions. How much would we care about him now if hackwork for the magazines had drained his energies?

Today our political health is threatened by the image building used by candidates, from the county to the national level, to evade tough issues, and posturing always threatens the self-respect of anybody trying to stay honest. Twain suffered from his self-contempt. Furthermore, success breeds its own problems. Like the hustler in Budd Schulberg's *What Makes Sammy Run?* Twain learned how much effort it takes to hold the lead against the endless string of contenders and to try topping each previous triumph. As an unexpected cost, his control over the public increased his depressing suspicion that the damn fools hold a majority anywhere. But whatever the psychic strains, he projected the ideal of autonomy, which can subvert clichés, idols, habits, ideas, and systems that have outlived reality. In positive terms he dramatized an incorrigibly spontaneous individualist who tacitly accepted the need for social forms but drove them toward renewed vitality. We can admire those dramatics without conceding that they conjured up a fake Twain. Like George Santayana, I believe that "our deliberate character is more truly ourself than is the flux of our involuntary dreams."[12] More truly ourself, also, than the elevated feelings and ideas we keep private.

CHAPTER 3

A Blood Relative

MANY OF THE OBITUARIES agreed that *The Innocents Abroad; or, The New Pilgrims' Progress* (1869) had lasted as Twain's most popular or, in effect, his most characteristic book. Along with *Tom Sawyer* and *Huckleberry Finn* it was the title commonly worked into cartoons. In 1910 a series on "best sellers of yesterday" came to it second, after a pious romance, and called it a "vital book" that still won more readers than any competitor in travel literature. From just 1905 through 1907 Harper and Brothers sold forty-six thousand copies, about five thousand more than *Huckleberry Finn*. In Twain's lifetime it sold at least half a million copies, many of which were passed around to several readers. The newspaper world—crucial for the book's genesis as a series of paid "letters," for much of its basic attitude, and for its promotion—had continued to show special affection for it.

Twain's reputation had drifted east by 1865. *The Jumping Frog of Calaveras County and Other Sketches* (1867) helped it along with a sale that crept toward four thousand and the prestige of hard covers, and his sketches for eastern newspapers often rated reprinting along with a warm headnote. The *Quaker City* letters had led to more lecture dates and a commission for political columns from Washington. In November 1868 an insider wanting to see the *Atlantic Monthly* "far more popular" had suggested that a "writer named Mark Twain be engaged, and more articles connected with life than literature." We can only speculate whether this shrewd easterner realized how strongly Twain was tied to the newspaper world for self-advertisement as well as standards of writing and especially whether he appreciated how far Twain carried the spirit of a breezier pattern for approaching the public. That pattern involved a "much louder, laxer, stagier relation between writer and reader," encouraging a "performer, entertainer, star" who aimed at consolidating an audience that liked to think of itself as a group with openly common emotions. Furthermore, at his best Twain had already bent that pattern to his own talents and needs. During his Nevada years he had promoted himself into a local "combination of celebrity and journalist," a "figure whose way of reporting the news, whose peculiar expressions, and whose very comings and goings were themselves news."[1] *The Innocents Abroad* raised that figure to national celebrity.

While leaving highly distinctive impressions, *The Innocents Abroad* proves elusive under analysis of the authorial persona and the real-life man who, readers know, operates behind him. It presents the typical puzzle of Twain's writings. Someone who signs the title page with the made-up name of Mark Twain describes the doings and attitudes of that mythical individual, who often in turn likes to tell free-flowing stories about himself. Furthermore, such texts abound with sweeping judgments that anybody with a touch for abstractions can extrapolate into some kind of system. Still working primarily as a journalist, however, Twain aimed at catching the flavor of persons, objects, and places rather than at symmetry of ideas or effect. He hoisted signs of that lusty pleasure in "characters"—that is, spontaneous, near-eccentric, cheerful, and springy individualists—that would contribute lifelong to the impression of his democracy in personal manners. Most basically he angled for the humor that made his chief stock in trade. As early as 1910 a critic saw the need to protest against taking the book as "terribly in earnest" beneath its haphazard comedy. During the 1860s Twain had experimented almost desperately with a gallery of poses.[2] Each of them incurred or rather exploited the ambiguities inherent in comedy that bother the orderly analyst but not the kind of public Twain hoped to gather.

He had already learned to shift those poses with a dazzling speed that only the subconscious could follow. In fact the quick-change artist got overanxious in *The Innocents Abroad*, which lacked the benefit of the reassurance and dependable cues that success sends back. Moreover, Twain's genius could adapt to just about every pose it tried. Too often without trying to grasp his intentions, critics of *Innocents Abroad* now key on the pose or persona they like—or detest—the most. Their readings differ from those of his contemporary public more than for any other of his books, except possibly *Pudd'nhead Wilson*, because some of the most firmly assumed values in *Innocents Abroad* have lost their currency.

On the business level Twain hustled to present himself as attractively as possible. Complaining that the delays in publication jeopardized his "bread and butter," he worried about the gamble in sale by subscription with its imperatives for pleasing a small-town or rural audience that could raise a howl about not getting its money's worth for an expensive tome.[3] In revising his newspaper letters, he angled at as many tastes as he could perceive and kept diversity a prime factor in both the contents and their sequence.[4] Many reviewers noted this tactic, standard from the first for mass-circulation ventures. *The Innocents Abroad* never lingers on any subject or tone and sets up no insistent pattern to burden the memory of its reader, who was expected to enjoy its 651 pages in snatches. Since the reader was also expected to linger over the illustrations, Twain took his first step toward having a major say about them—this time "234 beautiful, spirited and appropriate engravings," according to the come-on prospectus.

For the one and only time, he would appear in them as a run-of-the-mill figure, dressed at the start in conventional coat and tie rather than some kind of Bret Harte costume.[5] The fundamental dialectic pitted Americans against the Old World. Although magazine and newspaper critics talked about a new California school of writers, a stereotype of real-life character had not yet been developed for the scatterings of people out beyond the Rockies. Or, to oversimplify, *Roughing It* had not yet been written. James M. Cox sums up the matter best while arguing that *Innocents Abroad* shrewdly and boldly reasserted a national viewpoint soon after the Civil War: it came across as by "an American who, among other things, had been in the West."

Besides prospecting for fresh customers, Twain already had an investment—as a freelance journalist and a rising star on the lecture circuit—in the poses associated with his pen name. As to which ones *The Innocents Abroad* features, several can be soundly demonstrated by quotations before being challenged with other passages. For example, both the anti-sentimentalist and his fervid victim have their innings. Today the dominant reading makes the narrator embody a zest for honesty to the facts and for spontaneous behavior and a scorn for smugness and putting on airs or—more broadly—genteel, middle-class ideality. However, the Abelard and Héloise section in chapter 15 rings with outraged propriety. Indeed the chapter runs a gamut of attitudes: Victorian democrat, lover of the picturesque, man of solid learning, experienced toper, irreverent egalitarian, naif, worshipper of virginity, moral vigilante, chauvinist, and then mocker of florid patriotism.

When the *Buffalo Express*, with Twain as part owner, reviewed *Innocents Abroad* it presumably followed his wishes, probably slanted more toward what he wanted buyers to expect than what they got. While cheering humor aplenty, the *Express* touted his homegrown independence of vision, the keynote of his Preface in which he promises to "suggest to the reader how *he* would be likely to see Europe and the East if he looked at them with his own eyes," and declares, "I am sure I have written at least honestly, whether wisely or not." Twain had approved of his publisher's idea for illustrating the title page: "What they *expected* to see—and what they *did* see." The text validated its genuineness of response through a contempt for faking by anybody—Europeans of all ranks, previous travelers, cowed Americans, and even the narrator in his stabs at parroting guidebook esthetics.

The passages ridiculing Twain's own posturing in effect redoubled his attack on phoniness. Although rather scarce, they stand out because he had already learned how to make himself the comic butt with a margin of burlesque that accepted his readers as insiders to the joke and, like his informal tone, bonded them to him. Here, including them in the explicit field of discourse took precedence over style or the dramatic illusion of a scene.[6] Careful not to let his persona turn owlish he once even invoked the "savage" rather than the long-honored "gentle reader." Ordinarily he addressed simply "you" or "any man" or "people" or, most revealingly, the "public"—signifying a wide and respectworthy level of opinion. On the subliminal level his irony created a more active bond of kinship; it was obvious and stable enough that most readers caught it, enjoyed a shared joke on anybody who might not, and felt intimate with the author's cast of mind.

The broad attitudes like patriotism that the narrator shares find matching company in some common blunders. He too had fallen for the guidebooks that gild the down-home facts. Established as an elder in the brotherhood of fools, he can admit his ignorance about such fancy words as "recherché" and even confess his awkwardness as a writer and his trouble getting the right proportions. Semiconsciously many a reader could imagine himself doing as good a job or better. Part of the vitalistic feel of *Innocents Abroad* comes from his vicariously sharing some of the active decisions in putting together an account that will please its customers. Through such psychology this author emerges as more human and credible than travelers who cope with syntax as urbanely as with problems of the road.

By admitting an eagerness to please, the author cut free from having to claim an elevated purpose. But pundits on the subscription trade believed that its clientele wanted some solid information to justify the time and money wasted on reading. Willingly, Twain obliged with volleys of fact, because his upwardly mobile side was committed to self-education. Furthermore, he understood that the public likes to find wisdom in a personality it identifies with. He gave it reasonable chances to perceive early that his narrator is a shrewd, keen-witted man of experience who deliberately chooses to play the fool, not always just to get laughs. For good measure *The Innocents Abroad* weaves in a strand of Victorian moralizing such as the advice that "setting oversized tasks" for a boy will "infallibly weaken . . . his confidence in himself, and injure his chances of success in life" (chap. 59). At subdued moments the narrator turns into a neocosmopolitan almost jaded by experience who can verify that "human nature appears to be just the same all over the world." Although the review in the *Cleveland Herald* called him a "laughing philosopher," he had stern opinions on the French economy or the Roman Catholic church. From the start Twain's submerged audience felt vaguely certain that his humor drove through to worthwhile substance.

To clarify this montage of personae flickering across uneven minds, it has been argued that the prospectus—a booklet with blurbs and sample pages and illustrations—is the best inventory of Twain's popularity. But the handouts of publishers have special angles. While prophetic, only press agentry as yet could excuse the claim that "no other writer has ever been able so fully to interest all classes and ages" as Twain, the "People's Author." Hamlin Hill judges the prospectus as accenting "fairly low humor and burlesque of sentimentality, highfalutin airs, and erudition" emanating, therefore, from a "raucously anti-intellectual" persona. It also promised, however, to improve the readers' "ability to judge between truth and fiction" about the countries visited. Journalists quickly learn the salability of the inside story, but sharper perception was being promised, not muckraking. With supporting excerpts from reviews, the several versions of the prospectus puffed outright "instruction" and even a "high moral tone" from a "fine family book."

The newspaper reviews give a more objective survey of the contemporary reader's reaction though they were distorted by their eagerness to boost a colleague. If anybody manages to track down the "twelve hundred complimentary notices" that the *Buffalo Express* had counted, that sampling will be richer than some national polls played up by the media today. If the total turns out to have been inflated by fifty or even seventy-five percent, what is left will still add up to a remarkable success in commanding the attention of the press. The reviews available so far galloped off in most directions; but at least they agreed somewhat about which passages to quote, such as the high musing about the Sphinx. Both Twain and his publisher quickly recognized that he had hit the right mix of profundity, exoticism, and pathos. Although modern sophisticates would like to disown it or reclaim its eloquence as parody, it evidently did Twain great credit and helped validate his tone as a Victorian sage. Other serious passages, particularly those contrasting democratic enterprise with Old World autocracy, were quoted but seldom tagged as memorable.

Three comic episodes got frequent mention. The first, a festive dinner for ten that cost a dismaying 21,700 reis (or $21.70), used Twain and his cronies as cub globetrotters innocent about rates of exchange. Some reviewers emphasized the boyish qualities of the narrator and his pals, cheerfully impudent and forgivably vulnerable to a shopgirl who rattles their poise. But that fumbling tourist in the fiasco of buying too small a pair of kid gloves can snap back with a respectworthy humor about his blunders and fits of petty anger. The episode about finding an ancient playbill in the Colosseum could originate only in a mind confidently capable of wild flights; that specific device—still a favorite in college humor—of describing antiquity in the latest slang could arise only from a smug modernism. This effect also underlay the most celebrated passages, the several raggings of the Italian cicerone who expected Americans to revere anything associated with Christopher Columbus.

Twenty-five years later, apropos of nothing, somebody in a lecture audience startled Twain with its punchline, "Is he dead?" The enduring appeal suggests that it twanged several lines of tension, such as tourist fatigue aggravated by the strain of foreign accents, irritation toward the obedience exacted by guides, an instinctual protest against decorum, and embarrassment that the discoverer of America could not speak English and hailed from a backward place. Perhaps because practical jokes verge on cruelty, Twain did not appoint himself the chief decoy for the guide. Still, the narrator of *Innocents Abroad*, who can storm vindictively before pulling up short, often steered farce into aggression and emerged as a skillful foolmaker, even foolkiller—here of those who "take delight in exciting admiration" from tourists through borrowed prestige. More generally, Twain was already perfecting a synthesis of the practical joke (which often entails some kind of deceit) and not merely the ridicule of pomposity but the exposure of "humbug" itself, either personal or collective.

Ragging the guides gained effect because it built upon a continuing routine. Although a single, brief passage, Twain's fit of weeping at the Tomb of Adam would prove to have a yet more impressive impact:

How touching it was, here in a land of strangers, far away from home, and friends, and all who cared for me, thus to discover the grave of a blood relation. True, a distant one, but still a relation. The unerring instinct of nature thrilled its recognition. The fountain of my filial affection was stirred to its profoundest depths, and I gave way to tumultuous emotion. I leaned upon a pillar and burst into tears. I deem it no shame to have wept over the grave of my poor dead relative. Let him who would sneer at my emotion close this volume here, for he will find little to his taste in my journeyings through Holy Land. Noble old man—he did not live to see me—he did not live to see his child. And I—I—alas, I did not live to see *him*. Weighed down by sorrow and disappointment, he died before I was born—six thousand brief summers before I was born. But let us try to bear it with fortitude. Let us trust that he is better off, where he is. Let us take comfort in the thought that his loss is our eternal gain. (Chap. 53)

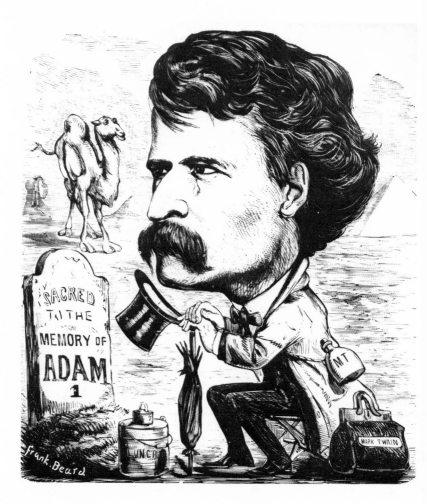

American Publisher (Hartford, Conn.), July 1872, p. 8

MARK TWAIN AT THE TOMB OF ADAM.

Harper's Monthly 50 (May 1875): 849

William Dean Howells' review would already refer to this as the "now celebrated passage." In 1876 Samuel "Sunset" Cox's *Why We Laugh* reproduced it as the acme of "serio-comic weeping and wailing," as the "humorous sublime." Twenty-five years later, a newspaper offered as a mock identification.

Who is Mark Twain? The man who visited Adam's tomb, the man who wept over the remains of his first parent. That beautiful act of filial devotion is known in every part of the globe, read by every traveler, translated into every language. Even the dusky savages of the most barbaric corners of the earth have heard of Mark Twain shedding tears at the tomb of Adam. By this time the ancient monument is fairly mildewed with the grief of Mark Twain's imitators.[7]

The lament deserves some of the explication lavished on less famous poems. Although preceded by a standard Twain paragraph of illogical logic, it comes after a gathering seriousness, and solemnity lies just ahead. Aside from comic relief and the recurring burlesque of guidebooks, however, it succeeds as a freestanding piece radiant with implications, starting from an indulgence in Byronic self-pity ("land of strangers") and phony excitement ("discover") on a worn trail. In spite of Twain's later complaint that too many readers believed he had actually wept, most of them must have caught a parody of sentimentality ("the grave of a blood relation" and "tumultuous emotion") and its bromides ("six thousand brief summers"), of pieties about "filial affection," and of funerary flapdoodle ("his loss is our eternal gain"). In the original newspaper text the mutual mourning was enriched by the modern regret that Adam "missed so much by dying young." No doubt Twain's contemporaries found fainter angles of meaning lost on us. His obituary in the *St. Louis Globe-Democrat* recalled a "denunciation of the pride of birth."

The core of the meaning lay in the daring burlesque of reverence itself. If not so sacred as the Biblical prophets, Adam ranked as a patriarch. Irreverence in the Columbus routine might slip by as genial fun, but many reviewers confronted it—with approval, edginess, chiding, or rebuke—in relation to Adam's tomb. Because the passage impinged on sensitive, ramifying values it became a birthmark of the often shifting, baffling Twain persona. The publisher of *Innocents Abroad* at first raised smokescreens over its subversive elements; he blurred his references to its "racy" or "spicy" tones by also promising enlightenment and even moral vitamins. But "reverent" or "irreverent" appeared in the reviews as often as any other key adjectives. Still tied to *Innocents Abroad* they cropped up in obituaries by newspapers as different as the *Springfield Republican* and the *Birmingham* (Ala.) *Age-Herald*.

The book did have its swatches of reverential antidotes. Whatever Twain's sporadic periods of faith, he had long since learned how low the threshold of indignation stood among the orthodox. In April 1868 his lecture dealing with the Holy Land raised a flurry of complaints about sacrilege. They help date his unpublished apology to a San Francisco minister claiming that he had "revered" the genuinely sacred places and had ridiculed only the "shams." By the time proofs for the book were ready he could share some of them with a devout fiancée, who must have expressed qualms. The breezy impudence turned a bit plaintive in the Holy Land chapters: "The commonest sagacity warns me that I ought to tell the customary pleasant lie and say I tore myself reluctantly away from every noted place in Palestine." His defensiveness never had sounder reasons. *The Innocents Abroad* "was in its very serious way a sustained act of irreverence and ridicule aimed at what many men still held in reverence, if not in awe."[8]

Ironically, expediency pushed Twain down the same road as his un-easily defiant convictions. As the profits mounted he exulted to his pub-lisher that the "irreverence of the volume appears to be a tip-top good feature of it." Between the literalist Christian majority and a sprinkling of skeptics hovered at least two sizable groups and an influential elite. The sale of *Innocents Abroad* indicates that many found Sunday school pieties duller than they might admit; they were matched by a layer of the genu-inely religious sophisticated enough to enjoy ridicule of lip service to some narrow creed. A chain of well-placed intellectuals disliked provincial dog-matism as a drag on mental or esthetic quality or, more grandly, "Culture." Scouting around for tolerance, Twain paid special care to reviews in the metropolitan dailies, urging for example that an advance copy go to the *New York Herald*. The result, he next judged, "will help the book along." After some ritual tut-tutting, the *Herald* sympathized with the narrator "forced to spend several weeks in the company of men whose highest delight is the singing of a psalm," obviously an ordeal for an American whose soul the Old World does not fill with "reverential awe" and who "merely insists on taking a comical view" that perpetrates nothing "so very irreverent."[9] For candidness the review ranked with a letter of recommen-dation.

The words "reverence" and "irreverence" were used well before their fourteenth-century baseline as identified in the Oxford English Dictionary, and they had continued to gain force. A concordance to Shakespeare will lead to revealing examples such as the *Cymbeline* passage on "reverence, That Angel of the world." For the nineteenth century the words still served in the arsenal of practical morality. Discussions of the underlying concept that did not cite classical or Biblical sources usually invoked Goethe's *Wil-helm Meister's Travels*, as Thomas Carlyle did in 1866. As for any idea widely current, the use of "reverence" often assumed that its transactional sense was clear to everybody. In broadest perspective it fell between "altruism," a left-leaning and do-gooder label, and "respect," which like "deference" or "esteem" too weakly implied a hierarchical order but which now comes closest to taking over for reverence, a casualty of World War I in its social mission.[10]

The secular usefulness of reverence had depended on a religious base that stayed firm, as in John Henry Newman's sermon "Christian Rever-ence"—which warned that Satan encouraged "scoffing" and the "light per-petual talk about him [a Twain habit] which is his worship." Near the end of the nineteenth century the eminent Phillips Brooks preached "The Wings of the Seraphim," in which reverence formed the chiefest virtue of a triad along with self-surrender and obedience. As an American he sadly admitted that his countrymen were the people most often accused of "inso-lent" irreverence—which even without the adjective had no champion on the plane of ideology, though ceremonial rhetoric abounded with tirades against a ranked society and haloes for a liberating rationalism. In *The History of European Morals* (1870), much admired on both sides of the At-lantic, W. E. H. Lecky, who conceded that false reverence could support "religious superstition and political servitude," classified reverence as the form of "moral goodness" to which the "epithet beautiful may be most emphatically applied." For everyday utility the *Cyclopaedia of Biblical, Theo-logical and Ecclesiastical Literature* (1879) defined it as a "submissive dispo-sition of mind arising from affection and esteem, from a sense of superiority in the person reverenced." So far not too oppressive but: "Hence children reverence their fathers even when their fathers correct them by stripes . . . hence subjects reverence their sovereign." Anybody who resented such ideas consciously or subliminally could get refreshment from *The Innocents Abroad*.

The principle of revering your superiors could work for social control by damping assertiveness or internalizing mores once enforced at the whipping post.[11] Of course the clique at the top of any system enjoy the awed deference; more important, it helps keep them on top. John Ruskin put the case too baldly in "The Future of England" during the same year Twain's book started its sweep. Alarmed at the rise of a class "now pecu-liarly difficult to govern," he lectured that the "lower orders" had lost the "very capability of reverence, which is the most precious part of the human soul"; still worse, "we have created in Europe a vast populace, and out of Europe a still vaster one [the New World?], which has lost even the power and conception of reverence." A prime culprit was the free education that the populace seek believing "they must become upper orders." In *Time and Tide* (1868) Ruskin had already declared "very sternly" that "a man had better not know how to read or write, than receive education on such terms." A footnote warned that "by steadily preaching against it, one may quench reverence, and bring insolence to its height."

Americans had naturally kept up on this vein of the anxious debate over democracy. Most notably now, Nathaniel Hawthorne joined it as *The Scarlet Letter* builds toward the climactic scene on Election Day. Behind a military escort come the "men of civil eminence":

Even in outward demeanour they showed a stamp of majesty that made the war-rior's haughty stride look vulgar, if not absurd. It was an age when what we call talent had far less consideration than now, but the massive materials which pro-duce stability and dignity of character a great deal more. The people possessed, by hereditary right, the quality of reverence; which, in their descendants, if it survive at all, exists in smaller proportion, and with a vastly diminished force in the selection and estimate of public men.

The passage proceeds to elaborate on "natural authority" founded by the "faculty and necessity of reverence." But Hawthorne then had a much smaller following than Josiah G. Holland, whose books of didactic essays would sell five hundred thousand copies. Sermonizing as Timothy Titcomb of *Lessons in Life* (1866), he found "nothing more apparent in American character than a growing lack of reverence. It begins in the family, and runs out through all the relations of society." He especially deplored the use of "light and disrespectful terms" such as "old Abe" for men of "place and position." Unsurprisingly, he would soon charge that Twain's content and tone were debasing the lyceums. Much of Twain's alleged paranoia simply reflected the real thing among his enemies.

His rise during the 1870s would encourage hotter charges that the United States bred a virus of irreverence, with its worst carriers the humorists—splendid in their "boldness," burbled Sunset Cox before feeling he should "reprehend" their "lack of veneration" if only because he ran for Congress every other year. Folk wit ordinarily shields a back row of irreverent wisdom, but the newspaper comedians had brought it up front. As Artemus Ward's reputation faded, Twain gladly took over the honors and risks of being ringleader. While promising a trusted adviser, "I *will* be more reverential if you want me to," he complained, "it don't jibe with my principles. There is a fascination about meddling with forbidden things." A Freudian may expatiate on immemorial totem and taboo, but Twain's contemporaries felt a threat to current establishment ways. In 1899 a high school teacher who was updating the literary pantheon could not help worrying if the "ignorant and irreverent person of vulgar tastes" behind *Innocents Abroad* was still the real Twain.[12] Until his death there was a touch of suspense whenever he was sounding reverential, and there must have been some relief at finally laying him in his grave.

Often at his prompting, reporters, whose trade inclined them toward irreverence anyhow, would continue to identify him with his first triumph. A regular complaint, which strikes modern taste as strange, was that his later books kept falling short of it. His ambivalence about its subversions therefore rebounded in other forms when he stared into the danger of looking like a has-been—a type he lampooned brilliantly. Also, as he prospered financially and intellectually, *The Innocents Abroad* began to seem crude. In 1904 he allegedly railed at it as "cheap, ungrammatical, and not fit for a gentleman's library"(†). But in 1908, before compromising on

"Stormfield," he wanted to name his last mansion "Innocents at Home" in honor of "my best-known book."

∗   ∗   ∗   ∗

The Innocents Abroad had also promoted his rising success along the lecture circuit though he calculated on a reciprocating action. In the fall of 1869 he urged his publisher to cook up "startling advertisements now while I am stirring the bowels of communities." Like *The Innocents Abroad* his lectures mixed froth with seriousness, which got the credit for pathos or bursts of eloquence. The reconstructed texts of the lectures do not catch the enveloping persona fully because, besides Twain's constant improvising, his delivery strongly affected the breadth of the recorded humor and the depth of any substance. Although the mere mention of strange places and customs probably sounded more educational than it was, the *Pittsburgh Commercial* (2 November 1869) reported that he had offered a "great deal of valuable information"—on the "habits of the people, the climate and volcanoes" of Hawaii—"interspersed with humorous passages." As a rule audiences overestimate the calories in an interesting lecture that made the time fly.

When still a newcomer on the circuit he clowned shamelessly. His offer to demonstrate cannibalism on a baby handed up to him excuses a reviewer for saying, approvingly, that Twain "sacrifices everything to make his audience laugh." A born showman, he loved to hear and feel the house roar. But to Mrs. Mary (or "Mother") Fairbanks, the middle-aged friend carried over from the *Quaker City* trip as an often ignored adviser on taste, he justified his instincts: "I *must not* preach to a select few in my audience, lest I have only a select few to listen, next time, & so be required to preach no more. What the societies *ask* of me is to *relieve* the heaviness of their didactic courses." Anybody condemning Twain's lectures as pop or pap culture should suggest how much to value the fact that they released an hour and a half of laughter in some dreary towns in gloomy seasons.

Less mercurial than in his sketches and book, his persona as lecturer became graphic in his physical manner, starting with a comic entrance. By 1868 he had a firm grip on a deadpan style that was not just impassivity but an "affected awkwardness and diffidence" or—said his friend and competitor Petroleum V. Nasby—a seeming "indifference" with a "deprecatory tone underneath." A highly artful damping of his normal ebullience, this style contrasted daringly with the current florid oratory punctuated by stock, almost menacing gestures. He set up a "sort of button-hole relationship" with the audience as he lounged "comfortably around the platform." That reviewer went on, "He is even willing to exchange confidences of the most literal nature," a sign that he would learn to convert his life into full-fledged public drama. Meanwhile, helped by his fraternizing with reporters, he was building the impression that a shrewd and "unaffected" individualist, as cordial as a blood relation, stood tall behind his antics and occasional tongue-in-cheek publicity stunts. The reporters could believe that the author of *Innocents Abroad* practiced the sterling loyalty its narrator shows to friends, no matter what anybody says against them. Overall, Twain had made so distinct an impression that the breed of his impersonators sprang up as early as 1868, probably.

Even before the splash of his book, Twain drew audiences surprisingly well. Growling that his lecture had bombed in New Haven, a hostile review conceded that "people clamor for a look" at him. Much of this clamor originated from reprintings of playful reviews and background stories by reporters with their own dreams of fame. A column, recopied with thanks to "the local of the Chicago *Tribune*," tried jocularity about "feet of no size within the ken of a shoemaker, so he gets his boots and stockings always made to order"; onstage Twain fell to "marching and countermarching . . . marking off ground by the yard with his tremendous boots."[13] Here the humor ignored fact, but only those who had already seen him would know that. It would take years for his description to settle down to reasonable accuracy—before starting a final cycle of respectful caricature based on his cues.

✳   ✳   ✳   ✳

That *Tribune* column began, "Mark Twain (Samuel G. Clemens) is a gentleman of some notoriety, and his effusions are constantly making the rounds of the press." Besides the Jumping Frog tale, his journalism from his western years was dug up and passed around while he supplied more copy. His heavy-handed newspaper map of the fortifications of Paris scored a lucky hit he coolly exploited through his new department in the *Galaxy*. In spite of such overlap he carefully distinguished between media: in the magazines "one takes more pains, the 'truck' looks nicer in print, & one has a pleasanter audience." He added the practical maxim that any writer who keeps cranking out copy will "tire the public, too, before long." From then on he would follow this principle, sometimes pacing his appearances in magazines as carefully as a Greek oracle.

For the *Galaxy*, a thriving monthly he rated "first class," he also hoped to get away from mandatory clowning. His first batch of "Memoranda" (May 1870) included magnificent tirades against snobbery ("About Smells") and racism ("Disgraceful Persecution of a Boy"). Still the *Galaxy* kept him alert to what it expected for generous pay by featuring the "Great Humorist" on its covers. Eventually the grind of deadlines dulled quality and the persona orchestrating it. However, the last full "Memoranda" (February 1871) ranged from literature to international politics judged by a compassionate, penetrating wit, as in his flaying of a fashionable preacher who had denied the supportive beneficences of a "ministry" in popular drama. The wrap-up verdict of the *Nation* that Twain had given "not very refined, perhaps, but on the whole harmless amusement to a large number of people" both reflected and encouraged a stereotype too narrow for the realities. The man behind the "Memoranda" established himself as clearly worth knowing, warts and all. In fact the persona of the newspaper and magazine writings, if taken collectively, would come closer to matching his public image than did that from his books alone.

Twain's decision in the meantime to buy into the *Buffalo Express* had resulted mainly from his plans to settle down with a bride. But the fact in itself of his becoming a part-time owner for $25,000 gave him a more substantial air. Besides, as he was determined to do, he went back into harness as a coeditor instead of an employee. He had picked his paper carefully, measuring his choices against the ideal of the "high-principled" *Hartford* (Conn.) *Courant*, whose owners—as they soon regretted—had turned down his feeler about buying in. The *Express* had to pass the test of a veteran reporter who in his old age still recalled the "deep shame" of working for the "washerwoman's paper" in San Francisco, the *Morning Call*. It is doubtful that Twain counted on using the *Express* to shape his publicity, though his mixture of idealism and insider's craftiness toward the newspaper world never stabilized. As an impassioned appeal to his future mother-in-law showed, he was looking for a more respectable career than full-blast comedian, one that would narrow the gap between his public and his private self, who—as suitor and then fiancé—was behaving more decorously than he had ever done or would do again. Flailing somewhat, Twain pleaded with her that "a private citizen escapes public scrutiny, & fares all the better for it—but my private character is hacked & dissected, & mixed up with my public one, & both suffer the more in consequence."[14]

During the months when Twain was trying hardest to reassure his fiancée's family, he must have stared with dizzying clarity into the gap between his showman's swagger and his parlor gentility. Still, basically delighted with how both his public and private lives were going, he intended to build the *Express* into a nationally quoted journal like Nasby's *Toledo Blade*. He laid out rules about elevating its tone by cutting back on garish adjectives and "thunder-&-lightning" headlines. At the enthusiastic start he ran off a variety of signed sketches—some highly political, others comic but pointed, a few limply farcical. He also contributed to the unsigned "People and Things," the *Express* caption for a then standard column of passing oddities, political jeers, bits of borrowed wisdom, and jousting with competitors. However, he did not work long or hard enough to add much to his reputation except the fact of having been a co-owner and editor, which at least the guild itself would remember well.

The money invested in the *Express* had come from the coal baron Jervis Langdon, father of the bride. Although Twain courted young Olivia in utter sincerity, a PR man could not have dreamed up a marriage that promised greater propriety. However, it also added to the Arabian Nights quality of the success of *Innocents Abroad*. Through the *Cleveland Herald*, run by her husband, Mrs. Fairbanks supplied details about the costly honeymoon house, and Twain spread the word to his old press cronies out west. Ambrose Bierce, never accused of a faint touch, started joking too harshly about Twain's long hankering for "some one with a bank account to caress."[15] Maybe referring more to book royalties, the manager for his lectures announced that the "fate of Midas" had led him to skip the winter season of 1870–71. As fillers about his affluence kept multiplying, he felt it necessary to demur to his sister that "we are not nearly so rich as the papers think we are." Sudden wealth excites more awe than envy, and Twain's admirers much preferred to see him rich—after having struggled, to be sure.

*   *   *   *

In October 1871 Twain's career started a new phase when the manuscript for *Roughing It* went to the typesetters and his residence shifted farther east to Hartford, Connecticut. Even after taking a loss on his *Express* shares, he could look back like a conqueror rather than a refugee. But he could also wonder just how he stood with the public. No pollster with a conscience could have pretended to give him a neat answer. The first biographical sketch meant to be serious (in *Frank Leslie's Illustrated Newspaper*, 16 July 1870) played up his adventures after being forced at the age of fourteen to earn "his own living, without the least assistance from anybody"; then it proclaimed him an "agreeable and accomplished gentleman." Twain knew that his image could fluctuate like the stock market and that some journalists considered it a joint property they helped keep saleable. The *New York Sun* (30 April 1870) was naturally quick to reprint a bogus anecdote from the *Comic Monthly* about his "Knowing Dog," who refused to let a newsboy give him a copy of the *Times* when his master preferred the *Sun*.[16] As a comic paragrapher Twain had himself played the game of harum-scarum invention to the hilt, and he watched it with tense-ness but not resentment.

The best vein of *The Innocents Abroad* had established a persona at-tractive for his brimming humor, spontaneity, honesty of vision, shrewd-ness, bulldog loyalty to his friends, and an irreverence that could rise into eloquently humane indignation. All these qualities took on force by op-erating through a somehow unified presence, to whom "we are required to accede authority . . . as the stylist of his own fascinating authorial per-sonality."[17] The route of escape from drudging as a madcap entertainer looks clear to hindsight. But in March 1871 *Mark Twain's (Burlesque) Auto-biography and First Romance* was issued along with planted rumors of or-ders for fifty thousand copies. Its three-legged stool fell flat, as it deserved to do. The account of his fecklessly criminal ancestors, one of whom hung from "Our Family Tree" on the title page, reinforced the crudest features of his image; it could explain why he soon wanted to destroy the plates. From the start, readers of the "Awful, Terrible Medieval Romance" have tended to feel that it deserves its burlesque title. The third leg, a cartoon sequence, satirized the Erie Railroad "ring" too minutely for casual amuse-ment. Only the hubris exposed in Twain's boast on 27 January 1871 that "my popularity is booming, now" could have lured him into this hurryup booklet aimed at diverging audiences.

Perhaps anxious about his blunder, he confided to his brother on 11 March: "I must and will keep shady and quiet till Bret Harte simmers down a little and then I mean to go up head again and *stay* there." Since he still looked up to Harte as a writer, the race that he imagined was for popularity, just as his schemes to hoist *Roughing It* into a "continental celebrity the first month it is issued" had royalties in view. So did his publisher Elisha Bliss, who fanned his anxieties in order to get quick help on the prospectus in April. Implying the ability of a syndicated columnist of today at detecting flutters in the mass pulse, Bliss noted gloomily that he did not find "as much of a desire to see another book from you as there was 3 months ago." No doubt this helped convince Twain, a day or two later, that the ebb tide had turned into a surge: "The papers have found at last the courage to pull me down off my pedestal & cast slurs at me—& that is simply a popular author's death rattle."

To the benefit of posterity, his self-confidence always sprang back. By 15 May 1871 he bragged, "My stock is looking up" with the "bulliest offers about books and almanacs" or "$6,000 cash for 12 articles, of any length and on any subject, treated humorously or otherwise." During the next ten years he would try many lengths on all sorts of subjects while often reasserting his autonomy and taking provocatively constructive positions. The effect would perplex those who needed to fix him into a neat frame. His admirers accepted him with pleasure, renewed surprise, and gratitude as more than a kindred spirit, as a brother under the skin.

CHAPTER 4

"The Mark Twain Mazurka"

THE MOVE TO HARTFORD was the sign of changes that would result in Twain's leading an impressively busy and mixed life embellished further by rumor. His expanding success would attract all sorts, from hustlers and also-rans to fellow artists, editors, fund raisers, and inventors. After September 1874 they swarmed to his new house, a monument to several of his images—self-made man, individualist, open-armed comrade, enigma, accelerating dynamo, and the pet of the goddess of luck. In 1871 a reporter for the *Brooklyn Daily Eagle* had overheard, "He's married three millions of money, and lectures for fun"; before the performance somebody else foolishly remarked, "He's got a baby that takes the humor out of him." With word of mouth helping the inventive press, fed by reporters competing for pay on the basis of column inches, catchiness far outran fact during the 1870s. Picking the most visible extreme, a friendly interviewer for the *St. Louis Post-Dispatch* in 1882 tried to set him going with, "The newspapers represent you as being fabulously wealthy, and as living in great splendor." Although he was already beginning to ignore such overdone cues, he had certainly helped to keep himself in the eye of the fascinated public and make it strain for a focus on his dizzying dance of word and gesture, reality and appearance.

Arresting inside and out, the new house was photographed or sketched frequently; Hartford soon used it as a landmark. It has often been treated as an eccentricity, something of a Twain joke on himself; a more specific cliché imagines steamboat motifs in the outside woodwork. But a fashionable architect designed it, and Olivia Clemens took pride in furnishing and decorating it while Twain soberly cheered her on. When a reporter for the *Boston Herald* added it to his select list of visits with authors he declared: "One perceived at once that its owner must be a person of naturally good taste and a devoted lover of landscape beauty." The detailed account had even stronger praise for the "library." Fortunately anybody can now judge the restored house for himself. Harder to judge is how the public, at second hand, pictured it then as part of the owner's personality, whether as evidence of his improving tastes or of the self-indulgence that sometimes galloped away with him. In January 1877 a magazine put out by a Hartford insurance company ran seven stanzas of a parody entitled "The House That Mark Built," describing him—among other things—

> *As a humorist not unknown to fame,*
> *As author or architect all the same,*
> *At auction or drama always game,*
> *An extravagant wag whom none can tame.*

Local readers understood those lines completely.

In the 1870s the top layers of Hartford lived smugly as a bastion of Puritan orderliness blessed by fresh wealth. Twain fitted himself in quickly, stirring up hardly more than the usual degree of clannish resistance. The *Quaker City* trip had given him pointers in behavior, needed after the raffish years out West, and the social amenities of lecturing introduced him to many a poised matron or an economic climber who had curried his manners. In moving up to the level of dresscoat Hartford he could feel he was merely regaining his parents' lost ground. Although his contempt for pretense would block either the appearance or fact of snobbishness and his lecture on the "American Vandal Abroad" lashed at those New World democrats "elaborately educated, cultivated and refined, and gilded and filigreed with the ineffable graces of the first society," this bear-hug for the complacency of his middle-class audiences still left much distance above the drifters in the mining camps with whom he swapped profanity and drinks. Especially proper types did wonder about the reach of his sociability, but they seldom confused him with his roughest characters.

The immediate neighbors among whom he settled his family belonged to an elite within the teeming camp of respectability. Justin Kaplan highlights their faith in a "dynamic aristocracy" and "their high responsibility, their earnest idealism, and their intellectual dedication." They are best understood as a vigorous side branch of the directorate of an American gentry, which for its blind spots and its panicky maneuvers (as it had to start retreating in the 1890s) earned the hostility that today goes with the epithet "genteel." Nook Farm, as this enclave was too pastorally called, tolerated unorthodox theories and put intellectual exchange ahead of formality. In basic patterns, however, it stood for moderation and stability. Actively in touch with the professional and literary cadres of the eastern cities, the Nook Farmers socialized locally with those businessmen and statehouse officials who shared their faith in the uplift that polite culture stimulated. Controlling the channels of stated opinion they stood watch on demagogues, fumed at both the irresponsible robber barons and butterflies of inherited wealth, and worried about shaping up the immigrants. They believed somewhat desperately that the standards exemplified by gentlemen and ladies would also teach the native populace to behave better and to choose politicians for their morality and character.[1]

Twain had liked Hartford from the first time he went there to confer about the publication of *Innocents Abroad*. While his wife, who had girlhood friends in Nook Farm, fitted quietly into its atmosphere of earnest striving toward ideals, the stories on Twain sometimes hinted at the dismay of his neighbors. The capable reporters, however, showed him as a voting-rights member who was developing into a prize exhibit of the enclave. He held his own in weighty debates of the Monday Evening Club for men and did more than his share among the clubs for ladies, young or portly. His speeches at spelling bees, his cavorting in amateur plays, and his contributions to Battle Flag Day or the Irish Famine Fund were more visible, that is, more newsworthy. Less welcome downtown but still bigger news were his caustic letters to the *Hartford Courant* about an unpaved street near his house or the spacing of the lampposts. Nook Farmers learned to realize that his influence depended on his humor and unconventionality but also that while his impulses could run wild he was privately conscious of his dignity. When some men out in the city organized Tom Sawyer's Gang and sent a mock-boyish dinner invitation signed—it said—in blood, he claimed to have other pressing business, but he probably took offense.[2] A British journalist whose Celebrities at Home series had snared many prestigious names came to Hartford just to see him. The interview, which American newspapers and magazines kept resurrecting for at least the next fifteen years, presented a gentleman of "calm directness and earnestness" fully at ease in his "charming" and "exquisite" mansion.[3] Only some other moods and masks saved him from rumors of going highhat.

At just as puzzling an extreme Twain sporadically reappeared in his role of buffoon. The naggings of self-respect aside, this raised fresh problems of how to shape his persona toward its better potentialities while capering, as he said of Artemus Ward, to "create fun for the million"— both of audience and profits. Giving up journalism had sharply cut his opportunities to use political or topical subjects. His age—he turned forty in 1875—made him less plausible for playing the blunderbuss who whines with astonishment when his behavior offends somebody. But a householder in Nook Farm could not swagger like a Westerner, and Twain's devotion to his wife drove underground the bawdiness which had no big market anyhow. While a pettily incompetent persona recurs throughout Twain's career, the 1870s brought some of his least attractive outings. The three McWilliams sketches about the baby's croup, a wife's panic over a lightning storm, and an erratic burglar alarm would prove that the irritations of a family man left a frame too small for Twain's dynamism. Only readers with a stark preference for the Twain of mindless play can now enjoy his biggest hit of this period, his "Punch, Brothers, Punch" based on a newspaper jingle. For adding a twist to a stanza of nonsense he got credit for later versions as its fad raged for months.[4] He milked his luck as long as possible, even entitling a booklet *Punch, Brothers, Punch! and Other Sketches* (1878). The linkage significantly added to the public's feeling that he shared its tastes, that he was as much a consumer as a voice of popular culture.

Looking ahead to *A Tramp Abroad*, he would have argued that he needed all the publicity he could get, since the income from his last three books had fallen short of his lusty expectations. Having banked on publishing by subscription, he accepted uncomplainingly its grubby realities. To a reporter who suggested that humor had stopped selling, he sounded resolute: "Is the writing that does not pay really humorous? . . . good writing of any kind always pays." Unlike some high-brow authors today, he rejected self-pity over the fact that the bound work of literature becomes a commodity submitted to the whims of the market. The tradition of the newspaper comedians included open, explicit admission of the desire to sell handsomely. Like Barnum, in his later dealings as publisher and as his own agent with the magazines, he never insulted the public for not buying what he thought it would like. On the other hand, accepting the status that the panjandrums of culture assigned to the subscription trade, he warned newcomers that the trade could promote "mighty few books that come strictly under the head of *literature*." Actually this understated the size of the saving remnant; besides *he* had raised the quality and prestige of the subscription tome. Still he offered no apologies for his basic mixture of topicality, information that looked more solid than it was, and unflagging entertainment. He would have smiled tautly at the agent for

Advertisement in endpapers of *A Tramp Abroad* (1880); first used as poster for *The Innocents Abroad* in 1869

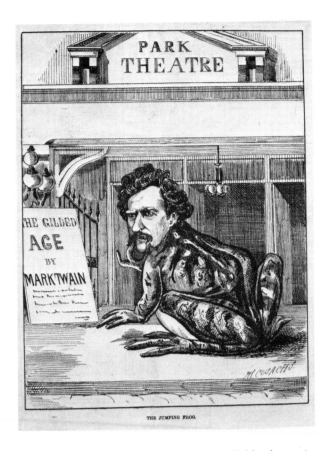

PARK
THEATRE

THE GILDED
AGE
BY
MARK TWAIN

THE JUMPING FROG.

New York Daily Graphic, 21 September 1874. Evidently an advertisement for the play that was soon retitled *Colonel Sellers* (copy from Mark Twain Project, Bancroft Library, University of California)

Tom Sawyer who sighed that Twain did not realize that her clients "were not the substantial kind he would like to have them."

He was also driven by fears that humorists face a short cycle of favor. On New Year's Day of 1871 a competitor already on the down swing wrote: "I am glad to see such evidence of your popularity, that augurs prosperity. The papers are full of you, from East to West and all delight in the genial Mark." But the chilling moral was to "make your hay while your sun shines." Re-alerted by such warnings, Twain judged a Bliss prospectus solely as a grabber for immediate results. In our time he would have tried test marketing. Evidently he did not squirm when Bliss concocted this silly blurb for *Roughing It*: "It is suited to the wants of the old, the young, the rich, the poor, the sad, and the gay." Intent on day-to-day soundings, Bliss never worried about a long-range, durable image for his prize author. At the back of *A Tramp Abroad* he resurrected an early poster for Twain's first book that had outshouted a pitchman at the circus: "The Most Unique and Spicy Volume in Existence . . . Large and Exceedingly Handsome Volume . . . Profusely Adorned . . . by Some of the Most Noted Artists in the Land." All this was centered on a Mark Twain in a mishmash of shirt-and-tie and Indian dress carrying a briefcase and tomahawk.[5]

He outdid Bliss, if possible, in the insistence on having "pictures enough" of any kind, preferably "eloquent." Unsatisfied with the decent sale of *Roughing It*, he blamed "mainly" the "engravings and paper." By the time he was ready to publish *A Tramp Abroad* he felt competent to recruit one of the illustrators. Later as his own publisher he did not need a reminder that his clientele expected his books to be "characteristically illustrated." Yet he accepted the pictures of himself casually. At first they were barely distinctive, partly because Bliss went for quantity over quality. Without aiming at detailed consistency from one volume to the next, they ordinarily dressed him in coat and tie. In *Sketches, New and Old* (1875) his face was noticeably lean for no good reason, and his eyes were sometimes styled as flashing with manic emotion. Four years later in *A Tramp Abroad*, however, some of the mainly nondescript drawings by at least five artists gave him a new degree of sedateness. The big change came in the frontispiece—an engraving from a stern-jawed photograph that clashed with the "war-path" ad. No doubt these extremes bewildered some readers while warning others to keep an open mind. Twain himself grinned when outside cartoonists took worse liberties with him, but he sat for his first oil portrait in 1876.

*   *   *   *

The same puzzling diversity of images weaved through his lecturing, especially as that evolved into a career as a public speaker. During his last full tour, the season of 1871–72, he drew much better than his second-level fees demanded. Sour about comic lectures, the *Danville* (Ill.) *Commercial* jeered that he could have cleaned up by charging twenty-five cents for the "suckers" who just wanted to look at him. No doubt his audiences preferred the relaxation of laughter far more than lyceum directors intended, and they spread the happy word ahead of him, almost by word of mouth. After considering even so bizarre (though latently anti-freedman and anti-

feminist) a topic as an "appeal in behalf of boy's rights," he kept falling
back on his old Sandwich Islands text for almost a hundred times until
December 1873.[6] His thinnest lecture, it projects a rover given to broad,
faintly risqué humor and quick at echoing smugness about primitive, dark-
skinned peoples. The best to be said for him is that he takes whatever
comes with a cheerful impudence which can flare into irreverence but die
back before committing a major offense. Twain was feeling his way, aver-
aging out the responses to a joke or just tone of voice, honing his routines
through an arm's-length, night-by-night course of trial and error that network television has now short-circuited. If the instances of a poor reception for his lecture made the public more dangerously perceptible than a
sit-at-home author can appreciate, the good nights fed his instinct to work
on developing a highly distinctive style. By the late 1870s he had earned
the wry experience of watching a young Hartford actor give impersona-
tions of two leading tragedians and him; the Twain part delivered the
Jumping Frog yarn with a heavy drawl. Even more startling than seeing
oneself on a home-movie, the performance must have stirred up as much
self-critiquing as vanity.

For the 1871 season Twain first switched to a sketch of Artemus Ward,
who had died in 1867. The most coherent of his scripts, it analyzed Ward's
deadpan delivery of outrageously loose-jointed humor—and therefore, in
a way, the very performance the audience was absorbing. Unsurprisingly,
metropolitan critics liked it better than small towners. His "Roughing It"
lecture went over more swimmingly everywhere. Its persona achieved Twain's
most effective combination, smoother than the American Vandals lecture,
of friendly jauntiness and superiority toward fools. Suspect of vices like
gambling at cards, the jauntiness professed a gusto for experience of any
kind, whatever the strain on dignity. On his other side the lecturer, never
owlish about his firsthand knowledge of Nevada, could satirize the complacency of lucky-strike miners who carried their "vast cargo of innocence"
to New York City and mistook a streetcar for a luxury-sized taxi. Overall,
straining less for stray jokes, this persona showed an ability to gauge human nature. More important, rather than loafing through the tropical islands of Hawaii he had taken a hand in hard work and danger in a bleak
terrain and had returned to mainstream society with his carefree spirit
strengthened. Twain projected manliness so naturally that most strangers
expected to meet a burlier figure. Likewise, among others, Everett Shinn
had the embarrassment, as late as 1900, of learning he had painted him far
too tall.

Reporters put more effort into playing up the "Roughing It" than
the Sandwich Islands lecture. Partly without ulterior motives Twain influ-

MARK TWAIN,
Too humorous to mention.

Graphic Statues (New York, 1876), no. 15 (by Theodore Wust)

enced many of the reviews because, while dreading the visits with local
dignitaries, he sought out journalists for conviviality and shoptalk; the
Chicago Post mentioned that he had spent two hours with them after finishing onstage. Other write-ups explicitly recorded his friendliness. Carried away by the offstage camaraderie, some undercut the broad virility of
the "Roughing It" persona with farfetched joking. Naturally these zesty
accounts were often reprinted, giving Twain's clowning still greater prominence than it deserved. The *Post* ransacked the fund of common similes

to cover the "lank, lantern-jawed and impudent Californian" with "nasal prow projecting and pendulous" who "bestrode the stage as if it were the deck of a steamboat" but also acted like an "embarrassed deacon" or "end minstrel man" or "disgusted auctioneer" or a "bereaved Vermonter who has just come from the death-bed of his mother-in-law, and is looking for a sexton"; and who furthermore rubbed his hands "like the catcher of the champion nine" and waved his arms "as if he were fighting mosquitos" but only managed to get "tangled in a bowknot."[7] Since Twain's manager quoted this burst of nonsense in his Lyceum Circular, its author had no cause for apology. Forthright respect for Twain's artistry as lecturer was rare until the news began flowing back in late 1873 that it had charmed London audiences. He had no corner on inconsistency, and his sniffiest critics at home tended, as hardcore Anglophiles, to jump through the hoop for British critics.

∗ ∗ ∗ ∗

When Twain "retired" from the lecture circuit in 1874 he was already beating his way to fame as a public speaker—"orator" would misrepresent his style. With relish he proved master of a stunning range of audiences, occasions, and themes. No group was too large or too small, too stodgy or boisterous for him to accept an invitation; no situation too minor or dismayingly visible; no proposed subject too serious or thin.[8] More diligently than his listeners cared to suspect, he never stopped refining a seemingly artless technique. Even after he was established as a leading author he would analyze oral performance much more consciously and astutely than the craft of writing. Supremely alert to the interplay with an audience, he tried to persuade himself to give up after-dinner speeches because they lie "miserably pale and vapid and lifeless in the cold print of a damp newspaper next morning." Although the biographers' fancy for the colorful stresses his few blunders, he set a superstar's average for hitting his target, whether it was his listeners' sense of humor or their feelings.

Some of the effectiveness his words lost in print was compensated for by the stories on how favorably audiences had responded. Still, his texts radiated enough of his humor and his evolving personality to command long quotation. To take extreme examples, in 1872 part of his speech to the Whitefriars Club of London appeared quickly in not only the *New York Sun* but also the *San Jose* (Calif.) *Mercury*; another London speech of 1873 could soon be enjoyed in the *Lafayette* (Ind.) *Courier*. After the *Cleveland Herald* reprinted yet another "after-dinner" from England, Mrs. Fairbanks wrote beamingly, "Everybody is watching you here." In 1877 the daughter of elderly Ralph Waldo Emerson assured Twain that he "has often asked us to repeat certain passages of 'The Innocents Abroad' and of a speech at a London dinner." The next year a British journalist judged that Twain's speeches "are probably read by a larger number of men and women in America than any public document, the President's message not excepted." Such exaggerations helped solidify the fact that he had already earned the greatest advantage of a speaker: the audience expected him to scintillate and itched to join the fun.

For years the passages that circulated through the press featured the wild jester, though alert readers noticed that Twain got invited to prestigiously serious functions too. His generosity with his time also stood out; even if he privately sniped at the eagerness of others to face an audience, it was obviously a good bet to approach him. Once on his feet he soared above pitfalls and clichés. He could honor a ceremonial affair without leaving a stuffed-shirt flatness, roar into eloquence yet come through as colloquial, ring the Liberty Bell but not too often or too long, play the family man while hinting at his masculine habits, wax personal yet squelch pomposity with self-ridicule. Above all he took chances, as with "The Babies" toast mainstage at the solemn Chicago tribute to Ulysses S. Grant or his repeated, sometimes acid irreverence at banquets honoring the memory of the Pilgrim fathers. Anybody who followed the reports of his speeches caught sight of a bold, rebellious spirit at the center of the pinwheel of clues.

More than his writings, the speeches kept scoffing at ossified piety, dull or plagiarized sermons, biblical fundamentalism, the doltish singing of hymns, and superficial notions of virtue. These assaults were mixed with a joviality that made it hard to isolate the offense of, for instance, his discovery from studying German that he had always mispronounced "dammit." Religion aside or apparently so, he joked about enjoying sherry cobbler or plain whiskey, winning at faro, or incorrigibly bending the truth. As for profanity, he grew into a connoisseur of its vividness, implying an esthetic scale that grittily reasserted its vitality as a folk art. He did control his liking for off-color or "blue" lines, and a quick gag that Jim Wolfe and he had "slept together—virtuously" as boys went no further than a stag dinner for an art magazine. When toastmasters assigned the topic "Woman" to him, he fine tuned his wit or eloquence to the situation. Nevertheless, before and after *Joan of Arc*, he would intimate the hollowness of the current myths about female wispiness and naiveté, so that his oratorial persona got credit for having a somewhat sharper knowledge of the ladies than did Twain the novelist.

An intriguing thread in the early speeches is the joking about ances-
try, starting with his own. Evidently he had often felt déclassé, particularly
during the Nevada and California years. Perversely, for introducing himself at lectures back east, he chose to invent a forebear whose hanging had
come off "very comfortably," though the sheriff's "speech was annoying."
Whatever Twain's tensions about lost status, his obvious fabrication laughed
at taking pride in the family tree. By harping on Adam as a blood relation
who should head any list of toasts because he was a "good husband at a
time when he was not married . . . and would have been a good son if he
had had the chance," he scoffed at pretentious genealogies and ridiculed
our common stock to boot. Sometimes, getting close to his adopted home,
he claimed a Puritan line while confessing its misdeeds too. In 1881 his
speech to the New England Society of Philadelphia went at the Pilgrims
as a "hard lot" who "took good care of themselves" but "abolished everybody else's ancestors." Demoting himself back to a "border-ruffian" from
Missouri, he also traced his line to an "early Indian" ("Your ancestors skinned
him alive, and I am an orphan") and to persecuted Quakers. The Pilgrims
"gave us religious liberty to worship as they required us to worship, and
political liberty to vote as the church required." Having already exhumed
ugly historical fact, he probed harder. "The first slave brought into New
England by your progenitors was an ancestor of mine." The intricacies of
friendly abuse get private and opaque for the parties involved. But the
onlooker who enjoyed such passages had to reduce whatever awe he paid
to dignity based on lineage and consider Twain a leveler in spite of his
fancy residence.

However complicated subliminally, friendly insult can establish the
aggressor's standing as an equal or insider, a leading motive behind the
once notorious speech at the *Atlantic Monthly* dinner staged in December
1877 to honor John Greenleaf Whittier. More particularly Twain asserted
that, as a fellow author, he had close, easy knowledge of the work of Emerson, Oliver Wendell Holmes, and Longfellow. After several newspapers
condemned his oral sketch about three tramps who crudely impersonated
those saints, he sometimes professed guilt, encouraging the view prevailing today that he had slipped into aggression driven by self-hatred for
courting the favor of New England. His sketch did implicitly contrast its
literary visions with the stinking grittiness of a mining camp. But, having
prepared for the occasion in good faith, he insisted, "My purpose was
clear, my conscience clean." His mind had focused on evoking incongruity,
the basic ingredient of comedy, fully aware that he was expected to shine
for a gathering of old pros. As he groaned to Howells, he had intended

"no disrespect toward those men I reverenced so much." He may even have thought that the punchline asking whether he too was an imposter left him the butt of his fantasy.

He had constructed the wrong kind of narrator for his sketch. Instead of a disarming naiveté or an imperceptivity too dense to resent, the miner who complains about the three tramps has a lively mind and sarcastic tongue. But Twain's chief mistake was to have missed the hidden agenda for the dinner and therefore get swamped by the tide of "reverence," the telltale word in the overt reactions.[9] It appeared prophetically in an open letter of regrets from Josiah Holland (who thanked the guests in advance for helping to "save the American nation from the total wreck and destruction of the sentiment of reverence"), in Twain's peroration, in Joseph Twichell's diary, in hostile editorials, and in a long letter to the *Springfield Republican*, which closed: "American social life . . . is in the formative period, and, jealous as we might have been of our political honor, a thousand times more jealous must we be of that most precious possession—reverence for that which is truly high." Twain's apologies, which included his now famous defense of himself as God's Fool, rang sincerely. After all, he *had* failed to warm up the house and give a welcome break from the encompassing fog of tributes. Still, his speech "Plymouth Rock and the Pilgrims," and other mocking comedy, came in the years immediately ahead. At a breakfast for Holmes in 1879 he stepped cautiously but stayed humorous, in colloquial language. Alert Twain-enthusiasts would decide that, as Jack Burden says of the judge in *All the King's Men*, "he hadn't scared." Free of self-depreciation, Twain's last sentence would shake hands with the *Atlantic* coterie as "my fellow teachers of the great public."

*   *   *   *

For the moment, the imbroglio did reactivate his fears of overexposure. He had enough inside experience to know how boredom can lead the newspaper wits to "blackguard" an old favorite. He advised Joel Chandler Harris to space the Uncle Remus tales three months apart, "for the ficklest people in the world are the public." But he also worried about sinking out of sight and not bobbing up again. Encouraged by wishful thinking, the umpires of taste were warning humorists that their night always falls early and fast. So he vacillated between trying to stretch out his season and making hay while his sun beamed. Either attitude supplied a rationale for seeking plenty of publicity after all. P. T. Barnum, spotting his eagerness at the game of hoopla, regularly proposed some kind of deal. Perhaps the Great Barnum had noticed Twain's comic endorsement in 1873

HARRIS & MOXLEY,

DEALERS IN

White & Fancy Goods,

SEWING MACHINES, &C.

12 Main Street, New London, Conn.

J. Emerson Harris,　　　　　　　Francis G. Moxley.

(Also used during the 1870s by a firm of "Plumbers, Steam and Gas Fitters")

of a fly and mosquito net; he must have wondered, as we do, how much Twain encouraged the tobacco premiums carrying his picture, the lithograph portrait given away by a "white and fancy goods" merchant, the stereopticon slide of him at work that was for sale, and the "Mark Twain Mazurka" published as sheet music and "dedicated" to the "Celebrated Mark Twain Cigars."[10] As early as 1873 he started pushing a trademark rather than copyright approach for protecting his name and writings from piracy.

In enough instances he so obviously strained after publicity that his showiness became in itself a stronger feature of his image. The very day after that comic-opera description of him as lecturer, the *Chicago Post* displayed Twain's mock protest, which set up a playful apology from the reviewer. In the fall of 1874, with long-distance walking still a fad, he persuaded Joseph Twichell to set out with him on a heroic hike; maybe his pastor-crony did think they could cover more than a hundred miles in three days. Well ahead, Twain telegraphed the plan to his lecture manager, who naturally gave it to reporters, who liked the humorous possibilities. The mutual hopes were fulfilled. After going a third of the way the footsore hikers ended up on the train to Boston, where Twain bantered with reporters, one of whom worked for the new Associated Press. When Twain pretended that they had given in so that Twichell could fill a date to preach, a New York City paper was quoted in the "exchanges" with, "We suspected that saving soles was at the bottom of it." The exchanges—a term for not just the out-of-town journals that came into the office but the choice items lifted from them—also featured the *Boston Transcript*'s puns because Twain confessed to hitching a ride on a hay-wagon: "Mr. Clemens extends no clemency to those wicked wags who trifle with his name and profess to find a marked wane in Mark Twain since his pedestrian failure. It was a marked wain indeed which had the honor to pick up that marked twain." Twichell's diary recorded that the affair caused "no end of talk." He pasted in clippings not only from Boston and Hartford but also from a Scranton, Pennsylvania, paper as well as the *Windham County* (Conn.) *Transcript*. Far from feeling used, he enjoyed the episode immensely as typical of the unpredictable twists associated with Twain, whose lecture manager liked this tie-in with the clergy. That manager, certainly with Twain's blessing when not with his collusion, was always diligent at feeding items about his star performer into the exchanges.

The next summer Twain surely expected that editors would fancy his letter advertising for an umbrella stolen at the "great baseball match" in Hartford. He offered five dollars for his property; for the suspect, a "small boy," he offered nothing if "in an active state" but two hundred dollars for his "remains." These passing stunts tended to highlight his manic side. A few months later, as a way of donating an autograph to a benefit for the Massachusetts Infant Asylum, he proposed to join a "thousand citizens who shall agree to contribute two or more of their children." Soon, "bitter" toward the Society for the Prevention of Cruelty to Children because "I have a baby down stairs that kept me awake several hours last night," he growled that he would not donate anything—of course doing so in the process and inspiring the paradoxical headline, "Why He Didn't." Curiously, such letters brought together his worst caperings and his Nook Farmer's "earnestness" about social problems. More provocatively, he yarned to a reporter about organizing an expedition to fix the "exact location of hell." The interviewers, incidentally, had started to hound him.

Some outbursts genuinely radiated the irrepressibility that ran to the heart of his private as much as his public character. Describing his parlor manners during the seventies and eighties, Howells affectionately recalled that Twain was "in some respects, and wished to be, the most outrageous creature that ever breathed." His gambits in print were so open that not just his faking but his mock clumsiness at faking added more layers to the fun, as with Mark Twain's Patent Scrap Book. His letter to his manufacturer was obviously aimed at the press; its disclaimer that he had invented the self-pasting gimmick "not to make money . . . but to economize the profanity of this country" was too blatant for hypocrisy. Exulting soon that the papers had toyed with the Scrap Book "all the time for months," he planned a "10-cent advertising primer"—a book of his writings to plug one without words. For it he executed a "Certificate" that "during many years I was afflicted with cramps in my limbs, indigestion, salt rheum, enlargement of the liver, & periodical attacks of inflammatory rheumatism complicated with St. Vitus's dance" until starting to use the Scrap Book. Any indictment that he peddled his dignity at cut-rate prices can rest on the Certificate, reproduced in his handwriting next to three pages of ads for the Scrap Book's seven sizes purchasable in twenty-eight variations. Even at twenty-five cents, however, the "primer"—*Punch, Brothers, Punch! and Other Sketches*—gave the public a bargain of 140 pages that included some worthwhile writings. (Today it commands a collector's price impressive by any standard.)

As "Mark Twain," selling out his dignity was still part of his business, but for nineteenth-century humor an effective "sell" cast glory for shrewdness on its manager. Also, far more visible than Twain's ill-fated mechanical typesetter, the Scrap Book would last as his most profitable business venture during his lifetime; the patent was worth updating as late as 1892. A steady moneymaker, its promotional leaflet soon boasted a medal from the

1878 *Exposition Universelle Internationale* in Paris; the leaflet also quoted the *London Daily News* as recommending the Scrap Book—appropriately to both parties—for newspaper clippings. More generally, the hucksterism was dimmed by the perception that Twain shared the enthusiasm for inventions and modern conveniences. Thomas Edison—just as much attuned to PR—and Twain discovered each other early.

No doubt Twain welcomed a clever pseudo-review, in so self-regardful a monthly as *Scribner's* (April 1877), which treated the Scrap Book as an autobiography.[11] While of course resenting solemnly faked facts that cut too close, he generally endured the jarrings of slapdash wit as a necessary evil. After the story that he had paid for a banquet in his honor circulated too often to let it pass, he denied it with poise, adding, "Where I was born they always hang a man who can't take a joke." With more columns of newsprint needing fillers every year, the countless paragraphs about him got reprinted at least as widely as their cleverness deserved. The press expected his full help. When the Clemens family returned from abroad in September 1879, the reporter from the *New York Times* turned grumpy because the "joker by profession and reputation . . . the pilgrim who was moved to tears while leaning upon the tomb of Adam" ignored the straight lines fed to him. The obituaries would prove how well Twain had succeeded at charming the press, but the ups and downs could mislead an editor so capable as E. W. Howe of the *Atchison* (Kans.) *Globe*, who grossly exaggerated on the last day of 1881: "Mark Twain's career is nearly at an end. The paragraphists have commenced to pelt him, and they will finish him before they get through."

Instead they built up a fund of stories that would resurface, often for no evident reason, during the rest of his life—river yarns, dusty anecdotes from the West, Hannibal lore that flourished as Tom and Huck grew famous, and fresh byplay in Hartford. The phony items outdid Twain in playing upon his ebullience. "Soliciting Mark Twain's Subscription," in the *Boston Transcript*, had him tantalize a book agent (of all people) for six hours before sending him away famished for both his lunch and a sale. In 1880 "A Few Epitaphs," which, bafflingly, would be resurrected when Twain started his world tour, staged him as sobbing while he declaimed his favorites in obituary poems like "By His Barkeep." Still cruder were three interviews in the *New York Sun*. The first (22 October 1876) opened with a description of his house as "architecturally midway between a medieval church and a modern game of baseball," and left him riding a mustang while shouting "Woe! woe unto Israel!" With details carried over, the second (26 January 1878) sketched him almost as wildly, named his book in progress as "The Mother-in-Law in All Ages," and ended with him

An advertisement for Mark Twain's Patent Scrap Book

exclaiming, "It is time for me to begin to gum" (the Scrap Book). "The Lookout of the World" (28 June 1881) had him spending his nights on the roof, vigilant to fend off the tail of an erratic comet with a pole.[12] In composite, the three sketches created a loony eccentric, though an analytic reader could also glimpse a householder with literary and scientific interests. The *Sun* meant no personal offense. Twain's image fluctuated so widely that third-rate humorists assumed he would welcome any sort of publicity or at least grant he was fair game.

*   *   *   *

As yet, the strongest direct source of his image continued to be his own writing—variegated in theme, uneven, fitful but growing substantial in amount. Appreciation of its collective impact must attend to more than the scattered reviews, must for example judge between the importance of his newspaper and magazine work. The latter, better known today, reached a much smaller audience, whereas his topical "A Curious Pleasure Excursion" ran in the *New York Herald*, then the best-selling newspaper in the world. The average reader, however, scans the dailies more quickly and less retentively than a monthly periodical, which goes to a higher percentage of opinion-makers. A sound estimate of Twain's reception must also confront a literary archaeologist's kitchen midden of reprintings and excerpts in prominent or bizarre, almost hidden places, ordinarily without his permission. His image benefited somehow from another source now distorted by both nostalgic charm and Sinclair Lewis's mockery—the parlor elocutionist. By the mid 1870s, judging from the cheap booklets of "Recitations" for sale, Twain's sketches were being declaimed semi-privately, doubtless as a relief from the preachy or esthetic part of a program.

Throughout his lifetime some of his denigrators refused to let him expand beyond the limits of newspaper humorist. For the 1870s that might still seem fair enough. In *Why We Laugh*, Sunset Cox meant well in placing Twain at the head of the tribe "with their spicy dialogues, practical jokes . . . little jets of fun." He steadily got offers to churn out such material and would have accepted more of them if his wife had not wrung her hands over his being "so persistently glorified as a mere buffoon." But while backsliding often, he moved far toward establishing himself, much sooner than his uncritical fans could realize explicitly, as relevant to substantive and national trends of ideas. In *Mark Twain as a Literary Comedian* (1979), David E. E. Sloane explains how his humor outlasted the hundreds of competitors because it more and more addressed the situation of the swell-

ing urban classes, took up the frustrations posed daily by large-scale organization which was engulfing them faster than they consciously realized,
and implied a fresh ethical system that fitted their own readjustments to a
corporate society. To be sure, we find his humor incomparably better written insofar as manner can be separated from matter.

Twain would have piled up a memorable body of squibs, editorials,
and topical articles for the post-Greeley *New York Tribune* if he had not
quarreled bitterly with the editor on private grounds. For those who prize
Twain as a fool-killer, he twice blistered the corrupt Shipping Commissioner of the Port of New York. Throughout the 1870s he kept firing away
on political subjects; while recognizing they were another sort of game
and another "sell" on public opinion, he saw socially important stakes.
Most notably he gave the *New York Herald* a staged interview supporting
Rutherford Hayes for president, then made a speech the *New York Times*
printed on the front page and seconded with an editorial, soon rebutted
by the *Boston Transcript*. The most partisan of his campaign orations, for
James Garfield in 1880, was soon followed, happily, by a victory speech
loaded with meat-axe irony. To the sharp eyed, Twain's civic commitment
shone forth, distinct from while indirectly affirmed by his burlesques of
sham fury from the politicos. In 1878–79 he mounted two suggestive items
in his patented scrapbooks: a filler sentence observing that among American humorists "MARK TWAIN especially has hit hard at the errors of
public opinion and the dishonest compromises of custom," and an editorial from his old *Territorial Enterprise* mistakenly welcoming his return to
running a "semi-political, semi-humorous newspaper." "Semi" was not half-
bad. Nobody would demote Twain's humor to merely an incidental quality
until decades after his death.

Like any professional writer, he measured the status of his outlets
carefully. Then far more than now, when the articles primarily form a bas-
ket for the ad spreads, moving up from the newspapers to the major magazines confirmed a large step toward belles lettres. The "awful respectability,"
as Twain phrased it, of the *Atlantic Monthly* marked the very top. After the
Whittier dinner the *Worcester* (Mass.) *Gazette* threatened that another offense "would cost Mark Twain his place among the contributors . . . where
indeed his appearance was . . . considered an innovation." The "would"
merely let off steam; Howells was still editing the *Atlantic*, and the reality
of how his business office valued Twain did not justify so much as a "could."
Furthermore, New England had the usual human variables and the on-
rushing generation that found its elders passé as models. Although Brah-
min enough in background and civic record, Sylvester Baxter of the *Boston
Herald* evidently believed that Twain belonged among the standard

authors. His at-home piece in 1880 stressed the "merciless" criteria Twain applied, often destroying a "whole day's labor as soon as it is written." Since this essay was quoted often in the decade ahead, it may have originated the notion common during his later years that he composed painstakingly; the image of a treacherously facile or divine amateur owes most to critics after 1920. Baxter closed with a tribute to Twain's qualities of heart and mind, such as an ethical fervor that "embitters beyond anything but laughter," lifting him above the swarm of comic journalists.

Just passingly unnerved by the Whittier dinner, Howells combined loyal friendship with priceless editorial advice. He virtually extorted "A True Story," a no more than lightly humorous melodrama about slavery, and his coaching deserves some of the credit for "Old Times on the Mississippi," treasured now as Twain at his high-riding best. Likewise, Howells either inspired or accepted Twain's most thoughtful sketches during these years: "The Curious Republic of Gondour," "The Great Revolution in Pitcairn," and "Edward Mills and George Benton," all with a firm, sociopolitical thrust. Still, the *Atlantic* gained as much from publishing Twain as he did, and it gave the more ground. His relief that it "don't require a 'humorist' to paint himself stripèd & stand on his head every fifteen minutes" can cloud the fact that it also carried some of his forgettable comedy: "The Canvasser's Story" about collecting echoes, "Mrs. McWilliams and the Lightning," and "The Loves of Alonzo Fitz Clarence and Rosannah Ethelton," which tried to have it both vapid ways with a courtship conducted by (the then rare) long-distance phone. Twain did tone down his physicality, his guffaws over the corruptions of the body: "Some Rambling Notes of an Idle Excursion," about the Bermudas, omitted a detachable yarn that is known now as "The Invalid's Story," a pungent mix-up between a corpse and a crate of limburger cheese. However, "Some Rambling Notes" heaved in a garish tale of soon-to-be corpses jockeying over a coffin. Anybody so refined as to read only the *Atlantic* got pretty much the total impact of Twain.

His next main book of sketches put "The Invalid's Story" back in. For that matter, the earlier *Sketches, New and Old* (1875) supplied a full cross-section that should have warned his admirers as well as his detractors to stay nimble. It included political satires from the *Buffalo Express*, an onslaught against racism from "Memoranda," the humane "A True Story," and "Some Fables for Good Old Boys and Girls," rejected by Howells for fear of offending the orthodox. These pieces in which the comedy digs down to substance had the dubious company of, at the emptiest, the flailing "My Watch," a longer farce about lightning-rod salesmen, a marathon pun about Twain stealing chickens ("To Raise Poultry"), and the loutish

"Curing a Cold." Overall the sympathetic reader could infer a Twain on whom nothing was lost, neither the speech of illiterates and crude folkways nor the experiences of an editor, traveler, secretary to a senator, and a householder familiar with decorous culture; yet a Twain altogether un-Jamesian, feisty toward pious constraints, and kinetically responsive. For a British critic his secret was a "tolerably open one. He is always wide awake, therefore he keeps you awake." Through a longer glass, however, *Sketches, New and Old* too often suggests a Twain committed to easy stereotypes and routines, reassuring the millions that a bond of taste lay beneath his zaniest or touchiest humor.

While less distinctly so than today, Twain's purely literary image was, during the 1870s, still rooted in the original books directed at the subscription trade. Focus that neglects his extra-literary activities has at least led to excellent analyses of the mock-author who lay behind those books and often inserted a Mark Twain into the narrative, a persona given to doubling on himself as he leaps off the page in an elusive chase. Because of Twain's quicksilver genius, disagreements will always continue. He shifted levels of discourse, switched masks so smoothly that the mind easily fails to count one or more. He shifted so often that only the dogmatic can always determine whether a given text blurs into a mishmash or coalesces into a tour de force. Nevertheless, some lines of analysis converge toward a consensus.

In *Roughing It* (1872) four main factors complicated, pleasantly, the impression made by the predominant persona. First, even without cues from the prospectus, the memory of *Innocents Abroad* disposed readers to find and like another irreverent, carefree individualist whose "Prefatory" promises the truth about his "variegated vagabondizing." Second, the author behind this persona was again openly eager to please while now and then implying he had only amateur standing; constantly changing the mood, he mixed in plenty of danger along with his dreams of sudden riches, and he spun tall tales and "sells" incorrigibly.[13] This last habit, combined with a zest for stretching any fact handy, went far toward solidifying Twain's reputation as a "liar," which he steadily enhanced thereafter with multiplying layers of irony. Third, *Roughing It* lay claim to some degree of substance as a rare inside account of Western mining life and the distant Sandwich Islands. Fourth, it took on a mythic aura by anticipating many psychic appeals of what would become the formula Western and its underlying dialectic between a civilized and a frontier culture.[14] Breathing with personality for those who felt no need to sort out their reactions, *Roughing It* cut in more directions than any single reader could coordinate.

The latest analyses center on Twain as a tenderfoot who invites ridicule while establishing the point that he survived to become an old-timer. But that pattern should not cloud the success story of the I-narrator, who eventually acquired a wide knowledge of the world, a certain standing and income back east, and an educated wisdom with a right to opinions on weighty matters.[15] To this should be added, again, the instinctive élan of most of Twain's writings. With no way to foresee how the phrase might strike the 1980s, Howells asserted that *Roughing It* first revealed Twain's sense of life as "a vast joke." The review in the *Overland Monthly* made the point more handily for our not confusing the narrator's past and present states of mind and for our appreciating both his vibrancy and his social thrust; it praised his humor for "its spontaneity and naturalness, together with an underlying element of sturdy honesty and rugged sense, antagonistic to sentimentality and shams." Perhaps Twain's contemporaries did not realize how deeply they appreciated *Roughing It* for implying a positive triumph over human inertia and the obstacles of history.

The *Gilded Age* (1873) linked his reputation with Charles Dudley Warner, just coming into prominence as a mildly amusing essayist. Twain's name was gathering such force, however, that he got most of the credit for the best passages, as he in fact deserved. For better or worse, parts of *The Gilded Age* also linked him with the socially respectable school of sentimental romance, that is, novels working within the conventions of chaste love plots and of moral fortitude blessed eventually with dollars. Elsewhere, besides the expected humor, it bristled with alertness to social and political corruption, dramatized with anger rather than cynical amusement. Its anger was acceptable, indeed praiseworthy, because it fed on proto-Populist attitudes: anxiety over the health of American democracy beset by the citified millionaires and waves of immigrants, resentment at the ballooning federal bureaucracy and corporations, fears that the efficiency of criminal justice was faltering, and nostalgia for the ethic of hard work. When the fans of Twain's travel books registered these aspects of *The Gilded Age* and others, such as its contempt for high society in the Capital, they had to admire his stretch for theme and genre. Then he devised a play with the same title that thickened his aura of versatility. For years the visionary, blithe Colonel Sellers seemed to have talked his way into the circle of immortal American types. Gradually, however, his likable sides merged into the image of Twain as either an incurably expansive spirit or just a courtly Southerner.

An unplanned book got into the act when a Canadian "pirate" saw that Twain's seven "papers" for the *Atlantic Monthly* between January and August 1875 added up to a compact, salable unit. Ironically, "Old Times on the Mississippi" is the most charming of all his I-spokesman narratives. Furthermore, it not only gave his pen name a native source, obliterating the British undertones, but also founded it upon the world of work, however romantic the circumstances. While the very fact that the papers had run in the *Atlantic* gave them status, they had their own core of sobriety: the cub pilot does persevere through a training that scours away his naive cockiness and demands competence in a trade more disciplined than prospecting for silver and more responsible than traipsing around the Holy Land as a journalist. This practical thrust was softened by the exoticism of a vanished, gaudy era on the mighty river and by the lone-eagle authority of its pilots. Above those perspectives hovered almost faintly a Hartford Twain now successful and cultured enough to comprehend them through a benign humor, which very much included his young self. Magically, it all came together, associating his name with a genius for superb entertainment that nevertheless left a sense of weight, if only as a historical record. The Canadian publisher had done Twain a favor with the public that he naturally failed to appreciate.

The public overrode Twain's waffling about whether *The Adventures of Tom Sawyer* (1876) aimed at children or adults with the grateful answer of "both." For the long run the book's magic established his trust fund of youngsters dazzled by his empathy with their fondness for disguises and their daydreams of confounding their keepers or basking in glory. Some were just as delighted by its intimations of a reality contradicting the literature prescribed for them, by its—as one recalled—patches of relatively unstilted, "life-like dialogue" or the Sunday school episode that "threw a new light on similar proceedings."[16] The adults could surrender with honor to the counter-current of nostalgia because it blended humor and self-indulgence through a narrator "fondling yet patronizing the world he evokes," a pleasant yet sleepy village with whose oldsters they need not identify themselves.[17] To all ages Twain, more seductively than ever before, intimated that the secret of coping was play, the spirit that burst through the workaday routine or reduced it to feckless confusion. Within these dominant patterns the implied author raced up and down the scale of voices, which could clash when sounded too close together, as at the opening of chapter 33, where he could swiftly be imagined to be irreverent or passably devout, antisentimental or boldly the opposite, folkminded or genteel, a learned ironist superior to clichés or a peddler of melodrama, a compassionate humanist or a devotee of crass success. In a review plugging *Tom Sawyer*, the ethically intense Moncure D. Conway bracketed its extremes by extending its appeal all the way to "poets and philosophers"—or Romantic fantasy and Victorian wisdom.

The least challenging of Twain's travel books, *A Tramp Abroad* (1880) made a much tamer effect than *The Innocents Abroad* though the prospectus naturally advertised a matching continuity. Without deserting to the other side, a stronger respect for European traditions and an underlying cultural relativism softened his screaming-eagle note. In fact the preface he discarded because it did not fit the contents implied that he needed to get away from the shabby underside of the New World. Explicitly, it had professed his intention to have a "good time . . . a satisfying, comprehensive and elaborate holiday"—a spirit more or less achieved in the adventures and the loose structure of the book. The finest passages are detachable yarns between which the rest of the text straggles like a windbreak. Its guiding persona again proved changeable, though not so much in the speed with which poses rotated as in the sharper lines between them. Insofar as he approached unity he had toned down his quick temper and meddling with touchy issues and had evolved toward a knowledge smacking faintly of refinement. Nevertheless, often flashing his invincible zest for the hour at hand, he seemed pale only by contrast with his earlier incarnations and some of those to come.

*   *   *   *

In May 1882 a third-rate humorist who fancied the pen name of Commodore Rollingpin spent a leisurely day with Twain that brought out his kaleidoscopic range.[18] When serious, they touched with occupational anxiety on their colleague "Q. K. Philander Doesticks," already neglected after a "world-wide" vogue for his extravagant parodies. Twain, however, legitimized by increasing popularity in England, had no cause to worry. Later in May, when his steamboat stopped in Muscatine, Iowa, "quite a number of our citizens, most of them from the younger portion, were at the landing to get a look" at him. What they thought they saw varied confusingly, with help from his press notices. When the *Chicago Times* reported that he had been "proposed as an independent candidate" for mayor of Hartford, it separated the details with lines from "Punch, Brothers, Punch." But there were signs that the comic paragraphers were missing a shift of attitudes. Elsewhere, the humor about him would increasingly radiate affection. In March 1880 a twelve-year-old from Dallas, Texas, sent him a composition on why Twain was the person "With Whom I Would Change Places." Rejecting the Prince of Wales, the schoolboy searched his mind for somebody "who has climbed step by step up the ladder of fame, until he stands at the top; the admiration and envy of the world." More specifically Twain qualified "because he is so jolly"; because, "worth millions," he "makes so much money and writes such funny and nice books"; because he has a "beautiful wife and children"; because, in short, "he has everything a man could have to make him perfectly happy." The covering letter, which testified, "I like Tom splendidly," sounded hopeful about getting Twain's autograph, though "I do not think Mr. Longfellow, Mr. Whittier &c. can stand a joke like you." (The boy got a memorable answer.) Twain's trust fund of young readers was already accumulating to save him from the fate of "Doesticks." In 1910, George Ade, who shared the actuarial gloom about their calling, could gloat that Twain had sorely disappointed those who "love to hold funeral services" over forgotten humorists.

More than at any other stage of Twain's career, even a wellwisher could reasonably feel free to pick from a gallery of images during the 1870s. He might prefer the barely educated clown that Twain sometimes willingly passed for to assure the plebeians he belonged to them. Likewise, Twain had already learned well that his irreverence was most tolerable to those it gored when it operated through a persona to whom they could feel superior. Yet he read so doggedly that any bright interviewer caught on to his drive for self-education and added it to the picture.[19] The *Boston Herald*'s man also caught a "passionate love of justice"—which might, however, almost disappear beneath the rancor of attacking a stupid regulation from the post office. What brought all the extremes together was the unique self generating them. The *Herald* proclaimed Twain "one of those authors for whose personality readers feel a really friendly regard." But he emitted individuality still more than warmth, projecting a "fascinating and complex character" whose "interest for the reader lies in the eccentric, acutely American complexion of mind which colors his perceptions and in his special role in a sometimes sketchy but always discernible dramatic situation."[20] He carried the drama over into his speeches, interviews, and social manners. More and more Americans visualized a Twain, pulsing with energy, who was instinctually, contradictorily, and openly himself in whatever he did. A fellow passenger to Europe in 1878 noted: "Every feature of the face, indeed, backs up the twist in his speech. There is no incongruity between the man and his work. Everything about him becomes droll, his humor being a part of the body as well as of the spirit within."[21] Trying to separate Mark Twain from Samuel L. Clemens was like distinguishing the tree from its branches, the dancer from the dance. Twain recklessly enjoyed dancing and grabbed every chance in Nevada or New York City or the Crimea. Far more exciting than a friendly author, he was winning his public with a robust mental dance, like a mazurka in its great freedom of figures and steps.

As a showy dancer Twain was expected to go too far occasionally, to slip and disgrace himself. Exhilarated by the lively tempo, he could be excused for sometimes leaping over the inhibitions that restrained an orderly, well-disciplined adult, for barging into humor that might strike second thoughts as crude or cruel. Furthermore, he varied his steps so quickly that the public had too little time to sort out the causes for offense or to decide what outraged it the most. Still, underneath the center that seemed not to hold, Twain's inconsistencies, missteps, lapses of taste, and gestures toward anarchy somehow added up to visible proof that he was functioning admirably and to intimations that his cohesiveness lay in that ability to keep soaring above rational, routine behavior.

CHAPTER 5

The Year of Jubilee

TWAIN'S IMAGES ALWAYS SOARED over any such neat boundary as a decade. The Nevada showman would again spring up as late as 1909; the makings of the elderly guru can be glimpsed in Twain's first writings. Nevertheless, three perspectives override the signs pointing in all directions. First, after *A Tramp Abroad* reversed a trend of declining sales for his books, he was, as Justin Kaplan says, "well on his way to achieving the eminence of a national institution." Although *Harper's Monthly* let a dissenter belittle him in 1890 as the "one man of all our newspaper harlequins whom Good Luck chose for its pampered idol," the *Book Buyer* obviously felt confident in describing him as "not only the most famous but one of the most popular citizens of Hartford." Second, the respect—not just attention or warmth—granted him across the country increased strikingly. While reporters were coming to operate within his terms rather than inventing freehand, he helped by straining much less often for a laugh at any price. His firmer standing gave him the nerve to create two major vernacular characters as first-person narrators in his fiction at a time when he had high stakes riding on his assumed name. Third, his fiftieth year in 1884–85 formed as much of a specific turning point toward positive images of him as can be found in his tumultuous career.

Some old patterns lingered as minor humorists still tried to use him as a springboard. The Ivy League graduates who started the satirical weekly *Life* in 1883 could not manage either much taste for Twain or cleverness at his expense. Its first biographical sketch merely inverted the facts as ridiculously as possible. Just as heavy handed, a second sketch jeered pointlessly at his affluence and at both his publishing by subscription and his recent leaning toward seriousness.[1] Both squibs were amplified by illustrations that had little impact because of their still minor source. Bound to be cartooned, Twain would help out occasionally, not even drawing as well as he could. For these years the most visible caricature—Thomas Nast's "Innocence Abroad (In Search of a Copyright)" for *Harper's Weekly*—intended a friendly touch. Sometimes he was meant to be identified simply by his thatch of hair, mustache, and nose—generally considered his most graphic features. Eventually a double master in the visual arts and in searching the magazines and newspapers will chart the course of his image in proliferating cartoons, photographs, portraits, and even rarer media.

As a more irritating form of recognition, the line of fake Mark Twains was multiplying. They may go back as early as 1868, surprisingly. While some were small-town confidence men who planned to skip out on a hotel bill, other "personators," Twain explained to an interviewer from the *New York Herald* (19 May 1889), were "actuated by a sort of idiotic vanity." Still others were probably carrying hero-worship into acted fantasy. They enjoyed the impromptu dinners of welcome, delivered readings or speeches, or, before the long-distance telephone cut their margin of safety, just strutted around for several days. Twain naturally expressed mixed feelings, in which an understanding amusement at such gall could be detected. Although he fretted about the harm the impersonators might do him, it was gratifying that several, evidently, got receptions so eager that obvious causes for suspicion were ignored and also that a Twain persona had emerged so distinctly that deceiver and deceived could agree on it.

Reporters who, as one said, conceived of Twain as a "sort of living and moving anecdote" likewise tried to hitch onto his star. In the dying vein of apocrypha the *New York Times* (21 November 1882) reprinted from the *Philadelphia Press* a wheezing routine about his servant Jacob, hired for his "deficient sense of humor" so that Twain could discard anything he laughed at. While this retreaded forgery surely did not fool those with any feeling for Twain's genius, guilt by association with his worst level was possible. More plausibly, the *Arkansaw Traveler*, to test a casual opinion that he had "ceased to interest the public," composed a crossgrained letter from 1859 over his name that was widely reprinted, or so it claimed.[2] In ordinary local papers, reminiscences—usually based on some slim truth—launched characteristic incidents on a wandering voyage. At Hannibal the romancing of an old playmate was gratefully started on a round of quotation. The *New York Times* credited the *St. Louis Republican* with a long yarn about how Twain's father had once restored order in his courtroom by knocking down the wrong man with a hammer. Although pure bunk,

t slipped into the channels of the newspaper exchanges. Knowing where
t drifted and combined with other flotsam has to depend mainly on whether
somebody keeping a scrapbook liked it or whether one of the very few
indexed newspapers picked it up. At least it dressed up Twain as a most
dutiful son who "selected and beautified" the burial site after his father
died at a ripe old age.

Out of sheer impulse rather than calculation he let the press in on
events that enraged or entertained him, as when a hundred and fifty letters
(soon inflated to four hundred, then a "bushel") from a network of friends
begged for his autograph on April Fools' Day. For a worthy cause he
could still fake such glowing vehemence that the papers quoted him in
full, as when he wrote to a group raising money to build a pedestal for the
Statue of Liberty. Ringing in an old standby, he began, "You know my
weakness for Adam, and you know how I have struggled to get him a
monument and failed."[3] That the United States had given liberty a home
after "she had been a mere tramp for 6,000 years, Biblical measure" led
back to Adam, who needed and also deserved a statue more because, though
he had brought on the "inestimable privileges" of heaven and hell, "Evo-
lution is steadily and surely abolishing him." This medley of patriotism,
irreverence, and dourness was lightened by bold fooling on how to re-
model the statue ("conceal the sex of his head with a fire helmet") and by
mock irascibility about the neglect of the "father of life and death and
taxes." Twain's letter enclosed serious cash, the public could also notice.

Although mixed motives pushed him into the limelight, he never pretended gentlemanly carelessness about profits. Primarily to combat Canadian book pirates he registered Mark Twain as a trademark with the Patent
Office. Not only generous but downright helpful with permissions to boost
noncompeting items like a new style of collar ("for I think it is time the
name should be connected with something useful—it has been confined
to the aesthetic and ornamental long enough"[†]), he kept considering
additions to his own lines of goods: a calendar decorated with fresh say-
ings by him, a pocket-sized perpetual calendar, or a "very small book for
railway circulation." When the public library in Concord, Massachusetts,
banned *Huckleberry Finn*, he reacted with, "All right, we may as well get
the benefit of such advertising as can be drawn from it." While that "as
well" sounds rueful, he pushed the ruckus as briskly as Howells thought
advisable. In 1890 he again got enterprising about the railway market—
this time proposing ten-cent pamphlets with large type for bumpy roadbeds.
Around then he also figured up the costs for a cheap edition of *A Connecticut Yankee in King Arthur's Court* because trade unionists could not
afford the subscription prices.[4] His go-getter approach offended fellow

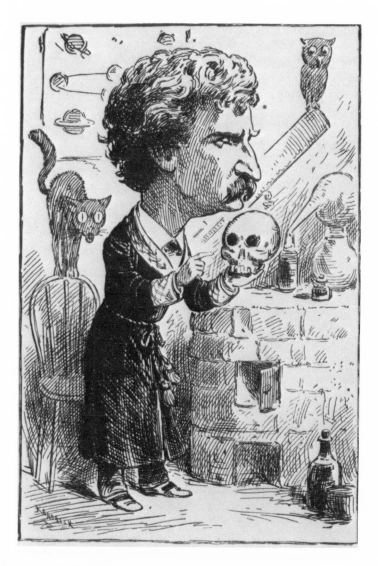

Life 1 (22 March 1883): 142

Life 15 (27 February 1890): 121

authors who tried to believe that they courted no one except the muses but who fortunately found it too embarrassing to criticize his crassness openly. The British critics who improved on his prestige at home never saw some items like the illustrated "biography" glued to sacks of Duke's Mixture tobacco, maybe without his blessing. But nobody doubted that Twain wanted to be rich and was not going to depend on book buyers—even of the Scrap Book.

*   *   *   *

The tour in 1884–85 with George Washington Cable, on which Twain set out frankly to earn ready cash and the fringe benefit of plugging *Huckleberry Finn*, brightened the golden glow around his reputation. At the start a middling box office moved him, as the financial backer and producer, to demand "louder advertising" for "The Twins of Versatility and Genius," as he had them billed, and even to consider sending out a squad of men in sandwich boards. But his loudest ideas died behind the scenes. The first circular for bookings had stuck to a moderate tone, and Twain gained dignity as well as headlines from the association with Cable, much in the news as a Southerner crusading for the civil rights of the exslave. This tour brought Twain's changeover from a baggy lecture to half-reading, half-acting out some mostly better passages from his published work, thus easing the emphasis on frenetic comedy and inching closer to "literature," his own along with Cable's. The joint result was an engrossing program recalled afterward as a classic of the platform era.

After one stunning performance, Cable reminisced much later, Twain groaned about playing the "mere buffoon" instead of giving audiences a useful experience. But that was not his dominant reaction, and he finished the tour at peace with himself. However chafed by watching the audience take his Twin more solemnly, he had planned for Cable to stir up pathos that alternated with his "irresistible drollery" in the "inimitable manner" promised in their circular. Under his coaching Cable shared bits of light stage business, but Twain often tipped over into clowning as the ice-breaker for his entrances, varying from a "side-long, awkward stride, amusing in itself" to a "funny little jogtrot, half-sideways, with a comic look of half inquiry and half appeal." His exits strain our tolerance for his ambition to lavish comforts on his family; Fred W. Lorch, a sympathetic judge, decides that he "often hippity-hopped" off the stage. Any regrets about demeaning himself surely applied mostly to such antics which, he had to suspect, the dull-witted mistook for his usual behavior. By comparison, his posturing in the interviews granted for advance publicity was mild, though it launched more nonsense into the exchanges. Only the shrewdest reporters as yet understood him well enough to angle for and get substantial commentary about books or social problems or even himself.

The tour honed still finer his gift for adjusting to the mood of the group in front of him and, if needed, notched the last degree of self-confidence. He had perfected the art of acting "natural," of being "as much yourself," marveled Howells, "as if you stood by my chimney corner." Howells and other friends could keep enjoying his performance because of the personality dominating it, a song without words filling the intervals between spoken content and redeeming any failed trick of manner. Impressive though undisciplined in amateur theatricals, Twain was a gifted actor, best at playing many versions of himself and eventually at simply radiating his "star" presence. At his walk-on appearance in 1889 for a program by James Whitcomb Riley and Bill Nye, the "audience rose in a body, and men and women shouted at the very tops of their voices. Handkerchiefs waved, the organist even opened every forte key and pedal in the great organ, and the noise went on unabated for minutes."[5] That audience was self-selected for humorists, but an imposing variety of admirers, primed to respond, turned up anywhere he might be heard.

Two aggressive patterns dominated the content of his speeches, already an institution on their own. First, he blithely assumed that his name carried a personality with a familiar history, based in the travel books but steadily enriched by his memorable anecdotes like those about the boyish prank with a skeleton, his soldiering, getting past an Irish doorkeeper, and pyramiding his discounts at a bookstore into a net profit. By relentless implication, that personality indulged in such lusty habits as drinking, approved of profanity both as a kind of vernacular poetry and a help in making appliances like the telephone function, took skill at poker or faro as an index of civilization, and honored irreverence as his supreme value. Twain merely did what was expected when he went full blast for a dinner in 1889 welcoming an all-star baseball team after its world tour, but he obviously feared no occasion or assemblage. Two years earlier his speech to twelve hundred at Forefathers Day in Boston had touched all the same nerves while mainly taking liberties with marriage, death, and political self-love.

Adding a second pattern of his taking charge, that foray, "Post-Prandial Oratory," also mocked the very situation—a banquet topped off with verbiage—and the gullible audience, which presumably would continue to fall for the clichés exposed by his "patent adjustable speech." He had seized the right of presuming that, as maestro of the art, he stood above the verdict of a particular gathering, so hypnotic that he could reveal his stratagems without giving them up for the future or even that night. "On Speech-Making Reform" (1885) had made the first of his open confessions that in his impromptu talks he plotted a "little finely acted stumbling and stammering for a word." Before the Fellowcraft Club he demonstrated how to bend any subject to fit the anecdotes in stock, such as his own. Converting self-revelation into social mastery, he luxuriated in a free-flowing identity that defied the ordinary reticences of either joy or sorrow. In May 1883 his text modulated into praise of death as "the refuge, the solace, the best and kindliest and most prized friend and benefactor of the erring, the forsaken, the old, the weary, and broken of heart." As his speeches added the darker tones they came, collectively, to embody his persona in its richest as well as most candid and genuinely confident mood.

Particularly good reading, the baseball text of 1889 was reprinted greedily. It upstaged his more thoughtful speeches like "On Foreign Critics," which defended American culture against elitists. Nevertheless, sober tints were seeping into his newspaper image, not so melodramatically as they would in the 1890s but strongly enough to make a conversion believable later by those who needed to deny his anarchic moods. More healthily, the facts settling out from the brew of newspaper and magazine stories were overwhelming the outdated features of his early stereotype. Besides, after the tour with Cable he never again tried so anxiously to generate publicity at any cost to his dignity. At last the reporters in the northeast were ready to measure him accurately, though out to the west they often did a doubletake on coming face to face with him. They did not expect the secretary trailing Twain on his trip back to the Mississippi Valley in 1882. Everywhere they were learning to watch for him to get off from the most expensive section of the train or from a private car if the family went along. Ordinarily that included a servant or two. In the summer of 1886 a *Tribune* reporter who caught the Clemenses at their hotel in Chicago felt it pertinent to mention a maid. Confessing surprise—"Mark Twain looks as little like himself as it is possible for a man to look"—the news story suggested a solid businessman on vacation by quoting Twain's relief at being "thoroughly cut off from letters and papers and the tax collector." He also came through as a responsible father of "three little girls, composed of three red gowns, three red parasols, and six blue stockings." Perhaps it was the same reporter who two months later visited the summer home of the "most refined humorist that America, and probably the world, has ever known." That was a compliment to make Hank Morgan say, "Well, I should smile." Relaxed in tone but without trying any nonsense, the *Tribune* story described a domestic circle living better than comfortably but decorously. It was becoming easier and easier to see that the Twain of the lecture and banquet circuit was a consummate actor, so professionally good at openness that perhaps it was under control and hid some enigma or at least depth.

*   *   *   *

Meanwhile the literary establishment was also learning to accept Twain. The indefatigably loyal Howells, whose authority rose steadily, gave his single most influential boost with an essay for *Century Magazine* in November 1882. Although Walt Whitman was still building rather than lending prestige (and privately rating Twain a lightweight), a reputable clique now looked after his comfort; they put Twain on their list of fellow authors to solicit. He contributed money at least twice and for the banquet honoring Whitman's seventieth birthday composed a letter so ecstatic about material progress that it annoys or mystifies some modern critics. For the eightieth birthday of John Greenleaf Whittier the *New York Herald* included Twain among the literary and political luminaries invited to send greetings. Totally solemn, he quoted from Whittier's poetry for a tribute to the "noblest citizen of the most fortunate land in the earth." By then nobody was likely to suspect Twain of trying to slip in a burlesque by a jealous outsider.

In 1888 a biographical sketch by Charles Hopkins Clark, the respected political editor of the *Hartford Courant*, proclaimed that Twain "has taken a leading place in literature, in society, and in business in America." The triad suggests that he had begun to compete with himself. From cap and bells he had graduated to looking not like one of the schoolroom poets but like a man of several important parts. Favoring gray suits as his red hair faded, he dressed more fashionably yet conservatively than at any other period in his life. His bearing hinted at confidence based on bankable reasons, and the begging letters long inspired by trust in his geniality now assumed he could afford to give away thousands to strangers. Bill Nye intended no burlesque either in describing him for the myriad *New York World* readers as the "Vanderbilt of literature" who "does much good by means of his wealth." Twain gladdened the hearts that treasured the myth of success. To prove that the "natural gifts of a man can conquer obstacles that seem impossible," Clark exaggerated his climb by grossly lowering the starting level: "At the age of 12 years he was a penniless, unschooled orphan, at 20 an illiterate pilot."[6] Instead of a jokester unworthy of literature, Twain threatened to prove, for the practical minded, too capable to waste on it.

Without any counterpoint the *Book Buyer* noted in 1890 that "there has often been talk of forgetting party and running him as a people's candidate for mayor." No doubt his tirades over a breakdown in Hartford's services encouraged such a risky notion. In more reasonable ways he carried out the later nineteenth-century ideal of civic duty so vigorously that his anti-imperialist crusade in 1901 should have surprised nobody. His activity in national elections peaked in 1884, when he gave three speeches and made his passionate stand known otherwise. The Republicans' choice for the presidency convinced him that the major parties had turned voting into a noisy farce whipping up symbolic issues to camouflage the pervasive corruption. After an election so close that many groups could claim to have turned the balance, he forever after branded himself a Mugwump. His civic profile matched that of many anti-Blaine crusaders.[7] Without their backgrounds of privilege and college education, he shared their disgust with machine politics, their uncompromisingly moral criteria for candidates, and their muted distrust of the wisdom of the masses as voters. The Mugwump leaders must have considered him an untypical but colorfully valuable recruit. Incidentally, other supporters of Grover Cleveland suddenly realized how deep Twain's intelligence went, and the comic weekly *Puck*, which was backed by Democratic money, soon praised him as a "thoughtful, sincere and suggestive literary artist." Just as naturally the opposition fumed that he had forgotten his place, but his commitment to idealistic politics left a permanent impression. In between crucial elections even some of the party faithful respect those who take a purist approach to government.

Whatever the balance sheet of Twain's identification with the Mugwumps, his highly visible link with a dying Ulysses S. Grant was refined into the solid gold of both income and emotional nobility. In fact Grant's fame would help Twain to match and eventually to surpass it. On his return home in 1900 *Current Literature* paired the "two great heroes" for climbing to the top on their own and for reascending a Golgotha of financial integrity after going bankrupt. In 1885 Twain, besides showing he could fully share the nation's sorrow, shone forth as a devoted friend and a benefactor who rescued the bereaved family with unprecedented royalties from his marketing of the General's *Personal Memoirs*. With those two handsome volumes coming on the heels of *Huckleberry Finn*, he shot into prominence as a publisher, and the newspaper fillers of the next five years abounded with rumors and facts about his firm's new books, most notably the authorized biography of the incumbent pope of the Roman Catholic church. His record for earning money was surging off the chart. To a reader's query whether Twain was "still writing," the "Funny Side" department of the *New York Press* (20 January 1889) responded that he was "mostly confined to writing on checks." Commodore Rollingpin had admired his "breadth and depth of philosophy . . . which might be profitably employed in directing the practical every-day affairs." Now he had validated the "practical" along with the "profitably." Confronted with Clark's testimonial in 1888 to his "extraordinary good sense in business," he would have found it hard to look modest.

✳   ✳   ✳   ✳

Daily mulling over large figures, he counted on only his books for income from writing. Still his short pieces, originating in impulse or an immediate problem, hit a high average of quality and therefore impact. The *Century Magazine*, which now blended its solemnity with much broader appeal than the *Atlantic*, got the prize of the lot—"The Private History of a Campaign That Failed" (1885), which brilliantly defused some grumbling that the publisher of Grant's memoirs had fought for the Confederacy. Of course the shrewd businessman was retransformed into a pitifully callow recruit, basically a throwback to one of Twain's oldest poses as a hapless victim. Beset by feckless, painful, ridiculous, and finally tragic mishaps in the field, he won the chuckling sympathy of Unionists while the Twain who signed the sketch impressed anybody who could appreciate his boldness at once more snatching his valuable reputation from the jaws of a damaging rumor. *Harper's Monthly* got the other topnotch piece, "A Petition to the Queen of England," which tickled democrats by beginning, "Madam: You will remember that last May" a clerk in the revenue office levied a tax on Twain's royalties. Rambling on with cheeky, masterful naiveté it pretended to cajole Queen Victoria: "You will not miss the sum, but this is a hard year for authors; and as for lectures, I do not suppose your majesty ever saw such a dull season."

His claque could find grounds for arguing that he was developing in sophistication. Both of those sketches were more subtly done than anything in his last collection, *The Stolen White Elephant* (1882), which was hobbled with other pieces almost as bad as the title story—a gasping satire on detectives who cannot see the obvious. Still it contained "On the Decay of the Art of Lying," which renewed his hallmark for somehow weighty irreverence in fleshing out its thesis: "No high-minded man, no man of right feeling, can contemplate the lumbering and slovenly lying of the present day without grieving to see a noble art so prostituted." More subtly, the essay reinforced his avowed reputation for incorrigibly deviating from the truth. On his straightforward side, his "1601," an earthy conversation at the court of Queen Elizabeth, had a tiny circulation in the first of the private printings that now clutter rare-book catalogues. But it started to gather its own constituency. Twain's versatility of subject and tone was impressive in itself and encouraged the conclusion that he was indeed the master humorist. Compiled mostly by others to trade on that prestige, *Mark Twain's Library of Humor* (1888) attracted nowhere near so many buyers as hoped. Nevertheless, a foreigner browsing the business and literary news could have thought Mark Twain was a gilt-edged conglomerate.

For the early 1880s anyway, his own books were still the backbone of his financial skyscraper, and he hoped that *The Prince and the Pauper* would surprise but not stun his public. While timed for the Christmas trade of 1881, it aspired to be, in Albert E. Stone's phrase, his "literary passport to propriety." The friends who fancied earning a vicarious glory had convinced him to reach up to a "worthy" standard, and his usual overflowing measure of response charmed them. Originally, as he explained to Mrs. Fairbanks, the "historical tale" was to appear "without my name—such grave & stately work being considered by the world to be above my proper level." After publication he insisted that sales counted as "very much less important" than the "approval of competent minds," whose verdict he waited for with such "anxiety" that he "couldn't eat or sleep."[8] However, he had again heightened his legend, if only out of a raconteur's penchant for drama. According to his yarning, this "maiden effort" at a "perfectly serious book" was unanimously reviewed as "just about the funniest thing to come off the press." Prompted by Howells, who regularly advertised a Twain improved with another ingredient, the consensus had instead hailed a "New Departure."[9] Critics especially approved its "generous and ennobling moral" from a "true philosopher" and its delicate artistry, which to our taste sags into clichés too seldom interrupted by robust comedy. Its anomalies hardened the unperceived yet faithfully observed rule that any essay on Twain had to discuss the weight and drift of his literary reputation, as if it were a freak iceberg endangering the transatlantic steamers.

The mediocre sale of *The Prince and the Pauper* indicates that his submerged audience cared less than the reviewers for his idea of a worthy standard, though because it was published by subscription its success depended partly on how well Twain's previous book had lived up to its billing. His keenest supporters shied away from children's literature even while accepting it as a higher genre than we do today and while giving credit for the diligent study that clearly lay behind Twain's tale. But *The Prince and the Pauper* probably did not swell his trust fund of young fans, who could sense a far firmer instructive tone than in *Tom Sawyer* and who might respect but could not thrill to its claims for an educative authenticity of details. The adult who mapped its socio-political bearings could find royalty both honored and ridiculed. Although British critics hooted the notion that an urchin could suddenly pass for a blueblood, readers hostile or envious toward royalty could enjoy the guiding device of the plot that it is clothes that make the man, indeed that set off kings from beggars. Still the novel went over best as a Sunday school lesson that the upper classes need to learn compassion toward the poor, who will then stay loyally grateful. It disturbed only those with totally conventional minds and those with fears that Twain had decided to narrow and subdue his persona, less visible here than ever before either as a hovering presence or an impulsive intruder.

More generally, *The Prince and the Pauper* raises the question of how well Twain's strictly literary and his broader images overlapped. In other words, how would someone conceive of its author if he had read nothing else by Twain and, improbably, had seen none of the newspaper publicity? That recluse's perceptions could also be heavily skewed if he saw only certain critics, especially those devoted to the ideal of self-development and anxious for Twain to demonstrate ethical "growth." The core of a thumbnail biography ran:

By genius and industry he has lifted himself high in the ranks of American authorship. He is not only a humorist, but he is a writer of rare and peculiar power. While his *Innocents Abroad* and other works have made him famous and rich, his *Prince and Pauper* will be one of the beautiful classics of the future. While other men are living on what they have done, Mr. Clements [sic] is continually progressing. He is a growing man, and each year he accomplishes some new feat in literature.[10]

This accolade would have been less worrisome if it had not ignored *Adventures of Huckleberry Finn*, published two years earlier.

Before then *Life on the Mississippi* (1883) had partly reassured the faithful with both its content and manner, with its lusty humor and even the frank patchwork common to his travel books. However, the now classic, fairly unified "Old Times" section and the loosely built other three-fourths each had a distinctive, somewhat divergent effect. As James M. Cox has argued persuasively—with only Twain's writings in mind—he invented himself with the cub-pilot chapters. At the least, in making his apprenticeship on the river a crucial stage of his legend, he projected his aura of glamor back further, practically to his childhood; he also solidified his and others' sense of his inborn naiveté, always ready, supposedly, to subject him to new surprises and mistakes. Whether cause or result, the leap in self-recognition from filling out a personal history brought a tighter level

of coherence, a vibrant wholeness that could inspire mastery when he en
tered fully into a youthful persona. That wholeness, furthermore, released
still greater subtlety and fluidity in manipulating the mask; it is mind
bracing to distinguish the various Mark Twains in the "Old Times" se
quence. But the persona of the last three-fourths did not insist on dynamic
self-fictionizing. At least by omission tamer than his counterparts in the
three preceding travel books, he came close to merging—apparently—with
the present-day reality, that is, with Twain's image as a successful author
lecturer, self-made personality, and businessman.

In the illustrations of *Life on the Mississippi*, the adult Twain, dressed
like a middle-class gentleman, suggests an air of handling himself responsibly; the exceptions rarely go beyond mild humor. The text yet more
firmly implies a poised citizen of the world, brimming with historical and
current facts, confident that his opinions on almost any subject are worth
stating. They spread themselves well beyond river matters, to economic
policy or the educated Southerner's sloppiness on points of grammar such
as the double negative (chap. 26). Obviously this gentleman long ago out-
grew the cub pilot in many ways. In the light of his savoir faire, the boyish
ignorance dissolves into a tribute to his willingness to exaggerate it and
his cleverness at doing that so winningly. Within either section the author
distinctly holds control, no longer making excuses for details he could not
whip into shape. When acknowledging the presence of the "public" or the
customer, he feels sure that all his constituencies will like what he gives
them. While new readers might have found the implied author faintly
smug, he did have his old robust tastes—two illustrations show him drinking at a bar—his gusto for tall tales now told mostly by others, and his
religious skepticism which can observe that the hinterlands cleave to an
"iron-clad belief in Adam, and the biblical history of creation, which has
not suffered from the assaults of the scientists." He was likable but not
memorable while the cub pilot bumbled his way into the national treasury
of characters and did more than Huck Finn, during the next twenty years
anyway, to associate Twain's image with the "majestic, the magnificent
Mississippi, rolling its mile-wide tide along, shining in the sun."

Despite close study of *Adventures of Huckleberry Finn* we know little
about how Twain hoped it would strike the hodgepodge of publics he was
acquiring. For both his psyche and the book's magic, much has been staked
on his decision to use a ragged, outcast boy as narrator; but the picaro, as
genuine rogue rather than just a runaway, was already an old viewpoint in
fiction with I-confession of vices and crimes far beyond Huck's powers.
The most challenging question is why did some reviewers attack *Huckleberry Finn* so sharply as coarse, vulgar, and even immoral? Perhaps Twain's

two previous books had raised their standard for him. More basically, however, it was another case of primness fronting for social conservatism. Much of the heat came in the cause of reverence, masked under the charge of "not elevating" or of "gross trifling with every fine feeling." One Boston newspaper, quoting another, explicitly cited that "spirit of irreverence, which, as we are often and truly told, is the great fault in American character."[11] Conversely a defender of the novel protested against the verdict that it was "flippant and irreverent." Along with the passages in which Huck chooses natural morality over a Heaven that blesses slavery, the anxiety for conventional values can in fact feel steady, almost habitual slashes at provincial smugness and at evangelical religion in particular, such as Huck's report that a dazed Silas Phelps "preached a prayer-meeting sermon . . . that give him a rattling ruputation because the oldest man in the world couldn't a understood it."

Ordinary readers, who stay refreshingly defiant of cultural traffic cops, liked *Huckleberry Finn* from the first. It serves up a feast of routines by a veteran newspaper humorist—farce, puns, comic misspellings, and parody of highbrow tastes. Currently a rage, local color also boosted the book, as did its genre painting or passages of kitchen realism. Besides the then rare pleasure of finding genuine vernacular in print, many savored its folksy touches sometimes entwined with bits of forgotten lore. These elements did not undercut Twain as go-getter; the era liked to think that its leaders and heroes were rooted in the village past. Any novel that lasts has also stirred the bone-deep appeals of narrative, starting with plot, and *Huckleberry Finn* keeps on the move with surprises and a changing cast. It can reasonably be called "lowbrow 'escape' fiction," a "pleasing and familiar package" in its "western locale, the picaresque adventures of its raffish characters, and the strongly subversive stance of its vagabond hero."[12] Unanalytic conservatives can accept rebellion when it is properly hedged, as with pathos, and even enjoy irreverence when brandished by an expert tactician like Twain. Whether or not readers approved, they got a strong reminder of his earthiness, his insistence on chuckling over seedy rascals like the King and the Duke. He went on again to grin at the putrefactions of the flesh: Pap's "tree-toad white" skin, Jim as a Sick Arab, Huck's brains oozing out from under his hat, and the funeral "orgies" for Peter Wilks particularly offensive to one reviewer. At the other pole a few readers—joined by more each year—respected the author for his humaneness verging on profundity or—in our time—pessimism about oppression, conformity, and other social evils.

Beyond the conflicting signals *Huckleberry Finn* surely had a composite effect in 1885. It strengthened the impression of Twain's energy that, along with his highly visible personal, civic, and business activities, could produce so good another book so soon. Excerpted in three issues of the *Century*, it assured the magazine public of his rising status while the surprisingly wide newspaper debate over the banning in Concord underlined his controversiality as well as his importance. The author behind Huck clearly had a heart quick to despise pretense, an eye quicker to spot it in gesture or dress, and an ear tuned to register devastatingly the gamut of platitude, whether delivered in flossy English or vernacular. A free spirit, he was sometimes willfully playful but usually left a sting of satire. He had a passion for honesty with oneself, and his robustness of mind led to pragmatic ideals judged as closely as Sunday-school morals. Politically committed he sympathized with the freedmen and, more generally, with egalitarian self-respect. He was firmly true to his native, American origins rather than imported literary standards. For all his principles or his contempt toward pettiness, he rang to the core with warm humor and, of course, a genius for comedy at many levels, racing up and down them with reckless agility. Still, a personage of rich experience, he convincingly managed to sound informed on serious matters. So deceptively offhand in his skill at penetrating the surface of manners that the victim could topple before feeling the thrust, almost threatening in the freshness of his perceptions, impulsively kind while skeptical about the run of people, the author of *Huckleberry Finn* was a man on whom practically nothing was lost and yet who must be engagingly if fallibly human.

Twain was surprisingly slow to name *Huckleberry Finn* as his favorite book, often seeming to go along with the expected answer when he did so. If, as he plausibly claimed years later, he got "letters of sympathy and indignation . . . mainly from children" when the Concord Public Library banned it, he did not as yet realize that his junior corps of defenders had gained many permanent enlistees. Before deciding on publication he had fought spells of uncertainty, symbolized by the "heliotype" of a sculptured bust of himself pasted opposite the frontispiece drawing of Huck. Judging from the hundreds of photographs we now have, he faced the camera like a witness under oath, and he posed for the always more frequent oil portraits with the gravity of a banker or statesman or aristocrat. In 1887 he purged a woodcut of himself from the *Library of American Literature* being prepared for his firm: "The more I think of the gratuitous affront of wood where steel is lavished upon the unread & the forgotten, the more my bile rises." So we must speculate why, just as *Huckleberry Finn* was ready for typesetting, he incurred the expense and bother of adding the heliotype of his severely dignified bust even if it held up the "canvassing" copies. He explained tersely: "I thought maybe it would advantage the book."[13]

Certainly it could remind subscribers that the author behind the barely literate boy had demonstrable status in the up-to-date world and could write in a style to match it when needed. If they should ask about the sculptor, whom Twain had supported for years of study in France, that would work to the advantage of both.

The presently favored view of *A Connecticut Yankee in King Arthur's Court* (1889) has Twain losing faith in the progress sparked by technology. Although he often charged off in several directions there should be no doubt that the book and its emphatic illustrations intended to not only support but also extend that faith.[14] The prospectus promised "most irreverent fun" of royalty along with instances of the virtues of "Republican government." In two leisurely interviews Twain pressed the same points. His Yankee—a more consistent, less introspective, terse, but habitually ironic younger brother of Twain—managed to imply quickly that they spoke for each other. Including Howells, none of the reviewers doubted that the persona and the author behind him had lined up for the bustling New World against the kingcraft and priestcraft of the Old. British critics, including even a youngish worshipper like Rudyard Kipling, took offense, but democrats chortled approvingly along a scale that stretched far toward the left. Reaffirmed by Twain's anti-imperialism later, *A Connecticut Yankee* gave his image as a radical such momentum that many a pamphlet and short-lived newsheet of the late 1960s featured quotations from him or, usually, his Yankee.

Much of the time *A Connecticut Yankee* exploited the basic humor of incongruities so arrestingly that we tend to stop at its surface, amused or offended by five hundred "mailed and belted knights" charging to the rescue on bicycles, for instance. Insofar as its contemporary readers reached deeper they found a devotion to romantic democracy passionate enough to abhor its shortcomings in New World practice. More distinctly than in any book since *Innocents Abroad* they could perceive behind it a progressive yet business-minded, humane yet ambitious American recklessly frank in a colorful vernacular (not dialect). They imputed to Hank Morgan's creator a total dedication to the feisty egalitarianism Twain had expressed off and on from his start. The uneasy reviewer for the *Boston Literary World* (22 February 1890) detected a "persistent teacher of irreverence for great men and great events." Hank refused so aggressively to bow before aristocrats and sacred customs in a "clammy atmosphere of reverence, respect, deference" that no example can catch the cumulative effect, though the first issue of the Camelot *Weekly Hosannah and Literary Volcano* (chap. 26) comes close. Twain's notebooks showed awareness that the cohorts of reverence had stayed touchy, that his recurrent burlesque of *The Idylls of the*

King would raise hackles. Presumably he did not know that Tennyson, complaining that there was "much less of the old reverence and chivalrous feeling in the world than there used to be," confided in 1886, "I tried in my Idylls to teach men these things."[15] Although Matthew Arnold's "Civilization in the United States" (1888) skirted the key word while venerating the "discipline of awe and respect," Twain and his fellow iconoclasts recognized exactly what it was prescribing for Americans, and his working notes put Arnold at the head of the party of "reverence." Anglophiles still detest *A Connecticut Yankee*, the masterpiece of a mini-genre dear to humorists from Artemus Ward to *Bill Nye's History of England* (1896) and later.

Twain had his burlesque well along before Arnold provoked an essay-speech on New World journalism as the archenemy of reverence. Much of that text ended up in *The American Claimant* (1892), sold first as a newspaper and magazine serial. Unfortunately this step up from subscription publishing involved his weakest novel, cobbled from a play that had failed quickly. It aroused very little stated response at home. Perhaps reviewers took the word of his firm that the "whimsical humor" of this "original and delightful romance" fell under "Light Reading." One of his rare long narratives with a realistic setting, it wandered into contemporary problems such as the rub between equalitarian ideals and the ambition to get ahead. But any convincing claim for its depth or impact remains to be made.[16] The original edition is still priced low in rare-book shops.

In June 1888, acknowledging an honorary master of arts degree from Yale, Twain defined the humorist's "worthy calling" as the "deriding" of "shams" and of "nobilities, and privileges and all kindred swindles" against "human liberties." Yet *The American Claimant* borders on the antidemocratic in both the drift of its plot and some almost irrelevant passages like the sneers at letting almost anybody be called a "lady" or "gentleman" (chap. 11). It did conduct his last major discussion of reverence within a concrete setting (chaps. 10 and 12), but his criticisms were repudiated by those characters with the highest ethical and intellectual standing. Veined as always with his gibes at the old saws and rigidities of respectability, nevertheless included plenty of secular devoutness. Likewise, while Mulberry Sellers may have anticipated absurdist comedy with his scheme of "materializing" the dead for colossal profits, a love plot in which his daughter charms a British viscount eventually set the tone. The best that can be argued for the image of the implied author is that the book did not harm Twain appreciably since its antidemocratic and hackneyed features aroused no complaints—or perhaps just no notice. The prime example of his instinct to retreat for a spell after hitting a peak of aggression, it may have comforted those frightened by the trashing of stained-glass windows in *A Connecticut Yankee.*

*   *   *   *

By 1891 Twain had livelier worries than his latest book. Driven by problems of cash flow, as he would have phrased it today, the Clemens family finished their engagement as a plush but earnestly happy household by closing up the Hartford residence and sailing for Europe in June. Inevitably troublesome, the move felt still drearier because the 1880s had gone so satisfyingly, for the father above all. Besides the financial prosperity, Twain's reputation—the image coalescing loosely from behind and within his books, his speeches, encounters with the press, and the uninvited opinions of literary critics or just ordinary people—had made gains more crucial than he could yet perceive, had accumulated enough pluses to transform quantity into a qualitative leap. If the leap can be dated, it came during his fiftieth year. *Adventures of Huckleberry Finn* was published then, the result of the converging strengths of his career but also a coincidence that would gradually turn into the leading event.

The fiftieth year had even started out auspiciously. In November he spent his birthday, still fresh, between performances with Cable during what, says Lorch, was "without question the most celebrated reading tour of the decade." Although one reviewer quipped that Cable supplied both the Versatility and Genius advertised, most reporters treated him as a junior partner. For a performance in Washington, D.C., a syndicated correspondent gave him hardly one-fourth of the space. The "pen picture" of Twain opened with the old jovialities, here comparing him onstage to a "mammoth interrogation point," but put most of its effort into the contrast between his current luster and his grubby days as a Capital freelancer in 1867–68.[17] Because of the correspondent's age, he had to crib from hearsay and back files for a patchwork of legend and fact about the exciting career through which Twain had shaped himself into a top-earning author and "international character." When the tour reached Cincinnati, a phrenologist found nothing comic about Twain's head, slightly smaller than that of the "average intellectual giant," and decided that the "fiber of the whole man is fine, close and strong." After obvious judgments mixed with howlers ("small love of gain") the analysis closed: "Knowledge of the world and interest in humanity are his leading traits and, altogether, he is a phenomenal man of whom Americans may well be proud."[18] Years later he would learn that in 1887 a father in Michigan had christened a son after him though, presumably, he never heard of the namesake who started out in southwestern Pennsylvania at about the same time.

In January 1885 the New York weekly *Critic*, edited by the brother and sister of Richard Watson Gilder of *Century Magazine*, added mainline prestige by admitting Twain into its "Authors at Home" series, which had so far visited only Whittier, John Burroughs, the then eminent George W. Curtis, and Holmes.[19] Twain was assigned to Charles Hopkins Clark, who began by apologizing that the "romance" of Twain's life "has been told so often that it has lost its novelty to many readers." The best known of American authors and indeed "one of the few living persons with a world-wide reputation," he by now conferred its chief fame on Hartford, where his "unique house" had set a model for a "good many" residences. Balancing the humanizing touches, Clark described him as a diligent pewholder in Twichell's church, an addict of billiards and strong cigars, and an inventor of salable products like the Scrap Book, which "must be pretty well known." More intellectually, Clark emphasized his reading in the "broad field of general culture," the friendships that elevated his house into a literary center, and the hard work put into his writing. All this confirms Howells' memory that when "hard upon fifty" Twain, still slender, projected an extreme mental keenness.

Eventually the news spread that Andrew Lang, the British critic who was virtually a man of letters, had composed an ode in honor of the fiftieth birthday which began: "To brave Mark Twain, across the sea / The years have brought his jubilee." But the *Critic* had planned ahead for its issue of 28 November 1885, which celebrated his "semi-centennial" because he "had done more than any other man to lengthen the lives of his contemporaries by making them merrier." It followed this up through the fellow writers it invited to offer greetings. Frank Stockton, then eminent as a whimsical humorist, briefly but warmly echoed its theme, which Charles Dudley Warner, a crypto-rival in his mind as well as Twain's, toned down with: "Few have done so much for the entertainment and good fellowship of the world." Joel Chandler Harris, all the rage as Uncle Remus, cooperated handsomely while hitching on a defense of *Huckleberry Finn* for its "lesson of honesty, justice and mercy." The prize wellwisher was Oliver Wendell Holmes, tottery and besieged by a drumfire of requests even more heavily than Twain as yet. Pushing aside twenty-three letters "all marked *immediate*," Holmes struck off eight witty, cogent quatrains. From Twain's drinking ("I mean in Nature's milky way"), they built up to specifying the formula of the "precious draught" he served to his public:

So mixed the sweet, the sharp, the strong,
Each finds its faults amended,
The virtues that to each belong
In happier union blended.

Twain bragged to Holmes that his wife and daughters were terribly impressed. So were many people after the papers treated the poem as live news; he had it framed and hung on the wall in the Nook Farm residence, just possibly showing it as an official pardon from Boston for any offense at the Whittier dinner. A letter from a local associate assured him that "the 'bubble reputation' has not been sought in vain." Still, Twain cared deeply how his family rated him as a husband and father. In March of 1885 he had felt "proud & gratified" to find out that his thirteen-year-old daughter was starting a biography of him, partly because she thought his public image deserved better.

When the *Critic* of 12 April 1884 tabulated a poll to choose "Forty Immortals" who might form an American Academy on the French model, Holmes stood at the top while Twain tied with Warner as fourteenth, just behind Cable and Henry James. So soon as November 1885 he would have done much better with the clientele of the *Critic*. In closing the chapter entitled "Mark Twain at Fifty," Albert Bigelow Paine quotes him as exclaiming, "I am frightened at the proportions of my prosperity. It seems to me that whatever I touch turns to gold." In certain moods he later felt that everything had turned to ashes or vagrant dreams. But during his lifetime that would never prove true of his image, which his contemporaries cherished to not only their pleasure but their benefit. In fact the expressions of gratitude for his boon to their lives could have been made stronger. Beyond the self-taught writer and self-made Midas, the shrewdest observers admired him as a knowingly shaped, self-promoted personality. Far more than the general public suspected, his touch with the newspapers would always help it to keep his laurels green, would add the service of making sure that it fully appreciated his gift of himself.

CHAPTER 6

"Working the Newspapers"

WHEN TWAIN SAILED for Europe in 1891 worried though not yet desperate about his solvency, he carried along an asset that would prove indestructible: the good will of the press corps. Beneath his long and wide acquaintanceship with its members lay a justifiable feeling of camaraderie as insiders. In May 1907, on a social visit to the office of the *Baltimore Sun*, he romanced:

> I guess I am beyond dispute the oldest journalist in the country, for, ever since the time I first began the business with my little paper in Hannibal, Mo., I have been in newspaper work, with scarcely any interval whatever, in one form or another—if not actively writing or making material for the press, then figuring in interviews or as the subject of newspaper comment.

If quoted precisely, he was exaggerating out of cordiality; and hometown loyalty soon nudged him to take the trouble of writing to the editor of the *Hannibal Courier-Post* that, having started as an apprentice almost fifty-nine years ago, "therefore I was a journalist; I have never been wholly disconnected from journalism since; therefore, by my guess, I am dean of the trade in America." Twain had in fact gone into service with the earliest generation of reporters sent out to actually find the news, but the guild eagerly compounded any credit he claimed. "He was the product of the American newspaper," eulogized the *Philadelphia Press*. "There he began.

There he had his training. To the end of his days his work had the touch and inspiration of the journalist, keen, actual, rapid and lit with mingled humor and the broader philosophy of life." California papers naturally liked to think he had "learned his trade" there. To touch off such self-congratulation an interviewer had now and then prompted Twain to expand on the "literary value of newspaper training." Unlike many a genteelist poet and essayist, he never felt resentfully competitive toward those marketing language daily to the masses.

In San Francisco his farewell lecture had thanked the "unusual generosity, forbearance and good-fellowship" of "my ancient comrades, my brethren of the press." Expecting, until he sold his share of the *Buffalo Express*, to stay a working journalist he had cultivated his eastern peers with jovial speeches at their banquets. He had moved to Buffalo eager, as they expected, to outstrip the competition, but the editorial feuding common at the time allowed an underlying bond of professionalism. After a social evening he gloated that the local fraternity of the press were "all good boys" who "will do the book up properly." Their counterparts across the country approached *Innocents Abroad* as a step up by one of their guild who had not forgotten his or the book's origin. Just about the time that Howells had one of his fictional characters apologize for choosing journalism over the study of law, Twain commented: "I always liked newspaper work; I would like it yet, but not as a steady diet." The basic point is that he kept his positive feelings about it, stated most engagingly by a passage in the "Roughing It" lecture that bobbed up for the rest of his life, usually under the title of "Mark Twain as a Reporter."[1] Along with some of his most daring social irony it ranked journalism as the "best school in the world to get a knowledge of human nature, and human ways." That must have charmed many a potentially quizzical editor. Even more than professors or small businessmen the press loves to hear itself praised.

Knowing how a harried staff slap together the next edition did not discourage Twain from consuming it avidly after he had quit their school. To sneers that the day-to-day content is mostly froth, Charles Dudley Warner had him objecting, "I cannot get along without my morning paper. The other morning I took it up, and was absorbed in the telegraphic columns for an hour nearly. I thoroughly enjoyed the feeling of immediate contact with all the world of yesterday."[2] To the hostile this suggests Thoreau's caricature of the American who sits up from a nap asking, "What's the news?" While Twain could express relief that the Bermudas of 1877 had no newspapers, he undoubtedly paged through the back issues when he got home; the fact that in December 1909 he wrote from the Bermudas that he had not bothered to open the New York City dailies signaled the

Bookman (New York) 3 (May 1896): 207. (Perhaps from the later 1880s or early 1890s)

weariness of his approaching death. Much more typically, when bored on a trip from Hartford to New York he bought some New Haven papers, and "there wasn't much news in them, so I read the advertisements." His subscriptions trailed him to vacation spots where he also ordered the local dailies or weeklies. Today he would have fussed with a pocket radio anywhere to catch the latest bulletins and would have attended the evening TV news as if sworn to it. Knocked back into sixth-century Britain, his alter-ego, having founded a wretchedly printed weekly, sighed that "it was delicious to see a newspaper again."

His lecture manager in Australia decided Twain was "addicted" to newspapers "almost as much as to smoking bad cigars." On the Continent he arranged for his favorite London dailies so as to get British and American highspots or reactions as freshly as possible. While doing full justice to the portentous stories on the front page he picked up on the latest joke or gossip making the rounds and panned the fillers for any kind of glitter. Eager several times as a publisher to back his belief that eyewitness accounts never lose their vitality, he instinctively enjoyed, that is, got engrossed in the human-interest stories, the amusing or pathetic or shocking incidents that thrust somebody into a passing notoriety. Bonded to popular culture he referred to "the paper" in a tone crucially different from Emerson's loftiness or Dreiser's wary skepticism, much less Stephen Crane's contempt (for "a court / Where everyone is kindly and unfairly treated . . . a market / Where . . . melons are crowned by the crowd"), and his autobiography often keyed on an item from the morning editions. The familiar photographs of him writing in bed are actually rarer than those in which he is blanketed with newsprint.

Beneath his enjoyment of the daily parade he thoroughly shared the standard faith in the benefits of a free press. Angry in 1907 over current scandals he jeered at the "fine . . . quite elegant phrase" that once was "on everybody's lips" both "day and night and everywhere": "The press is the palladium of our liberties." Still he granted that it had been a "true saying." His lifetime had paralleled the rise of the principle of nonpartisan, socially impartial, accurate and objective journalism, which he assumed was the fundamental working reality beneath obvious exceptions.[3] At the least he knew he had managed to get wide publicity for his antimachine politics and other crusading. He could never have created the character in Henry James's "The Papers" who decides, "The Press . . . is the watchdog of civilization, and the watchdog happens to be—it can't be helped—in a chronic state of rabies." When public opinion enraged Twain as dangerously wrong or when some newspaper had wounded him, he could sneer at "self-complaisant simpletons" who wielded undeserved power. But more than his inside experiences might justify, he trusted the press collectively as a high-principled, progressive force. To this social ideal the nineteenth century added a cultural mission seldom brought up today. Overheated while attacking a snob in his *Galaxy* "Memoranda," he defended the "thousand and one lessons, suggestions, and narratives of generous deeds that stir the pulses, and exalt and augment the nobility of the nation day by day from the teeming columns of ten thousand newspapers." For the sober occasion of dedicating a public reading-room in 1900, he trotted out the more reasonable commonplace that access to the printed word leads up "through the newspapers and magazines to other literature" and so the daily paper offers the first rung on the ladder to the highest culture. Even in his final years of glory he had no qualms about writing for a tabloid if it paid enough or his message needed that forum.

In that same speech he glowed over the speed with which the details of a recent disaster had raced around the "entire world." Committed to the persuasion that finds social value in the widest possible sharing of current events, now epitomized in Marshall McLuhan's global village, Twain naturally preferred American newspapers, the pacesetters for timeliness. When going abroad in 1878 he carried along some socio-economic grudges and tried to decide that the German model was superior. But he found it dull—indeed, the "slowest and saddest and dreariest of the inventions of man. Our own dailies infuriate the reader, pretty often; the German press only stupefies him." Much later he still jeered at it for wasting ink and ruining paper with "stingy little paragraphs of idiotic and uninforming information."[4] His mechanical typesetter, whether it might earn him a bonanza or force thousands to hunt a new trade, had the final justification of bringing the enlivening word to more millions of readers, who also gained political and cultural wisdom for fewer pennies.

However, his instincts and acquired ideals collided with operative realities. Impatient with routine and supervision and gifted beyond any of his editors, he could feel misused as a reporter. His own situation aside, he could march toward a dilemma. When he spun patches of American journalism to fit into a sketch or book, their effect was often disturbing, even to the lusty taste of Hank Morgan, because their vulgarity betrayed old, common ambivalences. Almost all his countrymen, back to James Fenimore Cooper and before him too, saluted the press as an unbridled weapon of protest when it attacked Old World tyranny. But many felt threatened when its leveling thrusts struck too fiercely at home or were offended when its freedom from censorship allowed pandering to the crudest tastes in ways taken over now by sleazily assembled weeklies. "The License of the Press," Twain's paper in 1873 for the Monday Evening Club in Hartford, would have pleased a Federalist with his distinction between responsible liberty of speech and intolerable abuse of it. A few years later he cheered a suggestion that nine of every ten American newspapers ought to be suppressed because of their demagoguery. However, this extreme rode on his own vice of overstatement. Besides, passions on what to "do about" the press can run hottest among those who enjoy it most. Twain's enjoyment, perhaps more than any other habit, marks his deep linkage with the popular mind and its interests.

A second ambivalence merged with the first, at least to later analysis. Twain's birth also coincided roughly with that of the mass-circulation or penny press, which began to discard the cultural standards and the criteria for newsworthiness held by journals catering to educated or affluent subscribers. The process and problems grew clear in England by the 1850s, and not only the Tories detested most newspapers for their political restiveness, lowbrow literature, and frivolities displacing the achingly solid columns of fact. Except for those examining the data as detachedly as rocks from the moon, every intellectual finally drew and draws some line of battle. For instance, the *New York News*, whose tenement-house clientele gave it the largest circulation of any American daily between 1870 and 1900, was so consistently snubbed by librarians that no file of it survives. On more than personal grounds Twain had writhed about working for the *San Francisco Call*, the "paper of the poor." While brilliantly exploiting the latest trends for his career, as a private citizen he still respected the guidelines learned on the *Hannibal Journal*. Apart from his practical ends, he leaned toward a familiar pattern: in the name of progress he approved the first wave of stretching those guidelines but he worried that further innovation would undermine the sacred mission of the press.[5] Still he took such deep-rooted pleasure in verve, color, up-to-the-minuteness, and human theatrics that even his late growling at yellow journalism sounded perfunctory.

His recurringly positive, most fundamental attitude defended the press as democratic in both audience and impact, as antihierarchical through its habit and right of irreverence. This function dominated his response to Matthew Arnold's accusation that "if one were searching for the best means to efface and kill in a whole nation the discipline of respect, the feeling for what is elevated, one could not do better than take the American newspapers." In *The American Claimant*, an editor of the *Daily Democrat* in turn accused his British counterparts of teaching submission to monarchy and the Establishment while his New World colleagues proved that a "discriminating irreverence is the creator and protector of human liberty." Although the "discriminating" warned that Twain would not sound this trumpet so loudly again for political warfare, he kept his faith in a free press as the spearhead against hollow conventionality and, ultimately, any social despotism. More specifically, he recognized that he had been allowed to use his columns in Nevada and California so freely as to acquire a reputation for attacking stupid legislators, grafting policemen, tyrannical bureaucrats, and incompetent judges. Although H. H. Rogers used him to help cool off the criticism of Standard Oil, he otherwise directed his anger publicly at the corruption the Muckrakers exposed rather than at their erosion of a stabilizing faith in the rich and powerful.

*   *   *   *

Twain's success in also marshaling the newspapers toward his profit never hardened into cynicism. Habitually he seethed at poseurs as the worst kind of hypocrites. Of course—as he would argue, generally—he did not always subject his own behavior to the standards he held out. ("It is noble to teach oneself; it is still nobler to teach others—and less trouble.") But he distinguished between the hidden snobs and the open Barnums, and he assumed that the good reporters saw through his tongue-in-cheek games which were parlaying his insider's advantage into a network of friendships that eventually took on the loyalty of a football alumni. Sincerely gregarious in most moods, he added recruits steadily or renewed ties with those graduating into the major leagues like Noah Brooks, who moved from the *Alta California* to the *New York Tribune* in 1871 and then to the *Times* before finishing up on the *Newark* (N.J.) *Advertiser*. This network spread through the magazine world to his benefit since most weeklies and monthlies ran a column of short commentary or a gossipy roundup by a staff writer, who helped the public realize what and who it found important. By the mid 1880s Twain had made himself such surefire copy that the press squad did all the chasing ordinarily. In a weary mood he could then warn his brother— an embarrassingly erratic spokesman, anyway—"I cannot abide those newspaper references to me & my matters"(†). Still, enjoying reporters for company and their off-the-record knowledge of the passing parade, he would always keep up a thicker chain of journalistic than literary friendships. During the summers in Elmira, New York, according to local tradition, he regularly dropped into an editor's office, chatted about the exchanges, and—the natural topper—dashed off unsigned items now and then.

It would be risky to bet that any big-city veteran, especially in the Northeast, was a stranger to him. From New Orleans he wrote to his wife that he had "breakfasted with some editors" and, three days later, that "we dine with the editors tonight." The press corps everywhere went in for luncheons, banquets, and smokers, and in two senses he weaves through its reminiscences. In 1879 he reported home that at 11:30 P.M. he had gone to a "beer-mill to meet some twenty Chicago journalists—talked, sang songs and made speeches till six o'clock this morning." A few days later, after the herculean Grant banquet he trooped to a cafe with them for a session which unsteadily founded the local Press Club; for his farewell they staged a printed-menu breakfast. In a roundup on his visit, the *Chicago Times* testified that Twain "has not forgotten his old newspaper days or habits" and that "much of his time in the city" was spent with journalists. Ever afterward some of the "boys" there felt protective about his reputation, though he did his share for New York, Boston, and other club festivities. Before leaving on his world tour in 1895 he attended at least two such dinners and made practically a habit of them abroad. At a Smoke Night in Australia he thickened the cordiality by declaring, "I have been a journalist a great many years, and still consider myself a journalist, since I contribute to journalism in America, at least." Such occasions struck editors back home as newsworthy and admirable, and New York City reporters would not have dared to give Twain the hatchet job they were doing (led by the *Sun*) on Stephen Crane.

With strong personalities involved, the interplay grew tense when it came down to business, however, and emotion could overrun self-interest on either side. The *New York Tribune* should have lasted as a prime contact for Twain up until the election of 1884 because it offered the best combination of a newspaper which he looked up to and which would raise his status, yet which did not look down on his level of political humor. In 1868 its Washington bureau served as his mailbox because most of his freelance sketches were aimed for it. Having seriously considered investing in its stock, he followed the fight for control after Horace Greeley's exit and congratulated Whitelaw Reid for saving it from a "tumble into the common slough of journalism."[6] Reid did apply such firm standards that hearsay had William Cullen Bryant worried about a challenge to his *Evening Post* as the "only paper for gentlemen and scholars." Given first in 1873 for a college audience, Reid's charge to intellectuals to get involved in politics circulated for decades as the classic manifesto of the civic spirit.

But the icily pompous Reid was bound to clash with Twain, who repaid any favors lavishly but kept bustling back for more. Since he occasionally wrote for the *Tribune* in the early seventies at bargain prices and threw in a couple of publishable letters to the editor, along with private advice, he began hovering around like an older uncle while Reid got annoyed. Twain wheedled one puff for *The Gilded Age*, then a stronger one.

Riding for a fall, he bragged to his publisher about an angle to advertise the book "from Maine to the Marquesas free of expense." Reid curtly drew the line when he wanted to pick the reviewer for the *Tribune*. As usual, a rebuffed Twain seethed with anger, all the more because Reid was willing to let him stay alienated. When another crony eventually seized the chance of the boss's honeymoon to have Howells do an abnormally long and of course generous essay on *The Prince and the Pauper,* Reid grumbled from Vienna: "It isn't good journalism to let a warm personal friend & in some matters literary partner, write a critical review of him in a paper wh. has good reason to think little of his delicacy & highly of his greed."[7] Twain never saw that letter, but the local press had its rich share of infighting. Soon another editor, who had left Reid for the *New York Herald*, encouraged the false notion that the *Tribune* was running Twain down regularly.

As Twain filled his notebook with ammunition for an insulting "biography," the rumors he highmindedly recorded about a robber-baron's financial control of Reid descended toward sneers about his sexual habits. Twain showed inside knowledge of Manhattan's press-row gossip with, he hoped, a vengeance. However, a slow thaw soon began, perhaps because the loyally partisan *Tribune* treated Grant's *Memoirs* handsomely. Since Reid and Twain kept meeting on weighty occasions during the 1890s, they patched up a civil front while the *Tribune* had to carry more and more stories about so colorful a personality. Two major institutions of public opinion could not ignore each other indefinitely. People in the know chuckled at how the old enemies tiptoed around each other when Twain got his Oxford degree with Reid intoning pride as ambassador to Great Britain. Once Twain had become a Mugwump he naturally criticized the *Tribune*'s politics yet, revealingly, not its quality in general. Except for the accident of jostling egos we would have a thick dossier of his dealings with the best of the Republican newspapers, but, impressively, he reached the summit of adulation without its help.

The *Evening Post*, which Twain respected the most of all, paid him the least attention—for reasons that suited his principles and therefore saved him from another head-on quarrel. He never complained, and he even admired the *Post* all the more when E. L. Godkin marched into full power during the early 1880s and Twain's newsworthiness shrank further there. In 1892 he labeled it his "favorite paper"(†). Before and after that firm judgment he must have occasionally recognized with a pang that he was generating the kind of journalism it resisted. The one worthwhile daily older than the first assault of the penny press in New York City, the *Post* had entrenched its reputation for integrity and substance with bonus strength in belles-lettres. Twain felt special pride when the *Post* "spoke highly" of his "Recent Carnival of Crime" and his serious side.[8] Although Godkin intended to give the *Post* a lighter touch, it trudged on its Olympian way as the only major evening paper, shaped for reflective perusal of close-set articles by an upper middle class devoted to Manchester Liberalism and willing to pay twice as much as its competitors charged. Its circulation finally crept up to 20,000 in 1892 when Joseph Pulitzer's *World* was printing 375,000 copies.

Godkin was more vocally self-righteous and still less sociable than Reid, yet Twain approved of his *Post* ecstatically after it emerged as the organ of the Mugwumps and bitterest enemy of Tammany Hall. It editorialized with such moral absolutism that Godkin's supporters believed he could stay independent toward J. P. Morgan, his chief creditor. While Twain found more warmth from and for Godkin's associates, the *Post* carried far fewer stories about him than did its competitors. Its sketchy, handwritten index does not mention him between 1881 and 1893, when the select Lotos Club honored him with a dinner. Stories continued very scarce though Godkin, by then semiretired, privately encouraged him not to "retract or explain or do anything except rub it in harder" when he stirred the wrath of the expansionists in 1901. The *Post* followed through with a roundly supportive editorial. Ordinarily disdaining interviews as gimmickry, it also staged a conversation with him to oppose Tammany in the fall elections. In 1908 it asked him for a letter supporting Charles Evans Hughes's campaign to continue as a reform-minded governor of New York. He had finally pulled even the *Post* into his orbit—on the basis of principle rather than conviviality.

* * * *

It became clear that, on a higher level than chasing fire-engines, Twain had indeed involved himself with journalism all his life. Furthermore, his delight in the latest edition from front to back, his trust in the ideals of a free press, his knowledge of the working realities from the legmen's side, his relations with editors that kept reminding him that fallible individuals sat behind the facade of the most imposing offices, his improving awareness as a businessman of balance-sheet imperatives—all these combined into an accurately rounded sense of the newspaper as an institution that both reflected and influenced the dominant forces. His billowing late pessimism did not blot out his faith in the at least fitful integrity of the better newspapers. Nor, though intensely personal in many other judgments, did he fall into the mistake of seeing the great papers as each the toy of some colorful owner. With better than a worm's-eye view he observed the pulsating interaction of the hierarchy of forces, from the molding of basic policy by a mortgage-holder down to reporters competing not only on behalf of their paper but also for catchy column-inches of pay and down even to the strategy of hawking the daily edition for a crucially different price in pennies. His balanced insight earned him the success he achieved in adapting the world of publicity toward his needs and goals.

Since nobody had yet developed the concept of mass media, much less a penetrating analysis of them, Twain never went so far as to ponder where the criteria of what is "news" came from and how the means of gathering it greatly influences what ends up in print. So far as the press affected his career, he accepted it as an established, powerful mechanism that by the nature of its functions shaped opinion on all matters that interested its readers. Maneuvering on his own without coaching from a public-relations industry yet to be founded, he saw no social harm in influencing the treatment of his lectures, books, business ventures, and standing as a celebrity. Without needing to invoke determinism he realized that the mind and eye often perceive what they expect. In *Life on the Mississippi* a fieldhand who had shrugged off a steamboat as "loafin' along" recalled, after learning its famous name, that it "jes' went by here a-*sparklin'!*" Twain's lead-in was: "Anecdote illustrative of influence of reputation in the changing of opinion." During the mid 1880s, unable to gauge that above the boiling currents his own reputation towered as firmly as the Brooklyn Bridge, he worked especially hard to correct or enhance stories about himself. With expensive deals lined up, he had to protect his credit rating, for one thing, and for another, while counting on his typesetter to soon dwarf his book royalties into petty cash, he needed immediate cash.

The definitive history of publishing in the United States crowns Twain as "certainly the greatest salesman of his own books until recent times." He tried to earn that title—perhaps even stated too cautiously—by continually refining his ideas about tactics. Disappointed with the profits from *Roughing It*, he concluded, "If one don't secure publicity and notoriety for a book the instant it is issued, no amount of hard work and faithful advertising can accomplish it later on." Next came the principle of not encouraging reviews because bad ones had hurt the sale of *The Gilded Age*. Then came the discovery that whatever the critic's verdict, "it is the *extracts* copied from the book that does it." Therefore, changing his mind on a side issue, he hoped the newspapers "*would* copy my stuff" from the *Atlantic Monthly*, which went to only the "select high few." Moving inexorably toward founding his own company, he decided that Elisha Bliss, once his oracle on promotion, "never had a bit of sense about working the newspapers." For *Huckleberry Finn* he took charge, inefficiently, of when and where the free copies were sent. Although his generalship would look inept in many campaigns, especially those more delicate than guessing which reviewers might promote his book, he won the war and the peace after it.

Once an insider on at least four papers, he understood that editors can wallow in urgent items today and scrounge for copy tomorrow. He likewise understood that aggressiveness, especially when masked by his wit, made a big difference in catching their attention. By the 1880s he began to think routinely about planting stories. Seven years before the publication of *Mark Twain's Library of Humor* he composed a puff for it beginning: "It is rumored. . . ." To plug the biography of Pope Leo XIII he searched for an idea which the "illustrated newspapers" would help along until it gathered the momentum to "appear in all languages & in all the newspapers in the world." This revived the approach that had infuriated Reid, but each of his enterprises got a warm hearing somewhere while increasing, on the balance, the solidity of his image. Not famous now for tact, he could smother his irritability with politic finesse. When the papers panned *Ah Sin*, a play written with Bret Harte, Twain granted the improbability that the "criticisms of the great New York dailies are always just, intelligent, & square & honest—notwithstanding by a blunder which nobody was seriously to blame for I was made to say exactly the opposite of this. . . . Never said it at all & moreover I never thought it." Then, since releasing this statement could look servile, Howells was asked to leak it somehow. Fame never blinded Twain to the fact that the press ultimately courts the favor of the populace rather than the lion, much less the gladiator. Because his rueful humor recalled some blunders so memorably, they distort his record for navigating many tricky channels and for handling the *New York Times* and *New York World* much more patiently than the *Tribune*.

Today the eminence of the *Times*, fortified by a network of retrospective indexes, brings it far more mention from historians than its influence during the nineteenth century deserves. (Far too few libraries have the *Tribune's* competing index during the course of Twain's career, even on microfilm. A rich set of leads to the *Times* also brings overemphasis on the newspapers of New York City as against those of Philadelphia and especially Boston, which are much less accessible than might be expected. As for the Midwest, the now almost forgotten *Chicago News* peaked in 1895 at perhaps the second largest circulation in the country.) By the 1870s the *Times* had started sinking toward its low point in 1896 of a circulation of nine thousand, practically invisible from the landmark tower of the new

World building. The incoming owners, who were able to drive a hard bargain, had no choice but to take the gambles that turned the *Times* around. Fortunately for both parties, its hostility to Twain raged during its weakest period. A graph would show early peaks of friendly interest in 1874–75 and 1877, the summit of exposure in 1881, and a nadir lasting from 1884 to 1895.

During the cordial years, which roughly matched the tenure of Noah Brooks, Twain often enough quoted the *Times* respectfully, and he generally looked good in its news stories or anecdotes, short and long. As late as December 1883 his letter on the Statue of Liberty was printed in full. Six months earlier, however, the *Times* had carried an interview in which he maligned the city's Shipping Commissioner to further extremes, such as that "Judas Iscariot rises into respectability" by comparison with him. The insults glowed with other distinctive touches, but when the victim filed suit for libel, Twain denied their accuracy and then tried to go on the offensive against the *Times* for the trouble it had caused him. After checking out the "stringer" involved, the *Times*' publisher felt doublecrossed and seethed to Twain's nephew, "They say that Clemens is in the habit of getting into scrapes & then backing down." It proclaimed total victory when a jury awarded six cents damages on each of two counts based on the interview with, the *Times* now said, a "Connecticut person."[9] This allusion was meant to be contemptuous, not cryptic. Gossip among press insiders must have combed through every belittling detail, and it is surprising that the affair left so little trace except in the *Times* of the next ten years.

The *Times* started in to take revenge with a review of the reading tour, rating Cable as a genius but Twain as "simply man after the fashion of that famous hunting animal, one half of which was pure Irish setter and the other half just plain dog." Calling him a cur hurt less than a headline the next month on a lawsuit about *Huckleberry Finn*: "Put Him on the Witness Stand / He May Make Another Extraordinary Exhibition of Himself." When an alienated friend, who matched Twain's claim to being an old journalist, sued in 1890 over the rights to dramatize *The Prince and the Pauper*, the *Times* slanted the news all in his favor while sneering at Twain and especially the real-life veracity of this "modern Munchausen."[10] It went so far that perhaps it vaingloriously itched to bring on another libel suit. But Twain, chronically litigious, exerted such astonishing restraint as to imply a guilty conscience though a letter to his sister admitted only a sighing patience, which needed to continue. For a public reading of his in 1894 the *Times* grumbled that when hundreds come primed to laugh "nothing can turn them from it—not even Mark Twain." Just as futilely its review of the play hacked out of *Pudd'nhead Wilson* protested that "people stopped reading Twain with zest after *Huckleberry Finn*."

Any objective journalist knew that people had stepped up their zest for the man himself and were taking his recent troubles to heart. The *Times* seemed to soften accordingly. On 13 July 1895—after an editorial conference?—it expressed sorrow over the reports of bad health, sympathy for his business losses, and best wishes for the valiant world tour to pay off his debts. A stream of pleasant stories helped him out for the rest of his career, and in 1906 his dictation of his autobiography used the *Times* for the morning news, a function it had already come to deserve. That it had peppered away at his anti-imperialism in 1901 could be excused by its convictions on foreign policy. By then Twain correctly reckoned that no paper dared to persecute him for purely in-house reasons. If a holdover from the pre-Ochs regime had suggested rubbing salt in old wounds, the managing editor would have in effect demurred as in Ring Lardner's story when an outraged sportswriter wants to muckrake a loutish boxer: "Suppose you can prove it. . . . It wouldn't get us anything but abuse to print it. The people don't want to see him knocked. He's champion." On Twain's side the restraint had been still wiser since, as his own feuds while a feisty reporter could show, public figures can win no better than a truce in a battle of insults with a newspaper, which manages to have the last word one way or another. Twain needed to remember that truth concerning the *World* also.

His relations with the *World* were complicated by changes in not only its standards but those of the press in general. A friend of both editors of the *World* during the 1870s, he occasionally made warm contact with the paper, which angled at a select if Democratic readership. It genially wished him farewell on his sailing for Europe in 1878 and cooperated in an interview from Paris pushing for tighter copyright laws. However, unsavory Jay Gould had sunk his financial hooks into the *World* as well as—rumor said—the *Tribune*. So Twain might reasonably have welcomed the advent of Joseph Pulitzer in 1883. Instead he reacted at once with the still unpublished "The Great Journalist Interviewed," which centered on Pulitzer's alleged habit of printing faked conversations with the famous. Evidently posted on the latest shoptalk, Twain agreed with the worry current among the entrenched group of editors that Pulitzer would defy even the lately relaxed standards for sensationalism. However, *Huckleberry Finn* needed promotion in the face of hostility from some solid New England papers. The *World* appeared on Twain's brief must-list for review copies, perhaps because it had done a long story (27 November 1884) on the progress of the novel.

Dismayingly, ironically, under a headline bewailing "Wit and Literary Ability Wasted on a Pitiable Exhibition of Irreverence and Vulgarity," the raffish *World* warned potential customers against "cheap and pernicious stuff."[11] Twain's notebooks started listing the repulsive crimes played up by the *World*, which every day—he calculated—reached far more people than his wildest dreams for a novel. Soon the *World* seemed eager to damage his publishing firm again. Not satisfied to hint that he landed the contract for Grant's *Memoirs* unethically, it next implied that Grant had a ghost writer. This "intrepid lie" had earned a libel suit, with "no apologies accepted . . . & no compromise permitted for anything but a sum of money that will cripple—yes, *disable*—that paper financially." When lawyers cautioned that the story had made no demonstrable impact, Twain consoled himself that, since the *World* "hasn't got influence enough to get its lies copied," suing it would just furnish an "enormously valuable advertisement for that daily issue of unmedicated closet-paper." Although the *Memoirs* sold hugely, in 1891 Twain exultantly snubbed the *World* by demanding pay for an interview it proposed. As far along as 1898 he gloated to H. H. Rogers that setting his price prohibitively high had put "on ice" its "feverish desires" to display his signature.

Still he could not afford to boycott the *World*. For one golden reason, it had boomed past all its competitors. He had already let its reporters have two thoughtful interviews before a long one on 12 January 1890 which both plugged and defended *A Connecticut Yankee*. Second, the *World* dangled big money, a fine lure after his bankruptcy. From Vienna he cabled a front-page byline account of a riot in the Austro-Hungarian parliament. In 1898 he actually offered it "The Man That Corrupted Hadleyburg," and it soon did feature his vintage sketch "My First Lie and How I Got Out of It." As his financial guide Rogers expressed surprise at the developing tie. Although always slow to crowd Twain he pushed that far because the *World* had established a populist-Democratic voice, which crusaded against the powers in Wall Street. Among the wealthy, some of the contempt for Pulitzer's yellow journalism masked their anger at his reformist appeals to the bottom layers. Twain apologized for thinking the *World* had grown "respectable," but he stayed on trading terms even after it opened fire on Rogers himself with editorials backed by cartoons. Against the tow of deep loyalty to Rogers, he reasserted his autonomy, his innermost core of integrity that self-interest never overwhelmed either. In 1905 he publicly admired the *World's* exposé of prominent citizens who were bleeding the major insurance companies they ran, and he made it his main outlet for agitation against King Leopold's atrocities in the Belgian Congo. Looking back at sunset, he should have felt grateful toward the *World*. A magically complete, master index would probably show that between 1890 and 1910 it carried more column-inches on him than any other newspaper anywhere. Collectively that mass of words, photographs, and drawings would support hard speculation about how his image evolved within a circle of readers much different from that serviced by the *Evening Post* or the *Tribune* and about what kind of impact he made on their ideas and emotions.

*   *   *   *

The tensions between Twain's practical and civic values, his schemes and cultural standards, his spells of craftiness and his impulsive, trusting intimacy with men far more calculating than he were dramatized most vividly in his dealings with the *New York Sun*. Despite some early ties with the *Herald* his friendships within its staff seldom went deep. Furthermore it had sooner passed as arguably respectable while within the ranks of the press a distrust of Charles A. Dana clung to the *Sun*, even as the *Herald* slowly climbed toward a norm which itself sank closer to the *Sun*'s practices. Better than either the *Sun* or the *World* the Hearst papers might have exemplified Twain's relations with yellow journalism, that ultimate notch of hoopla, hit-and-run handling of the facts, and deliberate faking. But Hearst, erupting on the scene just as Twain ascended to herohood, had

Life 29 (4 February 1897), centerspread. "*Life's* School of Journalism" (Joseph Pulitzer stands outside the door with a mudpie labeled "NY World")

too little to bid with besides money in a now kingly auction. Better than any other paper the *Sun* poses the question of how clearly Twain realized that journalism had grown into big business, millions of dollars distant from the weekly and weakling paper in Hannibal or the handful of young-bloods who put out the *Territorial Enterprise* or even the *Buffalo Express*, one-third of whose market value had stood within reach of his ability to borrow from his father-in-law.

Most simply, his relations with the *Sun* raised again the problems of plain human dislike. In 1870 it had ridiculed his signed *Express* editorial on Cuba, arousing his venomous, still unpublished "Interviewing the Interviewer." Dana of course could not foresee how high this upstart would rocket, though Twain soon had a hardcover forum ("The House That Jack Built" in the *Burlesque Autobiography*) for recirculating the rumors that Dana took payoffs through Tammany Hall. It was easy not to overlook the sins of Dana, an erratic and imperious cynic usually detested by those not afraid of him. As late as December 1882 a *Sun* editorial deplored one of Twain's speeches as "so low in tone, so coarse in suggestion, so trite in allusion, so foreign to the spirit of the occasion" that it ranked with "bar-room" humor or the "end-man of the minstrels or the clown of the circus." Yet entrepreneurs as lively as Dana and Twain inevitably found reasons for stalking each other. As early as September 1882, Dana had tried to com-mission articles at a generous price, tried again in 1883, and the next year made cordial efforts to buy two or three short stories as well as to get on a social footing. His best gambit gave Twain the entree for making a "clear $100,000" profit—he mistakenly estimated—by publishing the official bi-ography of the pope, which Catholics would rush to buy. Meanwhile, Twain was getting ready, he felt sure, to compete against the Linotype machine for the rich New York City market; besides, Dana had a posh billiards room. Eventually Twain attended two festive dinners at the home of Dana, who next spoke in appropriate terms at the Lotos Club banquet in his honor.[12] More routinely, even before the age of tax deductions for entertainment, the Manhattan clique of editors and publishers hosted each other often, with Twain welcome as both an associate and a prize guest.

The *Sun* also embodied in catchiest colors the pull between his ra-tionalist and viscerally spontaneous sides. In principle it continued to of-fend unforgivably the standards of Nook Farm. As Twain's mock interview of Dana charged, the *Sun* had quickly become notorious for milking head-lines from every sordid murder, while one of Twain's fixed ideas, which he later itched to explode against Pulitzer, held that publicity for criminals sets off a chain of lurid deeds by the weak minded. Moreover, in its politics the otherwise unpredictable *Sun* betrayed a habitual softness toward Tammany, and it had led the abuse of the Mugwumps in 1884 besides getting the credit (or blame) for reviving the epithet itself. On the other hand the *Sun* had a polished style—as the newspaperman's newspaper, some declared; and it was dashingly irreverent in its dislikes, which Twain could share on an ad hoc basis. As for its graphic detail on crimes, nobody granted more warmly than Twain, whether as a rank-and-file reader or the would-be founder of a magazine, the fascination of eye-witness accounts. The *Sun* daily made itself exciting if unreliable, and devotees jeered that many of its enemies enjoyed its beams in private. Sure enough, apologizing that the *Evening Post* served as her "guide," earnest, moralistic Ida Tarbell later confessed to having bought the *Sun* "because it amused her and she wanted to know what Dana had to say." Twain never pretended to ignore it.

On the tactical side his traffic with the *Sun* epitomized his current anxieties. Although eventually 1885 proved to be the turning point of his march to the pantheon, in the heat and complexity of the present he confronted problems that could seriously damage him if bungled. He insisted that his royalties would benefit from the minor sensation stirred by the banning of *Huckleberry Finn;* but a worrisome number of editorials across the country had seconded the judgment of the Concord Public Library. Still more important, undercutting the glory of his link with Grant, the problems in marketing the *Memoirs* had grown thick. In fighting off several misleadingly billed competitors, he quarreled with the Associated Press, which insisted that his news release disguised a brassy advertisement for profit. The stories about his helping the terminally sick Grant to provide for the family often went on to boggle at Twain's share of the profits and point out his agility for raking in the cash. This last point was degraded into his alertness at snatching the contract away from the company that had serialized the *Memoirs* and expected to publish the book version, his grisly good luck in Grant's timely death, and the false report of his pocketing a bonanza from a late bust of Grant sculptured by a Twain protégé. On 6 July 1885 he worried in private letters to two editors that he was "fast getting the reputation in the newspapers of being a pushing, pitiless, underhanded sharper," indeed the "craftiest & most unscrupulous business-sharp in the country." One Boston editor, he thought, was spreading that image most deliberately out of petty revenge, and Twain never minimized the effects of appealing to latent envy.

The undertow quickened to a visible danger in Philadelphia during the summer of 1886 as his firm pushed litigation to restrain its agents from discounting the retail prices it had set. Testimony in court and follow-up stories revealed the huge markups on the cost of subscription books and criticized the practices used by the firm to spur on its agents, the "weaker party." Editorials condemning the system to "keep the price up" raised quasi-Populist cries of monopoly and pleaded for giving the "consumer" a break. With detailed newspaper ads about its "public service" in charging less than door-to-door canvassers, John Wanamaker's famous department store contended that a "high wall" was still making the *Memoirs* too expensive for the common folk for whom Grant had written and was selfishly reducing his widow's income.[13] When Twain, long friendly with the "boys" in Philadelphia too, traveled down for a court hearing in August, the reporters wavered between local loyalty and affection for him.

During this harried period his base in New York City felt unusually shaky. Godkin's *Post* stood austerely above his kind of game; the *World*, known for its "proud claim that it had no friends," scrambled after stakes too huge to neglect in Twain's favor; though starting to unbend, Reid's *Tribune* would not tolerate being hustled while the *Times* quivered with hostility. No doubt he sized up the *Herald*, still a leader in circulation because it spent lavishly on gathering the news and because, some sneered, its "Personals" department accepted ads pandering to almost every vice of a big city. In 1867 and 1873 it had made persistent, flattering attempts to line up Twain, who did grind out a set of letters on a shah's visit to England. Nevertheless he steered away from it during the 1880s and would not have appreciated someone's reference to him as its "author-humorist." The old guard, remembering that the elder James Gordon Bennett had pioneered the X-marks-the-spot drawings for a murder, stayed disdainful toward the *Herald*. Much more important, the younger Bennett, self-exiled in Europe for shocking behavior, was notoriously capricious, close to demented. So Twain's field of choice had narrowed just when he had lucrative deals creating stickier patches than ever before, and even humble Huck's code of ethics was offending a few influential custodians of righteousness. In 1886 he belatedly warned his assistant, "It isn't good policy for anybody connected with our publishing firm to be under a fire of newspaper criticism this year." Meanwhile, the election of 1884 had cost the *Sun* close to half of its readers for quirkily antagonizing the faithful of both major parties along with the Mugwumps. It needed new allies too, and Twain soon was counting on its cooperation.

For instance, when sketching a second Prefatory Remark to *Huckleberry Finn*—which sardonically confessed that the suspect hero took after the "author's two uncles, the present editors of the Boston *Advertiser* and the Springfield *Republican*"—he intended for it first to "drop" into the *Sun* "with a mere quiet editorial comment." To defend the genuineness of the authorship of the *Memoirs* he planned to elicit a fighting "note" from the General to place in "all" the papers and particularly the *Sun*, which soon carried Twain's letter about the proper location for Grant's tomb. He composed a "D. Wahrheit" letter "To the Editor of the *Sun*" scotching another rumor that just might hurt sales. The immediate harm of discounting list prices, he felt, called for provoking a libel suit through a fabricated chat with a Wanamaker salesclerk "accustomed to low wages & hunger" who said that if his grasping employer "had been around just after the crucifixion, I should not have been oppressed with these life-long doubts as to what went with the body." He would relieve this cold insult with a comic rebuttal of the stories that he had dozed off at the court hearing in Philadelphia, and he proposed to "slam" the entire piece "in among the minor editorials." Somebody vetoed that scheme without wrecking Twain's alliance with the *Sun*. Later high spots included a leisurely, informative interview from Paris in 1895 and a review of *Following the Equator* that left him gratefully "delighted all over." When added together these instances do suggest a would-be sharper, but the *Sun* hardly needed lessons in looking out for itself. It had gained an increasingly prestigious friend, usually far more loyal than the *Times* could believe, and a potential contributor.[14]

Interestingly, not Dana but William MacKay Laffan handled the *Sun's* part in almost all those cases. His obituary in 1909 identified him as a chum of Twain, whose biographers have accepted that kindly label and have enjoyed items such as the twisted self-caricature he inscribed for Laffan: "To the pleasant barrels we've drunk together." Having first made contact in 1880, they were cordial within two years after Laffan, whose letters often talked billiards, visited overnight at the Hartford residence. He could have explained why Twain hoped to field-test the Paige typesetter first at the *Sun*. Obviously versatile, shrewd, and forceful he steadily gained budgetary power on the *Sun* while underlings and associates mostly thought him "mysterious" or even "sinister."[15] Melville Stone's autobiography insists that during the early 1890s the United Press was controlled by non-journalists through a "private and mercenary" triumvirate that included Laffan. Almost forgotten now because he avoided publicity, he had instant access to operators the magnitude of Republican "Boss" Tom Platt and J. P. Morgan, whom he represented in the financial regroupings of the Harper firm; to start with, Morgan stipulated that the Harpers must pay Laffan a commission of $100,000. His role as go-between carried over into the Harper reign of George Harvey, whose pre-sailing dinner for Twain in October 1903 invited Laffan, Morgan, Rogers, St. Clair McKelway (editor of the *Brooklyn Eagle*), and Stone (then head of the Associated Press). Even after all the Harper people are counted for the literary side, financiers and industrialists held the majority among the twenty guests at the plush Metropolitan Club.[16]

The edition of the *New York Sun* that Twain holds is dated 7 May 1901

MARK TWAIN (*to* BILL NYE).—What, in the name of Artemus Ward, is going to become of *us*, if this thing keeps on?

Puck 37 (10 July 1895), back cover. Part of a large cartoon captioned: "The New American School of Humor.—The Men Who Are Funny Without Knowing It"

The badinage between Laffan and Twain often led around to ways of making big money: a can't-lose contract to publish the catalogue of a wealthy Baltimore art collector, an exchange of shares in potentially lucrative patents, a "job for Laffan which will pay him $210,000 in ten or twelve months," a stepdown to syndicating *The American Claimant*. Throughout the 1890s their connection gathered trusting joviality: a scheme with a hoaxing newspaper ad for which Laffan "could have the exchanges watched and saved," a comradely grousing that he had failed to tip Twain off to prospects about "that Monotype Machine," a feeler that "Laffan must be prospering greatly, now, and will need a large house, and will want to rent his present one to a capitalist of high character" like Twain himself. This last group of items all involved Twain's correspondence with Rogers, who in 1903 decided to have Laffan's *Sun* (Dana had died in 1897) sent to Twain in Italy. Taking the positive approach, Rogers' letters made it a point of reference. The most interesting example ran: "You will see through the columns that Laffan is gradually getting around to a position that will justify his opposing the re-nomination of Roosevelt. John Hay is still in the minds and mouths of all the people as the most desirable man for the Presidency." If not inviting Twain to play at kingmaker, surely Rogers whetted his impulses to undercut Roosevelt's popularity. Curiously, the post-Laffan *Sun*'s obituary of Twain was just about the least generous one out of hundreds.

Puzzles like that entice the mind back to the farewell at the Metropolitan Club among the generals of influence, the printed word, loans, and large-bore expertise. Updating Tennyson's farmer we can hear the wheels of the private railroad car that Rogers sometimes loaned Twain drumming "capital, capital, capital. . . ." What was the main course at that dinner? Or even who? The smartest power brokers put nothing in writing (or on tape) needlessly. Aggression and greed crouched beneath the suave chatter around the table, and Morgan would later carve off a juicy chunk of Rogers' millions. How much or how often did Twain suspect encirclement of his genius rather than hearty male bonding? Over the years he registered many rumors about which financier was getting leverage on an editor needing a huge loan to modernize and expand. He surely heard in 1906 that Hearst—a wholesaler of black kettles—had publicly labeled Laffan the "mortgaged menial of Morgan." What price did Twain pay for his connection with Laffan, a crony of Rogers but Morgan's retainer and art expert and a fixer always intent on his share? Who was using whom? Although kinder than exploit or manipulate, the word *using* allows too little chance, however, for the genuine affection Twain could extend and maybe inspire. From his viewpoint anyway, "working the newspapers" suggests the truth fairly enough. Increasingly he did so with a tone of negotiation or indulgence rather than wheedling. A magazine published by the stony London *Times* referred to him in 1899 as "that eminent publicist."

Whatever Twain's skill at handling the engine of print, he had been lucky to get so grand a ride on it. Retrospect shows that the heyday of the newspaper started around 1870 and hit full throttle soon after 1900. While cynics will judge his relations with the press as ultimately naive or else opportunistic when measured against his contempt for hypocrisy and phoniness, four points can be argued to his credit. First, his spontaneity usually shone through and sometimes overrode his maneuvering. At his death the *World*, after estimating that no other artist including Sarah Bernhardt had "furnished more news," saw "nothing of the poseur about him"—a compliment harder to win from journalists than anybody else. Here it was meant not to deny the surface facts but to acknowledge his underlying authenticity. Second, the press corps accepted him as genuine also because he admittedly worked within a tradition of projecting a showy personality whose audience valued color and pleasing exaggeration without strict concern for the truth hidden in the private individual. Publicity, which at its most successful founded a personalized legend with an unpredictable lifespan, was the name of the enjoyable game for actors, impresarios, strolling politicians, and humorists, as well as many lecturers who pretended a more habitual dignity than Twain. Third, he showed great skill, much harder than it looks, at riding the whirlwind of publicity to the very end—outrunning any ripples of boredom at his presence and leaving behind a model of personality that some can treasure as part of the American and, evidently, the human heritage. Finally, his political career from 1900 to 1907 would act out a brave independence that, building on his old faith in the mission of the press, put his fame to work for humane, progressive goals. There has been mental weight-lifting over Twain's inner contradictions, but those of his encompassing society went just as deep, and he would attack some crucial cases, using his popularity to encourage dissent.

CHAPTER 7

A Domestic Tragedy

DURING THE 1890s the press corps could have decided, fairly enough, that Twain's financial recklessness had driven his family abroad or that he had misused his genius for humor by trying to play the capitalist, and it could have clucked that humankind has the right to expect better from somebody whom fate had endowed with so much. Nevertheless, while Twain courted disgrace with more blunders, his popularity continued to climb rather than just bobbing on the reservoir of good will. If only because of his past and future achievements, we can be grateful that most newspapers and magazines kept singing his praises on any occasion they could find. For a society bursting with more immigrants every year, they held him up as a winningly vivid proof of the shared past, a model of success, and the most attractive frame for self-definition. The conviction that he typified the American personality was nearing its flashpoint across the country.

The first book-length portrait—by William M. Clemens, at best a far distant relative—came out in 1892 and sold enough for a second edition in 1894. It doggedly treated Twain's career as a "romance" of surmounting the standard handicaps through perseverance more than talent though it understandably stitched in the catchiest anecdotes, such as one form of how he had just missed finding a bonanza out West and therefore never finding himself as a writer. Both in accuracy and in deference this biography improved heavily on the chapter in Will Clemens' *Famous Funny Fellows* (1882), which chuckled over Twain strictly as a newspaper humorist. The anecdotes that kept increasing the newspaper traffic had throttled back on zaniness, and naming a giant redwood after him did not necessarily sound like a joke. As an oblique sign of his eminence the *Chicago Tribune* (15 May 1892) interviewed his colorless brother Orion.

Not just the respect but the affection mounted like a cumulonimbus. When the Lotos Club, an alliance of the arts and professions, feted him, even the still hostile *New York Times* reported the demand for tickets as "something unprecedented." No lasting harm followed the fact that, after the chairman of the dinner introduced Twain as "brimful of wit and eloquence, with no reverence for anybody," he unloaded one of his tamer speeches. His leading competitor as the wit of banqueteers, Chauncey Depew, would recall arranging a dinner in Berlin to which the most exclusive guests came eagerly because Twain had "contributed more than any man, living or dead, to our individual pleasure, the happiness of our homes, and the joy of our lives." Primarily the elite just wanted to bask in his company and his fame, but this stiff bouquet had its roots in reality. He attracted friends from every side and class. At the memorial service for actor Edwin Booth in Madison Square Garden, where "all the distinction of New York was massed," he knew "half the people there" and found it like a "family gathering," he told his wife (†). The undistinguished millions likewise kept feeling closer to him, convinced of his cheerfulness and generosity. He was outreaching Charles Dickens toward becoming a "primary form of modern celebrity: the writer as a spokesman of the common sense and basic goodness of the mass of the people."[1] His incoming mail from strangers grew more and more fervid. Just as revealingly, his answers to the always thicker flood of letters, too often grasping or stupidly blind to the demands on his time, hit a high average of patience and courtesy. We enjoy his angry innings like a "Form for Literary damned Societies" that want firsthand material. However, its actual content was polite. The vehement, scathing answers went, if at all, to petty bureaucrats but not to common citizens, who regularly found in the newspapers some new burst of comic spontaneity such as his way of petitioning the secretary of agriculture to send American corn and watermelon seeds to a temporary neighbor in Italy. Strangers who asked for an easy favor like using the frontispiece of *Huckleberry Finn* to advertise an oil for guns were playing short odds because his reflexes favored the entrepreneurial spirit.

Inescapably he now and then got weary of the spotlight and the demanding audience in the shadows. Bruised by both sly jeers and misfired compliments—the Grant *Memoirs* had run him through the gauntlet—he tried to profess an "inflexible rule to be satisfied & content with anything & everything a newspaper may say about me so long as it confines itself to statements that are not true." Aware under this bravado that his vigor

MARK TWAIN LEAVING HIS LAWYER'S OFFICE

New York World, 12 July 1895, p. 4

and impishness, which would sit well on a sophomore, had finally started ebbing as he neared sixty, he especially welcomed the tributes to his gravity of mind, such as that from fellow humorist Frank Stockton in the no-nonsense *Forum* (August 1893). Gratifyingly the same discovery was announced so often that it soon met with complaints about stale news. But he no doubt welcomed all private as well as public reinforcement when the collapse of his publishing firm leaped into headlines far taller than it rated in lost dollars. In his embarrassment and anxiety he could not know that established heroes can add resonance by proving vulnerable to the limitations and sorrows of ordinary mankind or, more specifically, that the recently increased weightiness of his image would merely deepen the emotionality of the domestic tragedy that the press corps created on his behalf—with his fumbling help, to be sure.

✳   ✳   ✳   ✳

Twain's bankruptcy in 1894 made all the louder news because, according to *Publisher's Weekly*, "it was supposed that any enterprise undertaken by 'everybody's friend' . . . could not be otherwise than successful." He had built up a glittering reputation as a businessman. During the litigation over stage rights to *The Prince and the Pauper*, the *New York Times*, still in a hostile mood, emphasized his shrewdness at making money. Will Clemens' last chapter had bowed to a "literary Midas" whose gold piled up "not from luck, but from hard work," and a hurried postscript for the 1894 edition blamed Twain's "incompetent and inexperienced" employees. With the age of the toplofty, detached manager decades away, another apologist, stubbornly holding that "as a man of affairs he has been even more successful than as a writer," likewise argued that if Twain could have "given more of his personal attention . . . the outcome would have been different, beyond a reasonable doubt."[2] The other casualties from the Panic of 1893 also helped to buffer his image as a responsible capitalist. Still the press was crucial in unreasonably, sentimentally giving him more than just the benefit of the doubt. Twain himself may have been surprised. Always ready to believe that the tricky currents had turned against him, he must have noticed in 1890–91 that a few paragraphers circulated the word that prosperity had made him gruff. More concretely, there had been complaints that his new travel letters were dull and all too predictable.

Perhaps not even the reporters got to know that his wife and H. H. Rogers had to dissuade him from unloading his corporation under all the advantages of the bankruptcy law. Reared in comfort that left poverty an abstract and surmountable idea, Olivia Clemens tried to insist that the creditors had total moral claim on payment. Even while Rogers was challenging them toe to toe, he was advising Twain that his literary and his broader popularity rated as the asset to protect at all costs, that the high road would prove the most profitable in good time. Just as crucial in the short run were his repeated warnings for Twain to say as little as tersely as he could stand. Although *Publisher's Weekly* criticized some of his maneuvers as hard on the book trade and Orion's scrapbook mounted two vagrant newspaper paragraphs deriding the transfer of copyrights to his wife, the public heard little about the tough negotiations. When a creditor called Twain out of his sickbed to testify about the income from those copyrights, opinion ran still warmer in his favor, all the more because he had taken that sudden turn toward looking old. In 1894 a review of a reading by "dear old Mark" singled out "those curly grayish locks, that drooping mustache . . . the gentle expression of the mouth, almost melancholy, that historic dress suit, too, a relic of several decades ago" and added his "self-abnegatory way of speaking" before rounding him off to a "charming quaintness."[3] To be sure this journalist knew he was observing a bankrupt; furthermore, Twain was economizing on clothing while slumping under the role of a failed go-getter. Hard-nosed as ever about sparing nobody, the *New York World* (12 July 1895) jocularly implied that, since his family had lived at a "very expensive hotel in Paris," he deliberately chose to look "poor" at the hearing to "ascertain if he has wealth concealed about his person or elsewhere," as in a fake assignment of his royalties. Nevertheless, the illustration with the *World* story showed a stooped, careworn, and distinctly pathetic man.

That the decision to pay off the creditors panned out handsomely should not diminish the fact that Twain's barnstorming around the world made a courageous leap into the dark of unfamiliar challenges. Still it proved a most fortunate leap without a fall. The obituary in the *World* dated his highest fame "no doubt from that day when he took up the onerous task" of clearing the debts—at the figure hammered down by Rogers. As soon as his plans were announced the press started throwing an ever kindlier light on the bankruptcy itself, demoting him to a "member" of the firm who paid up for his partners. Parallels with Grant were extended beyond the truth, and recalling the fiscal nobility of Sir Walter Scott became standard. When Twain warmed up with an American swing, his manager's diary noted: " 'Mark' is finding out that he has found his friends by the loss of his fortune. People are constantly meeting him on the street, at halls and in hotels, and telling him of the happiness he has brought them—young and old alike." As early as April 1894, he informed his wife, a stranger "sent me a dollar bill and thought he would like to get up a dollar-subscription."[4] In July 1895 someone in the family clipped an editorial ending with the same idea. Perhaps improving on it, his housekeeper and later a daughter would recall a move for a "five-cent collection" to spare "his advanced years the terrific labor of starting his life of earning all over again." These heady, hard-cash proofs of idolatry would almost lead later to a debacle.

With the tour mapped out, Twain started referring cheerfully to the often tense dealings with some of the creditors, who by the time the *Baltimore News* interviewed him in 1907 had tamed into a kindly bunch who needlessly "offered to settle at a discount." Reaching this benignity would involve much backsliding. Meanwhile, his progress in clearing the debts stretched into the longest, most colorful of the continuing stories about himself dramatized for the public. The effectively touching prologue was his statement published on 17 August 1895 after he reached Seattle, poised with wife and a daughter to venture over the Pacific. But its precise authorship is clouded by a testy apologia written out for his nephew Samuel E. Moffett, who was sent up by the *San Francisco Examiner* to consult with him. While a covering letter seemed to assume that Moffett would rush the apologia into print "unabridged," the *Examiner* of the seventeenth carried instead a majestic declaration that, whatever the reliefs open to a businessman, "honor is a harder master than the law. It cannot compromise for less than a hundred cents on the dollar." Although a strictly first-person format surrounded this soon famous passage, Twain informed Moffett that the United Press had promised to put "your interview" on the wire. His daughter expressed still more pointed gratitude: "We all like so much the interview you wrote for Papa."[5] Widely circulated at once, it often resurfaced locally during the tour, and after a full reprinting by the *New York Times* it enjoyed another cycle of quotation at Twain's homecoming in 1900. Surely Moffett, a topnotch journalist later promoted to New York City, deserved some of the credit if not a byline for its ideas and even phrasing.

Twain's original draft for a statement, which the *Examiner* finally ran on the twenty-fourth, tried to be comic but turned sour about a creditor who "persecuted" him and defensive about that transfer of copyrights. Furthermore, while meaning to sound grateful it bragged about offers of help "here and there and yonder" from total strangers. Meanwhile, perhaps Moffett had written the much more winning *Examiner* editorial of the eighteenth entitled "A Man of Humor and of Honor," which a member of the family clipped out. Sonorous about Twain's "heroic" rejection of "technical evasion and the quibble" about debts not his fault, it cheered the prospect of his bearing to distant shores a model of New World character at its finest, the saucy independence of *Innocents Abroad* matured by integrity and a defiance of failure. At his death the *Muskogee* (Okla.) *Phoenix* judged that his tour began "his gradual rise in a figure taken in some sense to typify the American." Expanded in concrete detail by the *Examiner*, the calls for a lending-hand campaign drawing on mass appeal encouraged Twain to feel like a patriotic institution. For the time being the newspapers, along with his mail, were cueing him much better than his own sense about his image. His statement on the twenty-fourth, in which he had first planned to parade even his nephew, bathetically invoked his wife, who had sacrificed her last "penny" into the "bottomless hole" of the debts and "wanted to turn her house in, too, and leave herself and the children shelterless."

While aware of many editorials declaring, for instance, that he had grown "gentler and brighter" with the years and deserved "all the good things he would enjoy" (*Mackinac* [Mich.] *Standard Union*), he was in any case too seasoned to depend on unguided sympathy, and the interviews he tirelessly granted would continue to stress the motive for his tour. Still he had no reason to worry since the foreign reporters felt as cordial and found him as fascinating as the editors back home who regularly polished up his shining example by reprinting stories from abroad. On Christmas Eve of 1895 the *Hartford Post*, noting a "tribute" in the *New Haven Leader* keyed to a London *Times* story, reminded folks: "A man well past the meridian of life, in poor health and having sacrificed his fortune in an effort to settle honestly with creditors . . . turns again from the well earned rest and quiet of his home and sets his face against the world to rehabilitate his shattered fortunes." From this gaggle of appeals the *Post* pushed hardest the never-say-die spirit of this "unassuming fellow citizen" who "scarcely finds himself downed before he's up and well on his way to a second achievement promising to surpass his first." The self-remade man had a submythology in the gospel of success. Because of Twain's "hard work" the *Chicago Echo* hoped he "may soon be as rich as he ever was." Ultimately the glorified version of his comeback enhanced his reputation for taking manly risks, whether as a pilot, miner in Nevada, inventor-speculator, or audacious public personality.

From abroad Olivia Clemens confided to her sister that Twain, "ashamed" of barnstorming the equator, "never wants to go back to America," but the home press portrayed an unwilling exile courageously redeeming his IOUs and providing for his family. In fact Twain did evince physical and mental grit by his tour of 1895–96 through Australia, New Zealand, India, and South Africa, coping with the dynamics of strange audiences and with fresh problems of projecting himself. Even if he were willing he had by now accumulated too much distinction to play the low-brow clown, yet the crowds came for entertainment. Performing in formal dress he was treated offstage as a dignitary, yet the ticketholders wanted a live exhibit of his most typical humor. Once more he worked out a fusion of substance and frivolity finely adapted to the circumstances. Since his unruly hair, liberated into a mop curling over his collar, had softened into gray it waved not a red flag of eccentricity but a banner of self-privileged character, free either to unbend from dignity or stand on it, just as likely to turn more solemn than before as to strain the limits of irreverence. Cartoonists for the magazines adjusted gingerly, moving away from ridiculous poses while stylizing more subtly the face and figure now well known from studio photographs, stiff engravings, and pictures of more oil portraits. Although Twain never totally mastered the knack himself, even strong caricature can manage to imply respect or affection, perhaps visually better than verbally.

Any American keeping track knew that Twain's lecture, billed after careful sifting as an "At Home," pretended to outline a scheme for the moral regeneration of mankind. A shrewd choice, it gave him a firm opening gambit and reviewers a strong lead sentence. Besides it fitted the heroics—the "imperious moral necessity," in Moffet's phrase—claimed for his tour. Yet the provocative scheme itself—to commit all the known sins as a process of inoculation against them—mocked the old notion that lectures should be educative, and its logical pretext for a loosely connected series of anecdotes mocked the Sunday school practice of stories lumbering toward an uplifting point. Still, within his typical oscillations from solemnity to nonsense or from froth to corrosiveness, he expected to remind some of the audience that the debate over whether Adam's descent into sin had brought humanizing effects and whether untested virtue had strength in a crisis reached back beyond the origins of Christianity. As a matter of fact he often fumbled for the answers himself, and "The Man That Corrupted Hadleyburg" would soon indicate a few of them.

The world tour therefore brought into dominance one of his oldest and most intricate poses, that of a Moralist and Instructor to Mankind.[6] Psychoanalytic critics rightly wonder why he liked to toy with a persona of unearned or excessive moral superiority. From the audience's side the effect for decades was primarily a slyly impudent reference to his inability to go on for long without misstating or dressing up the facts, and his routine of comparing himself with George Washington merely teased the literal minded or the over-reverent patriots. Yet essays like "On the Decay of the Art of Lying" had left a pebble in the boot of righteousness. To theorize about the frontier talltale does not explain why his yarn—perhaps his own platform favorite—about stealing a green watermelon and then scolding the farmer for trying to sell inedible fruit should please audiences around the world and why Sigmund Freud remembered hearing it next in Vienna with delight. At some point during the 1890s Twain's posing as an expert on morality turned bafflingly plausible, enriching the complex humor. After recouping his financial and psychic losses, he made his Moralist voice still firmer, notably at a London dinner of 29 June 1899. Thereafter it rang out more frequently and transparently with only enough clowning to forestall boredom. A connoisseur of irony, *Life* complimented his "faculty of telling the truth by lying about it in such a way that is immediately self-evident." The larger point is that the jeers that emptiness lay at the heart of the funniest Twain just about died off.

The bankruptcy also catalyzed the emergence of Olivia Clemens, indispensable for the mounting of a satisfyingly rounded domestic tragedy. Although her influence on Twain's artistry teases speculation, she never forgot who had the genius, and, flowing with the mores of the time, she had effaced herself while smoothing his relations with friends as much as strangers. At close range her poised gentleness helped to soften his image before the *Ladies Home Journal* had invented the wife-behind-the-man or mistress-of-the-celebrity's-home genre. When Twain dashed off an essay in 1885 on how she mothered their three daughters flawlessly, she let him perceive her distaste for such publicity. Still his impetuosity did him credit with the worshippers of the dream of the perfectly intimate and loving family which had developed among an interacting cluster of forces—popular entertainment as an industry, a jump in the standard of living, and a margin of leisure time for the middle class.[7] To the extent that reality flowed without pumping—except for short boosts from his speeches—into the channels of publicity, her devotion as homemaker and his reverence for it had been doing him more and more credit.

In the spring of 1894 the stories about the bankruptcy of his publishing firm kept mentioning Olivia Clemens as the chief creditor. Conceding her new prominence, Twain discussed her health in brief interviews of 15 April and then 16 August. As his companion on the world trip she had to get hardened to photographers. Along with their daughter Clara, a "very pretty, modest appearing young lady," she formed a Victorian tableau typically noted by a smalltown paper: She was a "quiet little lady whose face, dress and manner show good sense and cultivation," and Twain "is said to rely implicitly upon his wife's opinions and to yield cheerful obedience to the 'sweet tyranny' of her wishes." In return "her watchful care and tender nursing" had "brought him through his most recent dangerous ailment." Although the *Petoskey* (Mich.) *Resorter* went on uneasily to wink that "Clemens [with no "Mr."] is in the best sense 'one of the boys,'" the public grew familiar with her as part of his entourage, unaware how diligently she critiqued the latest "At Home" and monitored the choice of his photographs. Her debut emboldened their old pastor to cap his essay in *Harper's Monthly* for May 1896 with six paragraphs about her as the heart of Twain's fireside circle. In total effect she balanced but did not outweigh or, given the double standard, even undercut the masculinity rooted in *Innocents Abroad* and *Roughing It*.

For reporters along the tour he twice ranked her with Howells as a critic of his work whom he listened to, and he enlarged on the dedication of *Personal Recollections of Joan of Arc*—"tendered on our wedding anniversary" for "her twenty-five years of valued service as my literary adviser and editor." To a Hearst emissary he insisted that she had stopped a "lot of things from getting into print that might have given me a reputation I wouldn't care to have." Keeping the point vivid the prospectus for *Following the Equator* quoted his assurance that the manuscript had undergone her "second revision." Among his contemporaries anyway, his respect for her taste and the openness of his husbandly devotion added a touch of nobility. His "visible distress" at the recurring illness that slowly led to her death helped to narrow any reservations about his crudeness. It was mean-spirited to look down on a man everywhere in demand who earned headlines such as "Mark Twain Cancels Dates to Nurse Wife" (*New York American*, 13 November 1902). His bereavement in 1904 was so touching that nobody who valued the institution of marriage could resist Twain's wearing his heart on his sleeve. An obituary of "Uncle Mark Twain" chose the twin climax that "he paid his debts and loved his women-kind with a fidelity less common than it should be among humdrum men." Anything he did tended to look bigger than life.

∗   ∗   ∗   ∗

Meanwhile an earlier episode of his domestic tragedy unfolded with melodramatic timing. Just as the redemptive tour had ended in August 1896, "great headlines," according to Clara, grieved that "Mark Twain's Eldest Daughter Dies of Spinal Meningitis." Although Clara magnified the newsprint, Susy's forlorn death back in the United States sprang a gusher of human interest, and the devastated father could not have hidden away his sorrow if he had tried resolutely. But for Twain the big emotions demanded a witnessing, even responsive audience, whose size validated their depth or importance. He instinctively dramatized, that is, exclaimed over not only his own feelings but anybody else's, from a housemaid to a president. In November 1897 *Harper's Monthly* carried his long, orotund poem of bereavement "In Memoriam." When the *Kansas City Star* commented on this new side of his writing, he responded to the editor, "I suppose we are all poets when we are under the stress of deep feeling." But he had long ago established a unique right to discuss himself with a candor breathtaking beneath the irony and burlesque. While the hide and seek never stopped, the newspaper public more and more believed that it peered into his innermost thoughts, his griefs as much as his triumphs, both of which had too much vitality to halt at the reticences called for in the middle-class code.

Susy's death helped lure Twain to the brink of ridicule as the family's mourning period in London fed rumors of his decline. On 28 March 1897 he noted getting a clipping from the United States with a five-column banner, "Close of a Great Career." Another story two columns wide, headed "Mark Twain's Poverty in His Old Age," led in with the news that, a "slave to debt . . . burdened with age and the woes of a broken heart," he was fighting poor health. This darkened into, "It is probable that the end has come." More certainly the "inspiration has gone," and insiders expected little from the book in progress.[8] While such reports surely depressed him further, their pathos also encouraged him to daydream about a bravo reception of a homecoming tour, with the tickets priced on a frankly inflated scale. After all, people ought to remember that he had mounted the stage to benefit some charity more times than he could list. The patchy record may even identify him as the mastermind behind a plan for performances "by invitation" in New York, Chicago, and San Francisco, each preceded by a rigged "auction of a dozen first-choice seats at Jenny Lind prices."[9] He toyed with refining touches for months before his wife vetoed his hopes to "go into history as the only lecturer who ever made so immense a scoop" (†). The scheme would have gambled boldly yet forthrightly on his capital of good will. His detailed manuscript for the lecture signed off with graceful joking about having retired his debts at the expense of those on hand. If carried out this frontal assault on the wallets of his admirers would surely have reduced the lately heroic side of his image.

His sense of the limitless sympathy for his troubles got the unneeded benefit of a smash witticism because, as the *Philadelphia Times* of 2 June complained, newspapers eager for a scoop had reported Twain "dying in poverty all around the globe." A day earlier the *New York Herald*, after describing him as "grievously ill" with his mind "shattered," had keened that "bravely and sturdily he fought up to the last." Skeptical, Hearst's London agent sent a legman over to Twain who, busy writing in bed, scrawled a note that a cousin had been sick recently, and "The report of my illness grew out of his illness, the report of my death was an exaggeration."[10] The reminiscences of the agent sound dubious about whether Twain's note was primarily geared to irony though we know he had begun joking about his funeral. Helped by the press the delighted public quickly overwhelmed any doubt by strengthening the key phrase to "greatly" or even "grossly exaggerated," as it now also goes on T-shirts. Of course Twain never disclaimed even the improvement, and in his fading months he tried twice to recycle what had already become a classic line for insouciance toward the horrors of the grave.

At the moment he charged toward a pratfall on the front pages of the *New York Herald*. Among the papers calling for some dollars-and-cents show of sympathy in 1895, it had shown the hottest enthusiasm, speaking for "millions" who "only wait a sign to come forward with any kind of assistance he might specify." James Gordon Bennett, Jr., had long yearned to lay an inside track to Twain, who as early as the spring of 1897 talked with a go-between about the *Herald*'s organizing a fund for him. After it had flopped, Twain would still openly admit having approved of it, and privately he cited precedents like the fund for Grant once proposed by the *New York Times*. Hindsight reveals that he badly underestimated the professional suspicion and jealously toward the *Herald* and overestimated the wand-waving, practical magic of his name even as enhanced currently by pathos. Still his so easily surviving the fiasco proves the resilient power of his prestige. As with his bankruptcy, the clear majority were eager to believe the noblest version—here that he had turned down any charity. Most of the rest simply let themselves forget overnight though Twain must have preached himself a reminder on the wariness needed in working the newspapers.

On 13 June he helped launch the fund campaign with an interview, which romanced that the bankruptcy had come "not by any fault of mine," a phrase that his claque kept echoing. The *Herald*'s biographical spread highlighted his worry about his fiscal honor but also reminded the sentimentalists that Susy's death had left him "heartbroken," a motif repeated on his wife's death and intimated as the cause of his own so soon after the drowning of his daughter Jean. Having blown his debt up to $200,000, or more than double the truth, the *Herald* argued that paying up for all the pleasure Twain had given to so many would constitute an act of fairness, not charity. Loudest on the patriotic note it called for proof that "republics are not ungrateful," that the populace can outdo aristocratic patrons. Since the staff of the *Herald* had alerted its friends and allies, it could at once reprint endorsements from seventeen other American newspapers, and its London and Paris offices lined up a little foreign support. Ominously, no other New York City daily joined the "world wide" appeal.

For two weeks the *Herald* pretended to gloat over a stampede to swell the fund. Along with editorials it featured a cumulative boxscore over a story patched together from the letters enclosing money. Unexpected, distractingly comic relief bubbled throughout the results, which closed at $2,938.45—$1,000 each from the *Herald* and Andrew Carnegie, $650 total from five others, and $288.45 from another fifty-five or so. Probably most burlesquable was the ten-cent level suggested for boys to thank the creator of Tom and Huck and for the poor to afford a symbolic part. Touchingly combining both constituencies, a "working widow" sent in the dime her two sons earned for a day of selling newspapers. But even traces of commercial self-advertising crept in, mostly for a mere dollar. Appropriate to Twain's origins, the irreverent hooked on to the growing absurdity. A practical joker contributed a dime over the name of somebody who then indignantly chipped in ten dollars; a long letter from "Selberry Mullers" struck a confusing mixture of clowning and warmth. Among the honest bouquets that of "all around literary athlete" may have caused the broadest smiles. Still, however thin, the dominant response, cued by the *Herald*, was patriotic loyalty to America's "most representative writer." Unless the *Herald* censored its mail, nobody had questioned or satirized that idea, which evidently had already joined the self-evident truths.

Twain, who—we should remember—had to wait for a copy of the daily story to cross the Atlantic by ship, held on doggedly while the *Herald* did print several surprised inquiries about whether it had his approval. By 16 June, Rogers cabled that "all friends think Herald movement mistake." On the nineteenth the younger Bliss, who was dreaming up a prospectus for *Following the Equator* that would state Twain had been determined to meet his debts "by his own labor only," warned bluntly: "Herald fund hurting you." That day Twain moved to call it off but did not insist until a week later. Under the *Herald*'s headline of "Mark Twain Declines Help," he spurned letting others share the load "while my health is good and my ability to work remains."[11] This bare-armed courage was quoted widely and appreciatively. With the "greatest pain and reluctance," just the obscure and somewhat off-beat *Chap-Book* judged him "apparently only too anxious to submit" to "indignity."

Defiantly if not pompously Twain had scrawled out a self-interview contending that the failure of the fund proved not that he lacked enough friends but that "they do not approve of this method." Warm but fallible after all, his intimacy with the press world should have told him that Bennett's competitors would not join in, though their tolerant silence in itself sounded a tribute to Twain. Likewise he should have expected many veteran observers to question the motives of the *Herald*, which did puff itself throughout the campaign; Rogers' second cable mentioned suspicions of another *Herald* "fake." No doubt wounding Twain more than Bennett, a scandal sheet in New York City perversely excoriated the "abominable assault" on his name, accusing the *Herald* of a "quite characteristic and cunningly conceived scheme" of a vague "revenge." Some glimmers of fact had also blunted the appeals to pity. Twain's self-interview acknowledged a rumor that he was "living in luxury," which did strike much closer to the truth than did dying in poverty. At the height of the campaign he got unprecedented pay to write up Queen Victoria's Diamond Jubilee for the *New York Journal*. Maybe hoping to stir up rebuttals, the *Herald* itself printed a letter protesting that Twain had bungled his financial affairs. Without panic he came to expect that the press would dance merrily on the collapsed balloon, as he would have done in his newspaper days. It could have turned his domestic tragedy into the death of a salesman of pathos. But, significantly, the *Chap-Book* was "trying not to see" a "groveling figure." Those who refused to look hurried on gratefully to some other event such as the Jubilee. At an embarrassing crisis the celebrity can benefit as much from benign neglect as from the most visible coups.

The debt itself still paid dividends in publicity. By November 1897 stories started circulating that Twain had squared the remainder with income from old copyrights and his latest books. Obviously, many persons among both those editing the news and those using it as grist for their conversation remained kindly intent on his affairs. By next January the rumors hardened into a proclaimed fact though details of the settlement took several months more. Eager to spread the final word, on 12 March 1898 Twain thanked a friend for getting the impersonal London *Times* to notice, "I have worked myself out of debt," and he gushed, "you could not have done me a greater favor"(†). He had already granted the *New York World* a short interview ("Mark Twain Proud and Happy / That's the Way It Feels, He Says, To Be Out of Debt—Longing for Home") in which

Life 29 (27 May 1897), centerspread. "Our Popular But Over-Advertised Authors: Do ~~They~~ We Need a Rest?"

Life 32 (18 August 1898): 129. (Probably by Theodore Wust)

he took pains to deny he was a "bad businessman." Howells would reminisce that Twain's course eventually "redounded to his glory among the nations of the whole earth, and especially in this nation, so wrapped in commerce and so little used to honor among its many thieves." His "old-fashioned" integrity elevated him above the dog-eat-dog present, which *Life* belittled sarcastically: "He has no faculty for business, having an obsolete idea that when a man fails he should pay his creditors, an unforgivable trait at the best." In total perspective, under the smokescreen raised to excuse his bankruptcy, Twain deserved some credibility for subscribing sincerely to the work ethic and for leavening his greed with the ideal of

Life 31 (26 May 1898): 438. Part of a text and series of drawings titled "Taking a 'Turn'; or, The Literary Cake-Walk"

self development. Images distanced from the test of personal acquaintance and grounded purely in hokum are an innovation of the 1920s. Although his success looked much swifter and more impetuously chancy than the classic trudge upward, it had built on years of effort and of hatching out salable products. And though his moneymaking quickened into grandiose projects he believed that it swelled the pool of accessible riches instead of reducing somebody else's share, that most capitalists created rather than monopolized wealth.

*   *   *   *

Twain's return to solvency validated his right to his triumphs in Vienna, then much more than now a symbol of aristocratic glamor. From late 1897 to May 1899 he was lionized to an almost unexplainable degree merely hinted at by his Berlin winter of 1891–92. Of course he cooperated by immediately building a bridge to the local press corps. At a meeting of the City Council he insisted on sitting with the "other" reporters, and he kept American correspondents cordial with inside stories. So his casual opinions were rushed to the United States along with tidings of the social honors from dignitaries finally capped by Emperor Franz Joseph, who invited him for a private visit. The *New York Times* stringer was especially diligent about dates and events while the magazines hunted for angles such as the doings of his family; the *Musical Courier* (7 December 1898) made Clara's piano lessons an excuse to report that the "name of Mark Twain is a household word here," and "feuilletons and anecdotes of him have filled the newspapers." He helped by both a decent knowledge of German and expertly humorous self-deprecation on the point. However, invited in March 1899 to lecture in Budapest by the Association of Hungarian Journalists, he even gained admirers who did not understand English.[12] The plain folks back home understood that his magnetism worked everywhere.

Quite reasonably they could have suspected him of going highhat. Although painfully sincere Stephen Crane judged that Twain had degenerated into a "society clown," the clear and present danger was still pomposity. Having sat for a frowning portrait reproduced on postcards over his signature, he used them himself. But any fears that the hobnobbing with aristocrats meant a defection from his barefoot past were shamed by his fervent public Americanism while the postcards, a kind of Yankee enterprise anyway, were balanced by his willingness to pose with a corncob pipe for another portrait. Overall his countrymen formed the impression he was behaving naturally, down to earth, without trampling the social niceties or clapping princes on the back; the time for swaggeringly confusing an earl with his butler had passed. They read that he considered his visit to the "most exclusive and conservative" of all royal courts "as a compliment not to himself so much as to Americans in general." In a tableau as vivid as a historical painting—according to hearsay—the "humorist's quiet, courteous manner, respectful but free from the cringing flattery with which the Emperor is wont to be treated, evidently pleased the ruler." George Ade later speculated that "much of the tremendous liking for Mark Twain grew out of his success in establishing our credit abroad," but Ade felt sure that anybody else who stayed away so long would have been "editorially branded as an expatriate." Like Ben Franklin and Will Rogers, Twain sensitively and self-consciously created the role of traveling exhibit for his national culture. He sanded away at the motto "I have filled the post—with some credit, I trust—of self-appointed Ambassador at Large of the United States of America—without salary."

His final eighteen months abroad, mostly in London, brought a lowering of dramatic tension—an effective lull before the mob-scene at his homecoming. Still, Americans got further episodes of a Twain equal to all occasions as a chum of world leaders on a steady basis, not just at banquets. Stooped—presumably for good—in posture and subdued by family problems, he had dared to accept the highest level of herohood and the vulnerability such exposure incurs. There are many more megalomaniacs than there is room for, but he had enough experience to gauge the burdens of apotheosis. He also had the shrewdness to realize that the methods that had brought him so far would not all work for continuing vibrancy, that playing it safe and freezing into the most loudly cheered patterns could be a mistake, that some of his clowning routines could turn counterproductive since their very success had finally raised him above them. Actually he did sometimes cavort almost as wildly as ever but in more sharply defined situations that made it clear he was doing an act or just an entr'-acte. More positively he perceived his chance to take another giant stride toward seriousness, thereby gratifying himself while aligning his popular dimensions more manageably, that is, bringing his dominant persona closer to his private attitudes while giving it a better balanced range. He joked more often about "practical morals in the place of theatrical—I mean theoretical—" but without stumbling into stodginess.

In keeping with his reputation for confronting the truth he also started to play openly with the fact that he was a highly privileged character, enjoyed for a frankness about even his weak or petty sides. During his tour he clipped out a news story about his impudently defending his attack on James Fenimore Cooper's novels with, "I got money for it." Although

The American Humorist.

Life 33 (2 March 1899): 173. From "*Life's Pantheon of Popular Pets*"

the strutting mood of the Twain persona broke into print less often than before, it boldly updated itself through his speeches of the late 1890s as his self-confidence found its old catlike footing. Defying false humility he responded at a banquet: "It does not embarrass me to hear my books praised so much. It only pleases and delights me. I have not gone beyond the age when embarrassment is possible, but I have reached the age when I know how to conceal it." He was developing that rare touch for a smugly personal tone, dangerously close to preening, that arouses interest or delight, not an uneasy rustle. Introduced as one of the "great" authors he demurred only that "they have a sad habit of dying off. Chaucer is dead, Spenser is dead, so is Milton, so is Shakespeare, and I am not feeling very well myself." That also became a famous passage at the time.

✳   ✳   ✳   ✳

Better signs agreed on taking Twain as a presumably classic writer. Too enthusiastic, the "Lounger" of the *Critic* declared him the most famous of living authors, ahead of Tolstoy, Zola, and Ruskin. In 1899 a poll for a hypothetical American Academy ranked him third though he still guessed that five-sixths of his sales came from "people who don't visit bookstores." When dedicating a library with the piety that "Literature and its temples are sacred to all creeds, and inviolate," he must have assumed that his own writing was unfit for the tabernacle; but that poll naturally made him wonder despite the nagging fact that his latest books, except for *Joan of Arc*, dissatisfied him by his own standards. Ironically, his raised status encouraged him to question the criteria which, he now suggested, had "misjudged" him "from the very first."[13] While mainline British critics continued to advance his reputation, domestic opinion, rather than just following their lead, was starting to argue that foreigners put his shaggy humor above his "true merits" such as a limpidly informal style even aside from the vernacular mode. The reassessments that the typical American essay or review had always felt obligated to make sounded more warily troubled than ever, more alert to a range of possibilities before and after his latest book.

The kindest effect that *Tom Sawyer Abroad* (1894) and *Tom Sawyer, Detective* (1896) could have had was to recall the two great "boy" books, while *Pudd'nhead Wilson and Those Extraordinary Twins* (1894) complicated more than it enhanced Twain's standing. Attempts to rediscover its greatness still run aground on the reefs left by the various drafts, written at a troubled time. However, more than might be expected, it was praised in 1910 for its comedy, vividness as a historical record, and "philosophy." Prone to euphoria that exaggerated favorable signs, Twain gloated that it was arousing a livelier response than any of his books since *Innocents Abroad*—in part because the *Century* had aggressively promoted the magazine serial with picture-posters. Furthermore the age liked its crime stories within a family setting. This also means that *Pudd'nhead Wilson* had a conventional ambience, thickened by the simplistic and racist illustrations; to a browser it looked like many a potboiler. On the other hand, readers encountered bitingly Twainian touches, and his hardcore fans could maintain that his fiction had grown profound. Since adults dominate the action its violence, pivotal device of miscegenation, strains of determinism, mean-spirited villain, and sustained irony cannot be laughed off.

The sardonic wryness was encapsulated by the chapter epigraphs or maxims, then the most fetching feature of the book. Soon the *Century* compiled a handout *Pudd'nhead Wilson's Calendar*, which it refurbished in 1897. Usually quick to spot the focus of applause, Twain developed a habit of spreading maxims around as a deluxe autograph. He refined new ones for *Following the Equator* and thereafter watched out for ideas, hoping to net enough for an entire book. After 1900 he cooperated several times with the marketing of postcards bearing his best-liked maxims. We now could not be less impressed that the public then saw him as rejoining the tradition of the newspaper wits, descended from the cracker-barrel sage of a rural America. But he was fully aware of the kinship with M. Quad or Josh Billings, whose "quaint & pithy maxims were on everybody's tongue" in the 1870s—to quote Twain.[14] Most nonliterary critics had his usually somber maxims in mind when they delcared that the presence behind *Pudd'nhead Wilson* evinced a reflective intellect, indeed a "philosopher." ("One of the most striking differences between a cat and a lie is that a cat has only nine lives.") Today the awe toward specialization resents so honorific a term for a catchy sentence or two distilling wisdom of the moment that sounds universal or, at its cynical best, triggers a psychic rebellion against a hollow commonplace.

Although *Personal Recollections of Joan of Arc* has disgraced Twain posthumously with several levels of readers, it met general approval in 1896. Even more than *Pudd'nhead Wilson* its tone and ending fitted the vibrations from his personal tragedies, which had reportedly darkened his vision but restiffened his courage. The leaky secret that he had tried to hide the authorship of *Joan of Arc* was mostly taken to prove he wanted its profundities appreciated even at the cost of royalties. He did settle for less money so long as the magazine serial did not carry his name. The cynics who suspect another stunt can find clues, mostly because he waffled for financial reasons and worried at first that his lecture tour needed more publicity. On the side of higher aspirations, to which he has at least equal rights, both his fame and his passing the age of sixty were impelling him to aim for that masterpiece which the Romantic poets had taught is the only reachable form of immortality. Anonymity would give the book a fair start with those who started to grin as soon as they heard his name. Also, his earthbound ego daydreamed about confounding the reviewers who had left as many scars on him as on any writer active for thirty years. How sweet it would be, after they had gone on record about the mystery-author, to stage a Tom Sawyer unveiling. Too late, a decent compromise occurred to him: S. L. Clemens on the title page instead of his trademark for humor.

His most faithful readers no doubt traced the continuity he felt with *The Prince and the Pauper*. Once more he had turned into a historian harvesting—the publisher's flyer fibbed—"twelve years of serious study." Others heard democratic echoes from *A Connecticut Yankee*; though sustained inferences for an egalitarian message from history will crumble under logical analysis, his Joan died a victim of priestcraft and the ingratitude of royalty. Qualitatively new was the sustained exposure of a Twain thrilled by patriotism and the holiness of maidenhood, thrilled into open sentimentality. One of the most elderly career-soldiers for the genteel tradition would recall, perhaps choosing his key word slyly, that *Joan of Arc* "struck the highest note of reverence."[15] A thoroughly comforting book, *Joan of Arc* treated inconsistencies like double-edged truths and blended Rousseauistic and Christian symbols into a misty moralism. Finding only glints of skepticism or loaded humor, Twain's lustiest followers must have feared that, like Isabel Archer, he was being "ground in the very mill of the conventional," of eloquent platitudes mistaken for refinement.

In stark contrast, *Following the Equator* (1897) was designed from the earliest scribbled note to boom as a subscription book. Like the appeals by the *Herald* fund, the prospectus, quoting a British "authority," pushed hardest on how Twain "expressed the sterling, fearless, manly side of a great democracy," on how he sees, feels, thinks, and "reasons like an American, is American." Softening the most provocative link with *Innocents Abroad*, it promised that he "has no reverence for things which in themselves are not reverend." The illustrations played just as safe with a humorist who was selling another enjoyable book but exemplifying the national virtues. While the frontispiece displayed his yachting cap and shaggy curls in a supposedly candid snapshot, he otherwise generally paraded through quasi-photographs in which the foreign milieu counted most. For renegade Trappists or anybody else ignorant of the tour, the book at least strengthened the image of Twain as habitually on the move and infused an exoticism stronger than that of the Sandwich Islands. Understandably, the text overstated his physical zip and his good humor toward the irritations of travel. With the press too quick at exaggerating his creakiness he needed to step lively, and his status no longer allowed the petty rages of a journalist baffled by Europe.

Following the Equator raises best the insoluble question of how concretely the unanalytic readers envisioned Twain's implied personae or distinguished among them and then of how heavily the broader image depended on his books rather than even his magazine writings. Insofar as the public Twain evolved out of the subscription trade, *Following the Equator* offered the most consistent poses. If merely because the text itself presented him as planning on a book all along, its author-traveler came much closer to what the real-life Twain was thought to be. Moreover this Twain had too much luster to pretend he was simply the buyer's roving ego. No longer appearing, much less threatening to pump a routine until he got a laugh, he regularly transmigrated, as the prospectus stated, into a "rough-and-ready philosopher." By then reviewers had a long track record to go by, and they did credit to their guild, though a worthwhile book never allows unanimity.[16] The sober *Chicago Dial* found an "eminently sagacious mixture of sense and nonsense"; the sophisticated *Critic* felt "as if traveling with a shrewd, kindly, sincere, and humorous man of the world who has kept only illusions enough to make life really living"; the centrist *Independent* valued most a "tolerance" that it elevated to a "large kindliness" and then to "sweet-natured." How many in the reviewers' own audiences, a small part of the great circle of buyers or borrowers, agreed with any of them was and will stay a puzzle. The most probable truth is that *Following the Equator* presented, once more, a mélange held together by a uniqueness each reader defined by his own lights. As much from the motive of helping Twain get needed royalties as from a growing tendency to blur his nonconformity, critics said much less than did the overall persona about imperialism and seldom mentioned his delight in the raucously irreverent Bombay crow. But Twain had in fact given himself a new degree of intellectual tolerance, making it even the tranquilizer of his contrast between true and false irreverence (chap. 53).

Intent on getting to Twain's *dämmerung*, biographers have undervalued his magazine articles during the 1890s, though a grudging observer conceded at the time that they "command a higher price and a larger audience than those of any other writer."[17] Giving them much care as a source of ready cash, he haggled over prices, and, in an era of heavy promotion by the monthlies, wheedled editors to step up the advertising; he encouragingly praised the posters for "The £1,000,000 Banknote" as so "inge-ious and seductive and beguiling" that they "made me go get that article and read it myself." Yet his professional standards had risen along with his fame. Reluctant about being associated with the high-paying but wide-mouthed syndicates that were springing up, he also guarded against the air of hackwork by not contracting for the "full glare of the big magazines too often." During a financially lean spell in March 1895 his rejection of a ten-day deadline from the *North American Review* jeered at those who "*puke* an article & think it's literature" (†). To one of the endless appeals for advice, he bragged on his practice of never submitting four out of every five manuscripts originally intended for the magazines.

The survivors reached a probably better educated yet bigger audience than his subscription books. As a serial *Pudd'nhead Wilson* brought him readers who scorned literature sold door to door. On the average his new essays and stories gave higher quality than his current books or a collection of his older short pieces like *Merry Tales* (1892). Surely they were more engaging and impressively versatile, ranging from the informal to the polemic with easy firmness about the general society, morals, or politics. "Is He Living or Is He Dead?" achieved thought-provoking farce (on the price of paintings), and "The Esquimau Maiden's Romance" came close (about cultural relativity). "Adam's Diary" revisited the Garden of Eden with a pathos that grew too shrill about wife and home during "In Defence of Harriet Shelley." At the right length on a feud later overdone, "Christian Science and the Book of Mrs. Eddy" charged into religious minefields. Although the press might well have carped at "Travelling with a Reformer" for the underlying snobbery—less explicit but more forceful than in *The American Claimant*—his narrative essay got, he exulted, "no end of compliments" for its system of jacking up insolent or slovenly clerks (†). "Stirring Times in Austria" proved that a plain democrat could observe European politics knowledgeably, and "Concerning the Jews"— still lengthening its list of reprintings as well as rejoinders today—displayed America's ambassador to the world as humanely analytical about racism. Closing out the decade, "The Man That Corrupted Hadleyburg" epitomized Twain's accelerating reputation for humor that somehow turned somber without losing its lift.

In 1891 he had re-identified himself as a working journalist by taking to Europe a deal for travel letters that included the *New York Sun* and the *Chicago Tribune*. Promoted as being on the "same Topic" as *Innocents Abroad*, the six letters had some jaunty illustrations of him as a brisk, egalitarian Yankee often frustrated by Old World bureaucrats. Beatified by his world tour he benefited financially when an intensified battle for circulation provoked in turn the traditionalists' "moral war" against the most "yellow"

New York World, 10 December 1899, Christmas Book, p. 2. Part of a spread for Twain's "My First Lie and How I Got Out of It"

papers, Hearst's *Journal* and Pulitzer's *World*. As one defense, Hearst bid in quality names like Stephen Crane and Henry James, with Twain a likely prospect also because Sam Moffett, who deserved the affectionate respect his uncle felt, had moved up to the *Journal*. Still Hearst had to pay Twain a premium rate for covering the Jubilee Procession. That led to talks about a lucrative contract, then to a handsome offer for excerpts from *Following the Equator*.[18] Although he apologized for not having Hearst bid before selling a dispatch from Vienna to the *World*, he also sold to the *World* "My First Lie" to highlight its Christmas supplement for 1899. Heartily favoring the war to liberate Cuba, Twain had not yet reacted against jingoism and would have taken more "yellow" money had he not signed a tight contract with the reorganized Harper firm.

∗　　∗　　∗　　∗

The Harper deal brought off the collected edition that had weighed significantly in his literary decisions since at least 1894. An aborted set in 1896–97 gave wellwishers a chance to cheer—and former scoffers a space to back around a little. Taking courage from the Oxford degree in 1907, William Lyon Phelps of Yale chose to "remember very well" when "mockery" would have greeted such a project. Unexpectedly, *Life* predicted that a "half dozen kinds of Mark Twain" would be "re-discovered" for their literary skill in "this array of imposing library volumes." It marked a quantum jump in prestige, "almost the only fact which looks like recognition of him as a real author," sniffed an essayist in the *Atlantic Monthly* who examined Twain's "vogue" as the vocal "type of multitude," as the American his admirers "would like to be were good manners and cultivation added to him."[19] By 1899 the mismatches of contracts from subscription and trade publishing were adjusted, and Twain could chortle that "President McKinley & other big guns" had ordered the deluxe, autographed set. For him the Uniform Edition, continually rearranged during the rest of his life and again made "complete," carried not a funerary but a festive air, sounded not a bugle of departure for Valhalla but stood as visible proof of his having arrived as Literature and having moved on from celebrity to Fame.

Instead of demanding the traditionally severe format, however, he took cues from the hottest trend in magazines, the monthlies geared by the advertising revenue from enlarging their audience through lighter and brighter content for less money. For example, a *McClure's* article on him in 1897 risked just enough text to ballast fifteen photographs; at two other times during the year it printed fresh shots rather than going to the files. Hindsight makes clear that the latest wave of magazines furnished a distinctly middlebrow entertainment and wisdom, a mold Twain could be pressed into without cries of sacrilege from either party. For a "character sketch" in 1898, *McClure's*, a bargain at fifteen cents, featured his surefire advice on how to get the job you want. (Evidently it rated him at that pitch of celebrity where true fans need a steady diet.) When the expanding *Ladies Home Journal* reached him fourth in its "New Form of Biography" series, it draped twenty anecdotes around seven pictures. (Vaguely embarrassed because some of the anecdotes "dribbled" into the Vienna newspapers, he renamed it the "Chambermaid's Home Journal.") Slouching toward our sinkhole of trivia, *St. Nicholas*, bought for juveniles by earnest parents, introduced "Mark Twain's Pets" in January 1899 with a photograph and engravings. He was only being practical in fussing over the nicest shots of himself and the Hartford house for the Uniform Edition, got up in handy, inexpensive volumes often with bright red bindings and with comfortably sized type appropriate for the "People's Author."

He likewise kept his Preface airy and brief. After a stab at a full introduction he settled on Brander Matthews, a friend who had gone on record generously and had certified his sensitivity to the magazine world yet could be billed as Professor of Literature in Columbia University. Heading volume one—*Innocents Abroad*, naturally—the "Biographical Criticism" hailed the self-sustained growth from a "sage-brush" reporter into an artist. It also hailed the maturing of a young jokester into an acute social observer who "transcends humor." Throughout, Matthews blurred Twain's long record for iconoclasm. The overarching motif was his embodiment of national virtues, summed up with an on-the-other-hand alertness to the pillars of the consensus:

Self-educated in the hard school of life, he has gone on broadening his outlook. . . . Spending many years abroad, he has come to understand other nationalities, without enfeebling his own native faith. Combining a mastery of the commonplace with an imaginative faculty, he is a practical idealist. No respecter of persons, he has a tender regard for his fellow man. Irreverent toward all outworn superstitions, he has ever revealed the deepest respect for all things truly worthy of reverence. Unwilling to take pay in words, he is impatient always . . . to see the thing as it is. He has a habit of standing upright, of thinking for himself, and of hitting hard at whatsoever seems to him hateful and mean; but at the core of him there is a genuine gentleness and honest sympathy, brave humanity and sweet kindliness.

Overanxiously, Twain also lined up an essay by Moffett which landed at the rear of a miscellany in volume 22.[20] While keying on the humanitarian and universal Twains it echoed the theme of self-development.

There was flagwaving galore when Twain came back home in 1900. A word-of-mouth rumor on 31 July had collected a pushing crowd at the pier, but in early October he announced the exact date of his return from what the press pitied as his "voluntary exile." In anticipating this "Hero as Man of Letters" the *New York Times* thanked him for putting to shame the "old sneers at 'Yankee sharp practice.'" That theme reverberated within the roar of welcome that rolled far beyond metropolis. His collected edition aside, Twain now functioned in his culture as an exemplar of character grounded in a sense of responsibility rather than as simply a personality in the looming sense of somebody noted for appeal or exposure, however devoid of social or moral content. The *Southern Churchman* believed that by demonstrating the strength of individual honesty over "materialism" Twain had benefited humanity "as much . . . as he has ever done in his writings." For happier glory he had a "record of triumphs won in all lands" by "so plainly an American of Americans that no amount of foreign travel can ever expatriate his spirit." The *Minneapolis Times* praised all his points down to his "well-known modesty." By then insiders needed a warning from the hero of "The £1,000,000 Bank-Note": "I might be joked about still, but reverently, not hilariously, not rudely; I could be smiled at, but not laughed at"—certainly not in Minneapolis and presumably not in St. Paul and Duluth. Another editorial professed "love" for this "sweetest-natured of our humorists" before closing with its relief that he was "at last

mancipated from even the most fantastic bonds of self-respect and con-
cience."
   The excess of such virtue had not swept Twain into a crushing classi-
al tragedy. Admired all the more for avoiding that, he became a truly
domestic hero. When the Twain persona had first swaggered into view he
was already presenting himself and others as habitually acting out their
ives with theatrical gestures and passionate speech.[21] Since then his career
had grown increasingly dramatic by any definition. However, until the
mid 1890s it had lacked the suspense of a sharp, huge crisis. In surmounting bankruptcy despite the shocking death of his oldest daughter, his life
had taken on the dialectic and symmetry of an actual play. Recognizing
hat, Twain would carry on his old game of publicity with a still greater
self-awareness and—as it turned out—an alertness to forestalling anticlimax or just a dwindling end. In nineteenth-century fashion he also made
sure to give his drama both ethical and social point.

CHAPTER 8

Moods and Tenses in Interviews

A SWARM OF REPORTERS waited for Twain's ship to dock at 10 P.M. on 15 October 1900. Today television crews would have jostled for the best angle. That night marked the crest of interviews with him, slightly higher than when he came back with his doctorate from Oxford University. Between 1879 and 1907 he was interviewed more often, evidently, than anybody else, including the most eager politicians. The three hundred or more texts (counting all versions of the same occasion) have left a mostly ignored attic full of his ideas and attitudes. His daughter Clara finally wondered how he "could manage to have an opinion" for the press "on every incident, accident, invention or disease in the world." In 1906 pride rather than weariness prompted his comment during a speech that the "New York papers have long known that no large question is ever really settled until I have been consulted; it is the way they feel about it, and they show it by always sending to me when they get uneasy." The collective result left the public feeling easy about his accessibility, more familiar with his presence, and intimate with his casual tastes as well as his convictions.

Amplifying his lectures and speeches, the interviews particularly helped to spread his personal impact beyond New York City, where the press knew him on sight by 1870. On his trip back to the Mississippi Valley in 1882 local reporters caught his reactions at the stops between St. Louis and

Minneapolis. For the tour with Cable he was happy to be interviewed in many small towns east of the Mississippi, north of the Ohio, and throughout New England. Starting the American leg of his world tour in Cleveland, he obliged half a dozen reporters whose accounts were reprinted as far away as Australia; he left an especially rich trail in the Northwest before sailing from Vancouver. His trips for private business or pleasure, to and through most of the major cities, rarely went unnoticed. The contents aside, the net of interviews signaled to the public that he rated prime space, swelled more and more often by drawings or half-tone photographs. It is easy to spot most items, all the more because editors waved his name in the headings of stories that involved him even tangentially.

The images aimed at or in turn suggested by the question-answer format enlarged several characteristics of the Twain presented within his writing and implied behind it. Above all, they confirmed that his spontaneity blazed far hotter than contrived literary effect. At his death the *Chicago Tribune* observed that after 1890 he "confined much of his more glancing wit to after dinner speeches and interviews"—the main sources of the quick jokes now passed around to his credit. ("How many cigars do you smoke a day?" "As many as I can—one at a time as a rule.") As kindred spirits of his joshing and cynical side, reporters egged him on. Of course, often paid by space-rates, they were prospecting for catchy bits and inflating any they could get. Nevertheless, except when skirting a deadly trap, he stayed loose and friendly, letting them into his bedroom with notebook and camera too. Someone on the *Grand Forks* (N.D.) *Times* would recall finding him "as easy to interview as the aspiring author of the poem published in the lower corner of the town weekly. He could talk on any topic, even the weather, and glorify it with his humor." Yet his way of refusing to stop and answer "a few questions" could also ignite a story that cycled through the exchanges and passed into the guild's folklore: "My editor asked me to come to the station and see you." "That's nice of your editor. Run along and tell him that you did." Most of Twain's duels with reporters were enjoyed by both sides as part of the game, newsworthy on its own. In December 1909 the *New York Tribune* decided that an uncooperative Twain must be seriously ill because he "always had something humorous up his sleeve to drop casually" when the press corps clustered around.

Some interviews gave the public its closest glimpse of the contemporary man acting interpersonally, that is, engaging in give and take and perhaps interrupting his answers to joke with a companion or cross-examine a waiter about the breakfast eggs. Other interviews evoked attitudes seldom expressed elsewhere, particularly about his own work. Because reporters continually nagged him, he now and then opened up about how his books had originated, what they tried to say, or which ones he favored at the moment. Likewise he chatted freely about his reading at the moment unless he was choosing to act the shaggy know-nothing. In composite the interviews fall into a rich if treacherous mosaic of his public image: the copy editors' filtering of poses, facts, paraphrase, and direct quotation—all colored to start with by the reporters' cues and shadings. The product sank into the minds of a clientele who seldom responded explicitly but discussed Twain with deepening familiarity and changing opinions. His willingness itself emerged as a dimension of his character. A hack safely estimated in 1901 that "probably no other living author has been so beset" by the press or "more amiable or liberal in his responses." The amiability made Twain look respectful of the public's right to know whatever might catch its fancy but clouded further his standing with the clergy of high culture. More fundamentally, either reaction recognized that an author who tolerated almost any question tossed at him was granting the profane world an unprecedented intimacy.

✳   ✳   ✳   ✳

The newspaper interview grew up in the bad company of vote-seekers and criminals and—to the British mind—Americans. Now it seems an inevitable step, though quibbling about its origins—the fascination with "firsts"—goes on. As early as 1836 James Gordon Bennett the elder began using direct quotations in the *Herald's* crime news. He also ranks as the originator in the opinion of some who tie its first use to politicians, especially President Andrew Johnson. Some amateur historians have broadened its pattern to include Socrates and Plato or else Samuel Johnson's Boswell, though Tories despised it as a garish Yankee vulgarity, an effect and also a cause of social leveling, and another crude practice sure to debase the press everywhere.[1] The cultural elitists started out just as hostile in the United States. Supervised by E. L. Godkin, the weekly *Nation*, itself a brash departure in other ways, deplored this latest vehicle for "spice" and the "sensational," for rubbing elbows with "notoriety." The key professional charge of unreliability, echoed by others, sounded all the more plausible because a discredited Andrew Johnson had used interviews to plead his case through a favored reporter and because the upstart *New York Sun* had gone in for them recklessly. Pushiness by newspapers slanted for a mass readership was the root of the broader complaints. On Washington's Birthday in 1870 Longfellow noted his inappropriately "disagreeable sensations" pivoting on having "been 'interviewed,' and private conversation eported to the public." Henry James would regularly satirize the "age of newspapers and telegrams and photographs and interviewers" like Henietta Stackpole, who snoops for a journal baldly named after her trade in *The Portrait of a Lady*. Chapter 16 of *The Bostonians* opens with a scathing portrait of Matthias Pardon, the "most brilliant young interviewer on the Boston press." Only in 1904, fittingly on his American tour, did James grant the first interview in his life. Although Walt Whitman, who still presented himself as their old colleague, got reporters to disguise some of his jottings as interviews during his trip west in 1879, he carried no weight toward enlarging the limits of tasteful behavior. Howells' *Rise of Silas Lapham* (1885) caught Bartley Hubbard in action as an interviewer in order to show that he was degenerating into a cynical opportunist.

Exasperatingly for those who prefer an incorrigible Twain he sometimes gave comfort to the old guard of journalism on this point of caution too. Always alert to the latest trend, he had published in December 1868 a jovial mock interview with president-elect Grant. But next, on the rise and feeling very professional, he concocted a jeering burlesque for the *Buffalo Express*, with the objectionable new term set in quotation marks, and he ridiculed the *Sun* for stooping to such frippery, which fell beneath his standards for building up a nationally respected daily and also those of the *Hartford Courant*, subscribed to by Nook Farmers and friends. By 1874 he had composed "Encounter with an Interviewer," eventually a staple of his platform repertoire. He later stated its basic pattern or point as, "Whenever you give the interviewer a fact, give him another fact that will contradict it." So a naive reporter, whose come-on pleaded that "to interview any man who has become notorious . . . is all the rage now," is fed one sillier non sequitur after another. Since the sketch amused all kinds of audiences, native and foreign, and appealed to several translators, it must have functioned as a display of Twain's humor at its wildest and, more subtly, as a rebellion against the strain of holding any rational colloquy. But it plainly made interviewers look foolish.

Twain could not have delivered it engagingly for over thirty years unless he had kept some impatience toward the interview, especially as practiced on him. By the 1890s he often felt he could get any needed publicity in some more effective way and could do the smoothest job of presenting his ideas, a modest attitude for him. Furthermore, a story about his turning down a reporter could assure the stiff-necked that he was no longer lapping up publicity. But his resistance sprang primarily from boredom with hackneyed questions and other assaults of ineptitude. Several times he sighed that reporters missed the wisest approach, which fitted his genius anyhow: do not interrupt once the respondent gets rolling on a congenial topic. Although Twain rarely resented some journeyman's attempt to compete with or even improve on him, readers must have groaned over humor that paled to ghastliness beside his incandescence. So that folly too could have impelled him to growl that the "poorest article I ever wrote and destroyed was better worth reading than any interview with me that was ever published." Finally, as the dailies swelled into big business he grumbled that they were getting something for nothing or "literary charity" out of him, something furthermore that—he warned his brother as early as 1887—"might be worth putting some day into my *auto-biography*."

Still his greatest irritations concerned the resulting image. Whether from remorse or prudence he usually regretted his quoted slurs at fellow writers, such as Bret Harte. At other times he was misquoted or had words put in his mouth; one exceptionally inflated item struck him as "a miracle equal to the loaves and fishes." Anyone intent on what Twain really meant rather than how he was perceived has to use the texts suspiciously.[2] Even at best, according to him, the intended meaning or effect failed to come through the page. This was especially true of humor, set down without crucial gestures and his expert timing. More fundamentally, he insisted, when set into print the modulations of speech get lost, not just in his case but invariably, because "print is a poor vehicle for 'talk.' " Near the end of a lifetime of experience he decided that "nobody can be reported even approximately except by a stenographer. Approximations, synopsized speeches, translated poems, artificial flowers, and chromos all have a sort of value but it is small." He tried to exact promises about not being quoted in the first person, but also concocted a classic example of how a flight of eloquence draggles its wings when deformed into "he-said" bits and snatches. Still worse frustration came from being surrounded by notepads open for a burst of witticisms that the subconscious refused to launch. Every offhand bull's eye meant that more "people are constantly expecting me to say extremely clever and brilliant things" though, as he openly confessed, his impromptu speeches took the longest grooming. It finally was not the expectations he minded but his inability to satisfy them all and the resulting aftershocks as measured on his extremely sensitive seismograph.

Whatever his complaints the irreducible fact remains that he continued to grant interviews after getting over the initial pleasure at such attention or his need to pull out of the pack clamoring for it. As one reason, he understood the reporters' side; if their paper was racking up millions they were just scrambling for a few dollars to live on. Familiar with anecdotes of his kindness toward some cub, those brushed off tended to sigh that it just had not been their lucky day. They knew where he lined up concerning their foreign critics. When the reporter from the *South Australian Register* (14 October 1895) apologized for the "ordeal" of the interview as an American invention, Twain rejoined that "an accurate interview is a good thing," treated responsibly by the best papers at home. In Vienna he teased a Russian for lacking the aggressiveness of his Yankee counterparts. Waxing unusually ponderous in 1907 he argued that, while lately overused, the interview serves well the "lawyer or business man, whose business is benefited through getting his opinions and interests before the public." If partisans of the proto-beatnik Twain mistrust that passage, its underlying receptiveness can be traced over decades. Before his essay "Concerning the 'Interview'" drifted into sighs of pain it granted that the average journalist, operating in good faith, "only thinks he is making things pleasant for you"(†).

To another apology from the *Times of India* Twain graciously conceded, "Everyone has his moods and tenses . . . but when I am going about at leisure . . . I would as soon be interviewed as not." More positively, he liked to rise above the safe dullness of "no comment," let his moods show, and broadcast opinions on any subject from the faddish to the immemorial. Sometimes a personal, even petty motive had him all primed for a reporter. Angry over a bill for $300, he threatened to let himself be sued and then "state my case to the interviewers," or he planned for a brief session that could be quoted in an ad plugging a health-food venture of his. A mixture of self-interest and principle regularly drove him into leisurely chats about improving the laws on international copyright. But he also submitted to plenty of interviews in order to promote humanitarian causes ranging from a children's theater to a crusade against atrocities in the Belgian Congo.

Unlike so many celebrities, Twain did not yearn childishly for both seclusion and ongoing visibility. During the 1890s, before and after the world tour, he often genuinely wanted to lie low within the bosom of his family. Nevertheless he gave no sign, hidden or open, of agreeing with the latest flurry of complaints that the press corps, armed now with cameras, was trampling the constitutional right to privacy at home and the human right to walk the streets uninterviewed and unphotographed. Instead, grateful for his popularity, he regularly obliged again the prying interest in his affairs he had helped stimulate. So the interviews kept rolling into print with some credit also due the reporters who knew how to wheedle the boon of "just one question," which hooked into another and eventually got him going. The experts fanned a fire from almost any spark, if nothing else enlivening him into a paragraph or two about his reason for refusing to talk. Even a tersely sardonic protest against performing free of

charge made a kernel for a story the editor would expect readers to like
In short, when they saw a heading about Twain and some interviewer they
looked for another showing of his fascinating unpredictability of role or
temperament.

＊　　＊　　＊　　＊

The interviews fall roughly into two sorts. From twenty to twenty-
five were prearranged, often with some proviso for checking the text though
nobody would later recall being censored; they generally portrayed Twain
as reflective and fairly subdued. Overall, the rest showed him as impulsive,
often on the move to somewhere, habitually jocular, and much easier to
identify with as he shared his problem of the moment, such as, on his
departure for Europe in 1878 or his return the next year, taking care of the
family baggage. During the tour in 1884–85 the press transmitted verbal
snapshots of horseplay at the hotel in Cincinnati, his lolling in the wings
while Cable held the stage in Detroit, and his wholehearted style of loafing
away the day in Rochester. When the University of Missouri awarded an
honorary degree in 1902, the St. Louis papers seized their chance at candid
sessions. The *Post-Dispatch* man rode east to share Twain's breakfast on the
train from New York, watched him gratify an autograph hunter and josh
the porter, and gratefully bagged two anecdotes that put the laugh on the
raconteur himself. Trailing him around the city, the *Star* recorded the same
comic self-deprecation—which happened to play up his laziness—but made
most of how the "tranquil, whimsical old man," avoiding both fake humility and preening, "took the adulation with quiet dignity." Thoroughly
charmed, the reporter added his bit to the notion that Twain "never penned
a line to bring the sting or blush of shame to any reader's cheek." It had
started hovering above him as a cliché but also a secular prayer, a denial
of reality that makes a good example of why Ernest Hemingway's generation detested official rhetoric. At Twain's best he exploited such tunnel
vision for healthy, realistic purposes. To insist that he should have brutally
corrected it takes unimpeachably high ground but also presumes he could
have done so without causing counter distortions. On almost as touchy a
point, he ordinarily refused to stroke local pride, responding irreverently
or frankly to the cue of "how do you like Our Great City?"

The best-known impromptu interview of Twain was done by Rudyard Kipling and published in the United States by the *New York Herald*
just as Kipling's exotic fame swelled up. Reprinted in one of his books just
as that fame crested in 1899, its currency was proved by steady references
thereafter to Kipling's regret that he had not stolen Twain's corncob pipe

as a keepsake. While throbbing with worship of a "master of tears and mirth, skilled in the wisdom of the true inwardness of things" inculcated by a "joyous and variegated past," Kipling took a fellow professional's interest in Twain's sermonette on copyright. The other chief Twain idea relayed to the public was his perplexity at the difficulties of being honest with oneself, all the tougher because the conscience behaves like a spoiled child instead of giving pragmatic counsel. Always competitive, the *New York World* had rushed out to get his reaction to the spread in the *Herald*. Cheerfully admitting or pretending he had not seen it, he went on to apologize for his absent-minded blunder of not offering lunch to a pilgrim from distant India. The most concrete effect was more publicity for Kipling's text, but both papers happened to show Twain at his expansive best in 1890, just before bankruptcy started to close in.

The most curious interview during the next few years ran simultaneously in the *St. Louis Republic* and *Buffalo Express* on 1 April 1894. It is probably authentic in essence though the date raises suspicion and only a tape recorder could have caught the exact rush of words. Whatever the source, it presented Twain at his most mercurial intellectually, darting from idea to witticism and back again; it set circulating a few vintage yarns, notably one about a bullpup with a glass eye. In passing, he joked grittily about his "lying" and his "success as a moral instructor." But an arranged interview in early 1895 distinctly modulated the tone as he philosophized in his Paris "studio" about French wit, the pitfalls for defining a national character, and the latest twists of diplomatic alliances in Europe. Those who saw both of these texts had to vacillate between taking him as complex and merely erratic, as a cosmopolitan observer unable to hold a straight face for long and a comedian trying to prate wisdom.

For the world tour Twain wanted steady publicity, which mounted up to include over seventy interviews. This group often touched on his literary tastes and judgments of his peers as well as of his own books. With deeper coherence than in 1884–85, he discussed the art and trade of lecturer, in the process making it obvious how hard he worked to give audiences the full value of their tickets. His opinion on dead and live humorists was naturally sought and was received with gravity.[3] But Australian or Indian or South African reporters wanted most to hear the saga of his career, especially after their curiosity was whetted by an anecdote from his piloting or western days, and he was inspired to spin a few items of fakelore that slowly drifted toward the United States. Clearly in control of any white-haired nostalgia, he could snap back to his concerns with the present or elaborate on his laziness, a warmly absurd idea about such a personage lugging a burden of voluntary debt around the equator. He flaunted his prosaic side further by itemizing his boils and other aches or revealing that he hauled candles along to fight the dinginess of hotel rooms skimpy on electricity. It is no wonder that so many millions believed that they knew him intimately, freckles and all. The people back home also registered the fact that he did not put on stiff airs for strangers.

His image as globe trotter centered on a posture of judicious responsibility in a tacit putdown of the British and, more lately, French visitors who had rasped American pride. The regular questions about a possible new book met with his regretful criticism of tourists who flit through a country but then judge it sweepingly. He was obviously making the effort to learn more about each of his stopping places, both its history and current problems. In Australia he inquired about free trade and recent prohibition laws; in India, poverty and famine; in South Africa, mining and the preludes to the Boer War. Balancing on the highwire of comparisons he diplomatically handled questions about America's penchant for personal violence, the plight of its blacks, or the rights of labor unions. His countrymen read that he had discussed local and international politics without either offending his hosts or tolerating discourtesy to his native land. They at least respected his call in Bombay for Anglo-American friendship when President Cleveland twisted the tail of the British lion over Venezuela. Once Twain had left the United States, no single interview created a sensation, and the columns in a faraway weekly stayed buried as a rule. Yet excerpts and approving bits of editorials inched through the network of requotation to form a composite portrait, sharper than the grainy newspaper photographs at that time, of an earnest citizen, a magnetic presence, a master humorist who continued to refine his touch for the occasion, a cosmopolite, and a self-trained intellectual loyal to his origins.

Somehow, the *Herald* fund did not spoil that portrait, enhanced next by the Austrian triumphs (which brought interviews in local German, Hungarian, and Russian—soon joined by Swedish and then Italian along with a Berlin item from 1891 and a French one from 1894). Before leaving Vienna in May 1899 Twain granted an interview to the London *Times*, which might have argued that the favor still ran the opposite way. This prestigious forum announced his plan for a prose-portrait gallery of his contemporaries too candid to unveil for a hundred years. Disarmingly, intriguingly, provocatively he justified excluding himself: "You cannot lay bare your private soul. . . . It is too disgusting." Back in London by June he told the *Chronicle* more about his "Doomsday" book and also proudly dropped some details on his collected edition and, poised between gratitude and Yankee uprightness, on his audience with the emperor of Austria-

Hungary. Surely the reporters asking Twain for an audience did so with increasing deference and expected less tomfoolery than ever.

*   *   *   *

But in May 1900, as his family was deciding to return home, he made a speech in which he joked about running for president in the fall. His text, which the *New York World* had sent by cable, was greedily reprinted, and Harry Truman's mother clipped it from the *Cincinnati Enquirer* for her scrapbook.[4] The kidding expanded into an interview for the *World* of 17 June headed: "Mark Twain Says He's Discouraged / Every Sort of Crank Except Himself Has a Presidential Following." Beyond doubt, the intimate of emperors and prime ministers had not stifled his irreverence and, furthermore, his sheer playfulness. Yet he was also, perhaps unconsciously, doing advance publicity for his impending return. On 28 September he forehandedly sent the *San Francisco Bulletin* his "Christmas greetings"—a mixture of "home feeling" for the West Coast and comic boasting as a "neglected benefactor" of its prosperity. Ready to sail in October, he let the *New York Herald* witness his quicksilver moods by clowning about the stiffness of the beds in London hotels and orating sonorously for Anglo-American solidarity in the bearpit of power politics. With the *World* which first hurried in a short cabled version but printed a long text on the fourteenth, he now stayed basically sober, reminiscing about his career as a reporter and *The Innocents Abroad*, reconfirming the facts on his "100-year" book, and speculating about the November election. Ominously, he declared for the first time that American actions in the Philippines looked very much like imperialism. The more than a dozen reporters at the dock in Manhattan had a rich choice of his leads for a question.

Since some of that bustling group worked for wire services and syndicates, the interviews were widely recopied along with an original, welcoming editorial. In their carefulness, tone, points of emphasis, and the space allowed they set up a comparative exhibit of the newspapers themselves. For instance the still ponderous *New York Evening Post* had just a news story quoting the political opinions it liked. One of the most orderly accounts (in the *Tribune*) remarked that Twain fielded questions for fifteen to twenty minutes; however, the time spent fencing with him usually seemed shorter than it was. His debts and world travels came up right away, naturally, with the resulting columns lengthened by the standard rebriefing for new or forgetful readers. While nobody hinted any doubt, Twain made it perfectly clear that his patriotism had survived all foreign seductions, and several reporters featured his swearing to a fellow passenger that he would break both legs to stop himself from ever leaving the United States again. Noteworthy also were his literary plans which marked an energetic, productive author rather than an exile creeping home to die.

In almost every interview the ebullient personality towered above the specific opinions. Leading the consensus that Twain, no longer stooped or quaint, magically looked younger than when his countrymen last saw him in 1895, the *New York Herald* presented him as exclaiming on the gang-plank, "I have had lots of fun. I have enjoyed myself . . . in every country and under every sky." Although joking further about a candidacy for president, he hit a memorable level in explaining his strategy as liar. The tolerantly skeptical questions about the book held over until the year 1999 triggered a set of paradoxes he had been polishing. The *Sun* carried this version: "I never yet told the truth that I was not accused of lying, and every time I lie some one believes it. So I have adopted the plan, when I want people to believe what I say, of putting it in the form of a lie. That is the difference between my fiction and other people's. Everybody knows mine is true." This flirted with infinite regression. The *Herald* interview gave a stronger effect of a desire to "disseminate facts" and "speak the truth." While the readers of any version may have found it primarily comic, some must have listened to him more keenly thereafter, watched still closer for irony, or even wondered if the truths that society took as self-evident could mask pompous delusion. The then much more common habit of browsing two or three newspapers left other diverging perspectives, but anybody who skimmed a favorite daily for headlines knew that Twain was back—patriotically touched by the ovation, eccentrically spry for his years, and as provocative as always.

His daughter Clara never forgot the "atmosphere of adulation," the "most sensational kind of cordiality from the public, press, and friends" which made every day like "some great festive occasion." When the family settled at 14 W. 10th Street in Manhattan, mistaken callers pestered a household at 14 E. 10th. Of course that made a hook for a brief interview in which Twain protested genially, "I could peter myself all out in two months by talking against a reporter's pencil so that I couldn't sell a thing." No doubt some of those callers had represented the press. Before the family managed to move from a hotel, a *World* artist cornered him at breakfast, wangled the liberty of sketches, and scribbled notes for her illustrated layout: " 'My Impressions of America' / and Kate Carew's Impressions of the Great Humorist / An Interview in Which He Refuses To Be Interviewed." Picking up from shipside, this noninterview began, " 'The trouble with us in America,' said Mark Twain, 'is that we haven't learned to speak the truth.' "

Competitively, the big dailies hung on his trail. The *World* shadowed him to a Yale-Princeton game where, adorned with a "huge yellow chrysanthemum," he at once set off several "Sis-boom-ah's" and later an occasional "Tiger" while the reporter stuck close enough to catch his reactions to football. In and near New York City, some *World* scout tracked him as keenly as a Natty Bumppo, and the following summer "after much persuasion, seconded by the kindly offices of Mrs. Clemens," its journalist-photographer could display him at ease in the Adirondacks. The *Herald* had already scored with "Mark Twain Bearded in His New York Den" (20 January 1901), another thin story fattened by snapshots. With the half-tone process now cheaply available, his photogenic qualities made him a prize subject for the gray, fuzzily defined prints that annoyed the elitists as another lowering of esthetic standards.[5] The farewell visit to Hannibal in 1902 rated top priority from a press squad with cameras aimed at retrospective, sentimental angles such as his "boyhood home" and "childhood sweetheart," while his spontaneous chatter kept his present self vivid. Thanks to his open confidences during the past two years about touches of dyspepsia, his digestion got more publicity than he may have intended. But the most touching moments and photographs of his parade through the land of Tom and Huck flew over the wire services, now well organized nationally.

A dogged loser in the scramble for beats and scoops was Hearst's *Journal*, fallen from Twain's favor on political grounds if no other. Its sprawling, heavily photographic story of 11 November 1900 meekly admitted that America's "most famous humorist" had refused to grant an interview. His pre-eminence had solidified into an achievement in itself, entitled to its willfulness. Swiping from competitors, openly eavesdropping, and playing up what seemed the hit of the homecoming interviews, the *Journal* had him posing as the "laziest man in the world" and as a habitual liar who "never had sufficient reputation for veracity to get himself convicted without corroborative evidence." Unabashedly it reported a typically disarming complaint against being hounded now by photographers too: "There are always more or less drawbacks to fame, as the man said when the sheriff was chasing him." In 1902 the tireless *American and Journal*, renamed after a major political blunder, faked a brief interview so well that "Mrs. Astor Injures Mark Twain's Feelings" could easily pass as genuine for its blend of irony, egalitarianism, sentiment, and yarning. Surely even more often than the record shows, the Hearst reporters went on jockeying for firsthand stories, pretending, for instance, to solicit his advice about the snags lurking for President Theodore Roosevelt on his trip on the lower Mississippi in 1907. There was no chance they might decide

New York Journal and Advertiser, 11 November 1900, *American Magazine Supplement*, p. 18

to ignore Twain. That would only hurt their image as news hawks when the rest jumped to his call. Between 1900 and 1910 the Hearst papers in New York City may have outdone even the *World* for column-inches about him. His name and face had undeniably made a deep impression at the tabloid level.

All sorts of journalists, from both sexes, kept approaching him hopefully in spite of rejections which twice included Theodore Dreiser, as pushy as any other freelancer. Having turned down offers of pay, Twain especially resented visitors who alchemized a chat into a salable account or invented dodges such as asking for a palm print and then retailed his casual remarks. Yet the cordiality toward his onetime guild lasted. According to the patient *American*, as he was being wheeled from the Bermuda steamer a few days before his death he turned and waved to "his old friends, the reporters, whom he always greeted jovially." Their hot pursuit had continued after the victory for a new copyright law and defeat—he thought—for Congo reform canceled the last two big motives of his interest in being interviewed. To be sure, the garrulity of old age could have taken over, but reporters are fired for turning in dull copy. As much as ever they expected lively material, and they felt that his final motive for obliging them was his now ancient camaraderie with the "boys," reinforced by his tolerance toward the public's right to hear more about whatever subject it wanted.

✳   ✳   ✳   ✳

Usually trusting as well as friendly toward capable interviewers, Twain had nevertheless tried to develop some rules for accuracy. On vitally important topics this led to his late practice of passing around a written text—a forerunner of the modern press release—offered sometimes on an all or nothing basis. It got placed more prominently, he found, and carried more force than his old letters to the editor; in 1905–6 he handed out several attacks on King Leopold. Likewise he started jotting down answers to questions that he allowed to be handed in or else anticipated, most notably for the Maxim Gorky scandal of 1906 and the garden party at Windsor Castle where he socialized with the king and queen. To lower the pressure of his daughter Clara's wedding in 1909, he prepared typed copies, with his inked changes, of an interview that some reporters submitted pretty much intact. Framed in questions answered by a lightly humorous "Mr. Clemens," it covered the likely points of curiosity, including the guest list, and slipped in a plug for the local "Mark Twain" public library.

Its proficiency suggests that Twain qualifies as coauthor of the interviews with him, taken collectively. Capitalizing on his training as a journalist, an ability to stay in the swing of and even dominate most situations, acute sensitivity to his listeners' reactions, and a lightning adaptiveness, he exerted much influence on the drift of the exchange and the write-up of his responses or digressions. An interviewer admitted in 1902 that Twain "had taken the wheel from the moment we came in the room, and piloted the conversation." Furthermore this was a self-feeding process since many reporters, consciously as often as unknowingly, were directed by what they had already read themselves. In reverse the interviews may have influenced Twain to choose a question-answer framework for some of his nonfictional pieces such as *What Is Man?* His unpublished boost to feminism, "An Imaginary Interview," is a direct instance.[6] While bare in structure it lets the journalist warn the "Lady" that his counterparts have the habit of taking over a conversation, and soon he does just that. In the *New York Herald* (30 August 1903) Twain talkatively pestered himself for a color story on the America Cup races. Besides fulfilling his assignment it slyly retouched some lately familiar aspects of his persona such as the "slave of truth" and focused his joking about being paid by the word, claiming here that his resulting flight from polysyllables had changed the standards of prose style. More certainly his affinity with interviewers had multiplied his challenge to the rules for the decorum of literary artists and had offered the genteel tradition a model for rapport with the masses it pretended to approach.

Even his owlish peers approved his unflagging readiness to discuss copyright reform while the wage-earning public surely respected him for his demand to get all the rewards of his literary labor. But many constituencies might have rustled uneasily at his "Mark Twain Interviewed," which comes up with "bronchitis and real estate" for the response to, "What is interesting you most, at present, among the great questions now agitating the public?" As the Young Interviewer fences to draw out a judgment on German resistance toward the Monroe Doctrine, Twain insists on praising the two houses he owns. Also, he grumbles about the "equities of the interview," which benefits a politician or an artist with paintings to sell but begs from authors their stock in trade. Only eventually does he challenge the Monroe Doctrine, which "will stand unmolested as long as we are strong enough to take care of it, but not longer" because it is "private property . . . not gotten up by advice and consent of the foreigner."[7] Still, Twain's own property may have been foremost in his mind. Anxious to unload, he had earlier approved a "Mark Twain's Home for Sale" listing of the Hartford residence after expecting that a simple ad "will probably bring out the interviewers & then I will tell them all about it"(†). If undignified to some, this attitude might have struck others as an honest recognition, like George Bernard Shaw's, that his fame carried such very practical advantages that ignoring them utterly could start to smack of pretense. Whatever his image as the fabulist of escape to a raft, he had mastered the dynamo of "newspapers and telegrams and photographs and interviewers."

Although "Mark Twain Interviewed" made a sales pitch, his mind pivoted on more than self-interest. For either-or thinkers his attack on the

Mark Twain in Italy, 1902–3. (Photograph from Mark Twain Project, Bancroft Library, University of California)

sacred Monroe Doctrine deserves consideration as his prime message, clothed in one of his trickier disguises; to play safe for profit he could easily have picked a demagogic or nonpolitical packaging. Moreover, any guess that the piece was shelved because of its dissent ignores his much harsher attacks on American foreign policy. It fits several ways into the pattern of how he connected his public and his private lives. It also typifies the more than three hundred published interviews—themselves a hallmark of demotic journalism—that brought millions still closer to Twain, confident that they knew his moods and tenses yet far from jaded and eager to hear more. They recognized that while he admitted to serving personal ends his genuineness and social concern were powerful too. On the world tour he had encouraged a smalltown cub with, "Sit down, young man! You know I am an old reporter myself, so let's talk shop for a while." But then, instead of guiding the interview into the heroics of his lecturing again, Twain used up the session with informed questions about politics in Montana.

CHAPTER 9

Statesman Without Salary

TWAIN'S LAST YEARS bonded social commitment into a sharp, permanent feature of his image. For a while his tenacity at bringing current politics into the adulation over his homecoming seemed quirky, but three strong reasons were pressing him. First, the foreign policy of the United States had expanded its reach, and the fall election of 1900 was cried up as a choice between world power and isolationism. Second, the choice excited Twain, educated by his tour along the equator, more deeply than any issue since the election of 1884. (On the dock he proclaimed he was still a Mugwump.) He would address it heatedly in the tones of his new herohood and with very little protective clowning. More generally, at some point between 1897 and 1900 he had decided to insist on the topical thrust of his humor, to function not only as the American ambassador to the world but as a "statesman without salary."[1] While a few editorials found it neatest to discuss "the new Mark Twain," anybody with much of a memory saw an intensified, more self-consciously focused drive of attitudes that had been perceptible from the start.

That an ordinary person of letters, anyway, would raise his or her voice on public affairs was no cause for surprise. The age expected it, if only because intellectual and material progress, though inevitable, deserved and would respond to guidance. Furthermore the elitist ethic taught its disciples they had a responsibility to enlighten the masses, who might vote foolishly if left to the demagogues, and also to set a model for the new-minted millionaires without training as gentry. This earnestness assumed that politics made sense at the overt level, that its terms had substantive rather than symbolic or diversionary reference, that elections confronted the operative forces rather than veiling the power of corporate business or the id or folkways. Convinced that civic decisions mattered, Twain shared them passionately, floundering into perplexities and ad hoc opinions phrased with a genius memorable on conflicting sides. During his last decade he was already being quoted along the range from robber barons to Marxists. An anarchist tract, *Direct Action: The Downfall of Capitalism* (ca. 1912), was quick to list his birth and death in its "Revolutionary Data" calendar. Even such claims to kinship had done him more good than harm. They expanded the impression of his teeming sympathies, which underlined the fact that his politics could not be wrapped up neatly—and therefore attacked with a single label.

If by some magic constrained to a pedestrian debate, Twain, I believe, would have argued that a politics which respects the ballot as the final authority accepts a calculus of the feasible adjusted by compromises and a taut willingness to "wait until next time." Between the poles of his enthusiasm for nobly strong leaders and his sweepingly stated moods of despair over human nature, he saw a hydra-handed tug of war to put together a majority in voting years. Except during the rough-and-tumble campaigns, zealotry could strike many as the wrong note, as intimated by a compliment in 1902 that he had "the spirit, without the self-consciousness of the reformer." Firmness had to stop short of petrifying into inflexibility, always a strategic blunder unless an upheaval diverts the thrust of history in the proper direction for a Cromwell. The rocklike dissenter on the left especially loses credibility with the pragmatic centrists and at best gets honored after retirement (like Norman Thomas) for having persisted in futile gallantry. Twain's rhetorical emphasis and his courage under fire in the early 1900s blur the fact that he steered a course that avoided or, taken more subtly, tactically exploited the extremes of both crystal principle and bending to light pressures. Beyond that he carefully planted enough episodes of humor to balance his heatedness. Asked by a reporter if the world was "growing better," he answered "solemnly": "Yes, I think so. You know, I have been here almost seventy-two years, and—but, really, you must not ask me any more on this subject. I am a very modest man, and prefer not to speak of my achievements."[2]

In the abstract, Twain himself jeered at compromise while rhapsodizing about his models for steadfastness, and he took risks in practice that strained his skill at working the newspapers and jeopardized his status. "He did not flinch," marveled *Collier's* in April 1910, "from facing the loss of the popular good will" by attacking imperialism. Instead, he gambled for and won that rare prize of admiration from the masses for daring to disagree with them. Still his luck depended heavily on recognizing his special problems of acceptability as a dissenter. Much of his old audience simply wanted more of overtly empty or generalized humor, and his new enemies were quick to complain of his overstepping his proper role. When he supported the licensing of osteopaths in 1901, a physician raged about comedians meddling in life-and-death questions; already hostile to Twain's anti-imperialism and perhaps remembering a grudge, the *New York Times* icily agreed on putting him back in his place. In spite of the triumphs his fiction stages for the individualist who defies yet dominates the mob, Twain as agitator stayed wary toward the combined volatility and stubbornness of public opinion, which no solitary voice can turn around through argument, and toward the normal weight of conservatism, which can kill overnight, especially if sharpened by journalistic wit and cartoons. Never substantially negative about fighting within the system, Twain waged a daring yet calculated campaign to keep being heard. American pride in the iron backbone of William Lloyd Garrison or Henry David Thoreau can survive the admission that Twain found the most constructive posture for his unique synthesis of talents, experience, and prestige.

Twain's training in political journalism lay so far in the past that eyewitnesses were scarce. Howells, from a similar background, credited him with a "constant growth in the direction of something like recognized authority in matters of public import, especially those that were subject to the action of the public conscience as well as the public interest." This argued far too sedately, particularly when compared with Twain's tirade in 1891 that he had worked as a "reporter four years in cities, and so saw the inside of many things; and was reporter in a legislature two sessions and the same in Congress one session, and thus learned to know personally three sample bodies of the smallest minds and selfishest souls and the cowardliest hearts that God makes." But even most of the pertinent *Buffalo Express* and *Galaxy* pieces were long forgotten. None of his collected volumes had preserved the acidity of that inside knowledge or the fervor of speeches nevertheless committing him to honest politicians and issues. The sampling in *Sketches, New and Old* had such motley company as to suggest that he grabbed any handle for salable humor. Although "The Great Revolution in Pitcairn," a minihistory of how a demagogue upsets a stable community, reappeared in *The Stolen White Elephant* (1882), the extravagance of the title story alone had made it hard for some to believe that Twain thought responsibly on the civil questions of the day and the future of the enveloping society.

Skepticism was aggravated by a split in his positions. He shuttled between romantic democracy and free-enterprise elitism, between heaping contempt on doubts, especially from a foreigner, about liberty and equality for all and subscribing to the harsher dogmas needed to manage a capitalistic republic. The underlying philosophy, Manchester Liberalism, insisted that rational thinking, education, upward social mobility, and laissez-faire economics would enrich everybody through applied science. When the voters supported such a system they were inalienably wise; when they defected, brutish or gullible. When a European country gave signs of adapting to capitalism more efficiently than New World egalitarians, an American Liberal perceived virtues in hierarchy and discipline. But when foreign conservatives resisted progress by belittling democracy, Twain as Uncle Sam thundered about natural rights and could send a Connecticut Yankee to update British thinking. The captive rather than the guardian of the inconsistencies, Twain stated either side so passionately yet amusingly that he often registered as more flighty than reflective, as a carefree on-looker rather than a marcher for liberated technology. Ironically, his vividly overstated praise for a position sometimes revealed its cruxes more starkly than his allies liked. And when he switched over he knew where to attack its lines, unconfused by alien rhetoric.

During the 1890s his stance finally looked fairly consistent though conservative. Well known as an entrepreneur and, according to some rumors, a millionaire, he socialized with bankers, industrialists, and the respected politicians. That his "Travelling with a Reformer" should demand courtesy toward the clientele of railroad dining cars (rather than, say, the patients of charity hospitals) seemed in character with his bearing, which implied that his ideas on financial or political matters counted more than those of ordinary people. His bankruptcy did not goad him to attack the economic system at home though *Following the Equator* criticized the extinction of natives in Australia, the castes of India, and land grabbing in South Africa. Between 1897 and 1900 he hobnobbed with the best of Old World society. His housekeeper recalled that "everybody knew what a grand time he'd had in Europe with Royalty and all the wonderful things that happened to him. Everybody, great and small, was proud of Mr. Clemens." She thought he "could just have and do anything he wanted to." Almost perversely, to those who suffered from the results, he decided to gamble his blank check toward humanitarian ends. Although the spectacle of injustice under every sun might have forged a modern Ecclesiastes, Twain brought home a demonstrative pity for the oppressed and a passion to rekindle the American mission of torchbearer for freedom.

* * * *

On the simplest level he intensified his habit of doing more than his share for charity. When he spoke, less than forty-eight hours after returning, at a "bazaar" for the orphaned survivors of a Texas hurricane, his irony about his "diligence" to regulate the "moral and political situation on this planet" lightened but did not hide his earnestness. Reporters soon got him to condemn hazing at West Point, a place he had particularly enjoyed visiting. His social conscience left a churning wake of actions and speeches, apologizing at a gala luncheon in 1902 that he must hurry away to "do some other thing—I don't know what it is, something for the furthering of the public good or the advancement of civilization." Unlike some reformers his standard for doing good reached a truly personal scale such as sending an inscribed copy of one of his books to a girl crippled at a railway crossing; unlike a modern president he acted without instructing his retinue to feed the *New York Times* its story, "Mark Twain Writes to Maimed Girl" (15 May 1905). Breaking out of tidy middle-class charity he donated an autographed set of his works to the local Salvation Army. If rumors of his private despair spread very far, they collided with hard proof of his social concern. Readers of *Harper's Weekly*, especially, got used to finding his pithy essays on how to stop "overspeeding," for example, now that the automobile ran smoother or how to protect young virgins by abolishing a legal "age of consent" to seduction.

In his most colorful action as everyday vigilante he filed a complaint against a cabbie for overcharging his housekeeper and followed through at a hearing before the Bureau of Licenses, where he jousted resolutely with the defense.[3] The turnout of the press included even the *New York Evening Post*, which placed this lesson to servants of the public on the front page (22 November 1900). The *Herald* had R. F. Outcault, creator of the "Yellow Kid" cartoons, dash off drawings that included a Twain in uniform because of his declaration that every citizen must serve as a "non-classified policeman." Approving editorials were copied by out of town papers while the *Springfield Republican* composed its own tribute for "An Act of Good Citizenship" in "making a 'kick.'" The cheers reached a more lasting level in not only the *Post's* alter-ego, the *Nation*, but *Harper's Weekly* and the *Century*, whose "A Humorist to the Rescue" was written by the venerable editor himself. Although Twain soon quietly got the cabbie's license reinstated, this foray in his "self-appointed task of reforming our national manners" impressed journalists deeply enough for an occasional mention up through his obituaries. More generally the *Critic* (January 1901) complimented the "public-spirited" returnee for "doing much to right the wrongs that he has seen about him on every hand in this city."

Cabmen might lack friends among those who could afford the next notch above streetcars, but Twain was not picking just safe targets among the working class. In 1903 he again impugned Mary Baker Eddy's sanctity, provoking the Century Theatre Club to disqualify him from presiding over its booth at the Actors' Fund Fair. He jabbed at exorbitant fees by lawyers and at businessmen whose notion of a fair exchange was to "give one and take ten," and he joined the crusade of *Collier's Weekly* against medical quacks by scolding the prominent citizens who signed testimonials for them. Howells, who had often encouraged Twain to shoulder some cause, now guiltily wished he would quiet down and produce more books, but the public probably fancied the deal it was getting. In any event he could not pull back, as Clara saw: "His interest in all important matters of the day never flagged and his instinct to reply in print to reports of evil acts in the daily papers was as compelling in these last years as it had ever been."

The prize-winning modern biography by Justin Kaplan discards this social conscience as the mask over a spirit tortured by self-hatred and drifting into emotional bankruptcy. Presumably judging results and not just tactics, a biography confined to Twain's final years more sternly decides that the white-haired gadfly was indulging himself while almost reinforcing safe attitudes by making them feel nonconformist. To be sure, selective reforms can meanwhile accept so much of the encompassing system as to be merely helping it function more efficiently for its masters. The revolutionary dilemma agonizes that to alleviate misery will ease the pressure needed to shake the footings of the establishment. Still, twentieth-century history has not yet demonstrated whether untended suffering brings the day of reckoning more quickly or whether demanding a clean sweep gets more done than appealing to popular assumptions for support. Although cinders in one's own political eye hurt the most by far, an editorial suggested a noticeable friction with soft consensus when it acclaimed Twain as close to "an Aristides for justness and boldness as well as incessancy of opinion, a Solon for wisdom and cogency, and a Themistocles for the democracy of his views and the popularity of his person." Disagreeing in advance that he had prostituted himself all over again, it added, "His sound, breezy Mississippi Valley Americanism is a corrective to all sorts of snobbery. He cultivates respect for human rights by always making sure that he has his own."[4]

In an era that still liked Greco-Roman facades on its banks, a more
frequent comparison invoked the image of Diogenes for Twain's insistence
that truth must be pitted against communal error, not just savored in seclusion. Some reviews of *The Man That Corrupted Hadleyburg, and Other
Stories and Essays*, published in the late summer of 1900, managed to discuss its most challenging items without surprise. Almost as a leitmotif, his
speeches now referred to "my natural trade—which is teaching," going on
ordinarily to announce his specialty either as a "moralist in disguise"—on
a pledge to uphold simplified spelling—or as a "professional moralist."
While objecting to any divorce of social from personal ethics, he let private
habits alone (and escaped a sure conviction on the charge of petty hypocrisy); his examples came from human interaction and customarily from
civic sins such as lying on tax returns, which he rebuked before well-heeled
audiences. Sometimes he explicitly implored them to carry their Christianity along to the office and the polls. Whether sly or momentarily sincere
the appeals to piety made fine protective coloring.

*   *   *   *

Of course many a preacher on many a somnolent Sunday morning
went about as far as most of Twain's moralizing. However, when he sallied
forth against the imperialists he knew that fierce counterattacks would
erupt. Once stirred by the prophets of an American trade empire himself,
he realized how easily they can turn pugnacious toward the skeptics at
home. Furthermore, watching the South heat itself up to secession while
he favored peace had taught him how quickly and hotly mass opinion
crashed down on those opposed to a war. While stocking up on facts for
challenging the new conquistadors, he must have sardonically welcomed
tributes, as in "Mark Twain, American" (*Harper's Weekly*, 15 December 1900),
to his "incarnation of all the virtues of civic life," and he missed no chance
to second the testimonials to his patriotism. The fervors of war with Spain
had created a pressing demand for avatars of the national virtues, and
Twain filled it admirably. A nonpolitical citation stated: "A stern sense of
duty and of honor, a seldom absent sense of humor, inexhaustible energy,
dauntless pluck, unfeigned simplicity and abiding sympathy and fidelity,
are the salient characteristics of the typical American—of Mr. Clemens."
His image as the new Uncle Sam hardened into a granitic commonplace,
suiting both his thoughts about tactics and his sincere pleasure. Therefore,
no cynical discount need apply to his giving the most patriotic speech of
his career while chairing a fund raiser for Lincoln Memorial University on
11 February 1901.[5] Also, he had introduced "The Battle Hymn of the

Republic" as the "most beautiful and most sublime" product of its genre the "world has ever known." When he scrawled an anti-imperialist parody of it three days later, the motive was outraged faith.

Once settled into New York City he had started to reveal the surprising depth of that outrage. The news from Vienna had instead featured his spunky defiance of Old World cynicism by blessing the crusade to liberate Cuba. But feeling betrayed by the Treaty of Paris, through which the United States acquired the Philippine Islands, he transferred his idealism to the anti-imperialists while lying fairly low at first, aware of avoiding the flak that dissenters were catching. In January 1901 his notebook recorded, "Hoecake opinions (bread-and-butter) on religion and politics"—the gist of his essay "Corn-pone Opinions" that sighed that we trim our beliefs to protect our livelihood. Or, to put the case more kindly toward naysayers, Twain's career had taught the running lesson that sticking his neck out drew an unusually strong vein of ad hominem ridicule; he probably felt no surprise when his testifying against the cabbie brought a few sneers at his stinginess "in beating down charges . . . to the extent of a quarter of a dollar." While likely to have done so anyhow, he cagily dusted off friendships with editors and reporters, speaking as soon as 27 October 1900 to the Women's Press Club and letting the New York Press Club hold a jovial reception for him on 12 November.

His handiest forum was the banquet hall, watched diligently by reporters as well as his admirers. On 10 November a VIP audience at the Lotos Club got a dazzling medley of wit, sentiment, camaraderie, tomfoolery, and barbed criticism. After praising the Cuban crusade and American actions in China it modulated to, "We started out to set those poor Filipinos free, too, and why that most righteous purpose of ours has apparently miscarried I suppose I shall never know." Although already sure of the answer, he still restrained himself to a quick thrust in his speeches as the anti-imperialists, staggered by McKinley's re-election to the presidency, scrambled to recruit a superstar. In the face of atrocity stories about how the Chinese had turned against foreigners, he soon declared before the Public Education Association that "the Boxer is a patriot," the "only patriot China has." A few days later he composed:

A Salutation-Speech from the 19th Century to the 20th, taken down in shorthand by Mark Twain: I bring you the stately matron named Christendom, returning bedraggled, besmirched & dishonored from pirate-raids in Kiao-Chow, Manchuria, South Africa & the Philippines, with her soul full of meanness, her pocket full of boodle, & her mouth full of pious hypocrisies. Give her soap & a towel, but hide the looking-glass.

Like the "Baxter's hog" mentioned in his western journalism, he was setting out in "a gang all by himself."

After the Salutation appeared in the *New York Herald* on 30 December
it was widely reprinted in various ways including small cards to pass around.
Meanwhile he had pondered a full-dress statement and the risks it entailed.
A both reassuring and troubling pat on the back in the *Nation* (29 November) praised the "bold utterances" of this "old-fashioned American" but
charged that the press mostly ignored them and also that other men of
letters who opposed empire lay silent because of their dependence on the
favor of the public. He must have felt easier with the *Harper's Weekly* salute
to this "highest type of the American citizen, the man who hates hypocrisy." This both conferred near-sanctity and, perhaps unintentionally, touched
on an aspect of imperialism he hated deeply; it surely helped to outweigh
the warnings from friends that an all-out manifesto gambled more than
even his bonanza of good will could cover. Answering a fan letter about
the Salutation, he agreed that a "universal reign of terror" as well as "error" was repressing criticism of "our theft of the Philippines & of our
assassination of the liberties" there (†).[6]

Actually he had shown no fear on 12 December after young Winston
Churchill, lionized as a hero of the Boer War, paraded over to promote
Anglo-American unity. Twain seemed the ideal choice to introduce him
before a fashionable audience of twelve hundred at the Waldorf Astoria.
But his polished sentences, using the term "missionary" more disrespect-
fully than most realized as yet, laid down a maze of irony before emerging
with the epigram that South Africa and the Philippines had created a "kin
in sin." Embarrassed silence betrayed a full awareness of his aggression
though he suffered no doubts reminiscent of the Whittier fiasco. Perhaps
pent-up anger at his agility helps to explain the heat he elicited next by a
single sentence, practically an aside before the City Club on 4 January
1901: "I know enough about the Philippines to have a strong aversion to
sending our bright boys out there to fight with a disgraced musket under
a polluted flag." By 11 January a friend had to assure "the 'indignant' patriots who are demanding his explanations" that they would hear soon. An
inner circle knew he was concentrating on an essay, presumably finished
by the fifteenth, when his wife and he started a social visit in Boston or
else by the twenty-first or the twenty-second, when he caught up on his
mail—serenely acknowledging the "round of cursing I have got from one
end of the country to the other" and chuckling that he had "thawed some
of the frost out of the pulpit," especially in the West(†). The cursing, secular or religious, swelled into a roar when "To the Person Sitting in Dark-

MARK TWAIN TALKS OF CABMEN TO MAYOR'S MARSHAL ROCH E.

New York Herald, 23 November 1900, p. 4

ness" led off the prestigious *North American Review* for February.

Without visible trembling Twain expected a "diminution of my bread and butter" or cornpone. His crony Howells, who had once braved icy winds for the sake of the Haymarket anarchists, predicted worse, and the essay lastingly enlarged his reputation for courage. It is true that the anti-imperialists, who counted on two former presidents and much blue-ribbon support along with some mass attitudes, ran less danger than anybody in the United States opposing World War I after 1916. Still Twain's popularity invited the risk of implosion. The bloc that instinctively reveres de facto authority towered behind a letter to the *New York Times* (10 February) warning that his sturdy behavior in paying off his debts and demanding the "punishment of a dishonest cabman" earned no right to "false statements concerning the Government." More specifically the Republicans claimed a mandate from the recent election. Several kinds of volunteers for enjoying the white man's burden likewise trumpeted that the majority had expressed its infallible will, and armchair warriors, cocky after the "splendid little war" in Cuba, keynoted the special loyalty that armies bleeding in a foreign field can command. In late February another physician resisting osteopathy raged, with Twain on hand: "When he came back from his trip abroad he talked of a dishonored flag; we did not take him

eriously. If we had, some of us might have mobbed him, and rightly too."
A supposedly moral indignation boiled just as hot in the missionary camp,
which would field the most dogged adversaries.

Someone arranged to flank "To the Person Sitting in Darkness" with
a critique of this "entirely American" author by Howells, who briefly praised
his politics too. But without naming anybody for support and without
defensive clowning, Twain had charged head-on into the most emotional
ways of posing the issue. Bypassing the logistics of governing distant islands

Minneapolis Tribune, 14 February 1901, p. 1. Bottom caption: "Better quit your
foolin', Mark, and go back and work at your trade."

Life 37 (28 February 1901): 166. "The American Lion of St. Mark's"

or the spacing of coaling stations for the navy, his essay likewise ignored the dry constitutional questions though his correspondence probed the legal holes in the jingoists' armor. As in almost all of his anti-imperialist skirmishes he tried instead to wrench the Stars and Stripes away from the opposition, having learned from watching the Republicans make the Democrats defensive about loyalty ever since the Civil War. The chauvinists must have cursed the opening that the Lincoln University fund raiser in Carnegie Hall soon gave him to revalidate his red, white, and blue credentials.

His other fist pounded on the moral crux, most specifically the dishonesty of official rhetoric when it was measured against policies and actions. Although his cohorts had agitated the point, it drew on probably his deepest motive for resisting expansionism, his disgust toward lying to oneself with rationalizing that alchemizes guilt into complacency. Whatever his motives, the kudos for "To the Person Sitting in Darkness" stressed its cutting to the "marrow of an oleaginous and canting humbug," its exposure of "hypocrites." The ceremonial accolades to him had often sounded that particular motif in recent years. This essay made it almost obligatory in the future; and deservedly so, for he had carried off his main device of pretending to favor a smoother job of whitewashing the greed behind the scramble to civilize weak countries. In 1904 Thomas M. Parrott, later a distinguished expert on Shakespeare, would typically emphasize how Twain's "unrivalled powers of ridicule have been steadily directed against conventionality, hypocrisy, affectation, and humbug." His purest delight in 1901 came from pointing out, both directly and through biblical echoes from the title onward, the hypocrisy of the imperialists' steely enthusiasm for bestowing Christianity on the pagan. Opening with an explicit reminder of the Christmas season, he seized next on the enormity that an American missionary had not only supported bloody retaliation against the Boxers in his pastorate but had reportedly collected thirteen times the cost of damages. This pillorying of the Reverend W. S. Ament broadened the sins of the United States beyond the Philippines and in effect lumped it with the European powers which it had condemned self-righteously for a hundred years.

"To the Person Sitting in Darkness" inspired at least six editorial cartoons at a time when few newspapers used them as yet, and *Life* (28 February) showed a confident, lithe "American Lion of St. Mark's" from whom all prey fled in terror. Timidly omitting the section on Ament, the New York Anti-Imperialist League reissued the essay as a pamphlet, as did a matching group in Boston.[7] While its flashing humor ("righteous fun" to Howells) still reads well, its impact then depended heavily on Twain's prestige. The *Nation* gloated that the "ordinary epithets" could not be emptied on this "typical and whole-hearted American, who stepped from the pilot-house of a Mississippi steamboat into first a national and then a European fame." Echoing the other main chord in the air it rejoiced that the "merciless swish" of his satire exposed "sanctimoniousness and official humbug." Americans of 1901, incidentally, were still very slow to expect smokescreens and lying from their elected servants.

Just about every major newspaper took notice. For example the *Chicago Tribune* quickly regretted that Twain had "run amuck against national expansion as seen in all its modern forms." In another of his firsts for classic authors, he had learned to hire a clipping service, and he now studied the returns. The stunned enemy mostly hesitated at first, letting the *Evening Post* overstate the "magnificent tribute of significant silence which Mark Twain has received from the Imperialist press." More accurately, the *Nation* dismissed as "laborious grinning" the *New York Sun's* terse comment that he had gone on a "spree" from an "overdraught of seriousness." The *Springfield Republican*, about which the *Sun* had recently mocked that "Sambo" Bowles "wept his usual gallon over the Philippines," asked why it had so little to say. The *New York Herald*, still hoping to qualify as Twain's most favored trading partner and trying to pass as politically neutral anyhow, likewise went slow, finally judging that "Mark Twain May Be a Funny Man, but He Isn't a Statesman." Cautious tut-tutting dominated even the letters to the McKinleyite *New York Tribune* though they included a threat that the "foundation" of his recent herohood was "not granite." As his busiest critic, the *New York Times* wondered if his success in beating down the cabfare had gone to his head; after building a geopolitical case its editorial also jeered that "what has been called the swish of Mr. Twain's lash is only the tinkle of the bells on his cap." When a reader with an eye for symbols hurried in a rebuttal signed "A Christian Patriot," the *Times* huffed that Twain's essay was "amusingly perverted" or "'smart,'" the only result "his literary habit and temperament" cared about. Nevertheless the *Times* saw a business need to cover his ongoing speeches and activities, some of which obviously contradicted its slurs. Smalltown papers followed and, collectively, magnified the metropolitan pattern though the *Hartford Courant* felt intimate enough to condescend to Twain as the "spoiled child" of American letters, petted in spite of his political tantrums. To young radicals, however, the anti-imperialists as a group looked practically quaint because they invoked the old-fashioned ideal of a mission to remake the world by example alone.

Uncowed by more threats or cheap insults in the mail, Twain jotted an expanded note for "Corn-Pone Opinions," which soon would climax almost ungratefully: "We all do no end of feeling, and we mistake it for thinking. And out of it we get an aggregation which we consider a Boon. Its name is Public Opinion. It is held in reverence. It settles everything. Some think it is the Voice of God." His high spirits shone through the thickening furor somehow. *Harper's Weekly* pictured him in a snowball fight "Having the Time of His Life," and a cartoon in the *Minneapolis Journal* that clothed him in a leaf skirt, armed with a manuscript, asked, "Can the Missionary Reach This Old Savage?" With convincing aplomb he confided that the enmity of "goody-goody people" amused him "more than I have ever enjoyed hot water before." He had unleashed a lifetime of qualms about urging Christianity upon every continent and race. Even while still committed as a Liberal to the march of civilization, he had judged foreign missions skeptically. Long influenced though less openly by the free-thought school, he drifted further toward cultural relativism during his world tour and also came to suspect that missionaries, more handily than most of them realized, served as a lever for intrusion abroad and a rallying point at home. Pictured by themselves and their corps of supply as "noble bands of self-sacrificing men and women," they put the seal of morality on any expansion decreed by Manifest Destiny.[8] Their cry of personal libel as a response to Twain's essay clouded the issue menacingly while skewing its focus.

Although he understood he was provoking what the *Louisville Courier-Journal* regarded as "the most powerful organization of religious workers," only a smalltown, evangelical congregation can today appreciate the pious effort—Sunday school pennies, sewing-circle fund raisers, special periodicals, and summer retreats with a veteran of exotic travels—that fed money and recruits into a worldwide network. The missionaries might well have rated as the sentimental favorite in a slugging match with Twain. According to one reminiscence, his wife "begged him with tears in her eyes" to stop.[9] The American Board of Foreign Missions, which had sent out Ament, counterattacked with its flags flying. Its director, Judson Smith, D.D., demanded a retraction and next went public in the *New York Tribune* (15 February). The same page carried Twain's brief rejoinder composed at the last minute in place of a complicated argument. As the pressure mounted he drafted two more long answers but held back from debate in the newspaper, where he might be overwhelmed through numbers while granting a kind of equality to anybody who chimed in. Then Twain's charge that a missionary had made the populace pay thirteen times the amount of the damages done to Christian property was reduced to a reporter's cable error for one-third extra. Smith's troops felt sure of a rout because Twain stayed uncharacteristically silent under a drumfire of demands for penance. Even-

Minneapolis Tribune, 20 March 1901, p. 1. Bottom caption: "The G.O.P. 'Wow! Yah! Yah! Ho! Ho! Oh, wow! M-M-Mark you—Oh, Lordy! You always was a funny fellow.'"

ually the editor of the *North American Review* announced that the April number would print his response. This moved the *New London* (Conn.) *Telegraph* to an editorial on "Mark Twain's Coming 'Recantation,'" which warned, "No prudent person will excite him to loquacity when he chooses to be quiet." Across the part of the clipping he ominously scrawled "Good." In fact, the connoisseurs of his platform art could have noticed that he had stayed feisty, almost truculently toying with fellow banqueteers who, as editors, had criticized his essay. Nobody fully observant could have thought Twain was backing off and offering a passive target.

"To My Missionary Critics" justified his decision to bank on a leisurely, detailed essay that struck a posture of regret at being forced to prolong this line of the discussion. Controlling his heightened contempt for missionaries, he waxed folksy, at times self-deprecatory with the air of encoring an honored routine, but essentially condescending in a delicately overdone surprise at the inability of the American Board to grasp the key point. That the penalty exceeded the damages by merely one-third inspired his deadly quip about the woman who excused her illegitimate baby as "such a *little* one." The Board's main brief, an appeal to Chinese precedent, attracted his sarcasm back to the paradox of Christ's ministers using armed forces to collect those damages. In a battle of words the enemy seldom collapses, yet rebuttal of Twain's second essay was thin and partly frustrated in tone, angry as ever but fumbling for a fresh opening. While also dissatisfied he let this sector rest, tearing up a squelch of a private scolding: "It is such a disappointment. From the tone, I supposed it was God; when I reached the signature I found it was only you."[10] But many a friend and foe remembered his standing up to an eminently sacred army without offering even the rotten-apple concession on Ament's behalf. To at least the anti-imperialists he had acted as a hero rather than a handshaking celebrity, had dared to convert his popularity into leadership.

His fighting mood intact, he declined later in the year to speak at, as he objected, a "peaceful, courteous, social, non-political occasion." The label of treason had rankled most of all though it had little chance of sticking when a newspaper could entitle an editorial in mock surprise, "Mark Twain a 'Traitor', Too!" The superpatriots surely regretted having waved the flag hardest at his homecoming. For the Male Teachers' Association on 16 March 1901 he persisted in defining patriotism correctly before relaxing the audience with, "I will not go any further into politics as I would get excited." However, a week afterward at a dinner given martial tone by Rough Rider Teddy Roosevelt, he vigorously protested the ongoing cry of treason raised against his side. As the army "pacified" the Philippines the rhetoric did cool down, but Twain would continue to wrestle

MARK TWAIN IN AN ENGROSSING MOMENT

New York Herald, 23 February 1902, sec. 5, p. 5. (The book at the bottom is labeled "Looting Through China")

with the dilemmas of loyalty to one's country during an unjust war. A late interview with the *Brooklyn Eagle* (24 November 1907) charted in detail the traps and misuses of patriotism. Nobody had reason to see him as wrapping himself in the flag mindlessly or self-protectively.

His most provocative warning against misuse was touched off in the spring of 1902 by the return of General Frederick Funston, who had captured the leader of the Filipino insurgents through a questionable trick. The welcoming banquets had reheated the attacks on treasonous thoughts being voiced while the army bled overseas. Fumbling for a humorous yet dignified persona, the ironic "Defence of General Funston" (in the *North American Review* for May) orated on the "real," George Washington kind of patriotism that had ennobled the United States into a "*real* World Power, and the chiefest of them all, by right of the only clean hands in Christendom." In relation to the kind Funston practiced, Twain branded himself a traitor after all. In 1906, when Funston returned to the front pages as administrator of relief for the victims of the San Francisco earthquake, the *Hartford Courant* finally chose to demand an apology for Twain's "contemptuous and malignant" essay. Meanwhile, after the Denver Public Library banned *Huckleberry Finn* later in 1902, he blamed the influence of Funston, the new commander of the Department of the Colorado. Although the *New York World* soon described Twain's accusing letter as "famous," that greatly exaggerated the notice given an ill-tempered misstep which his wife was too sick to prevent and which must have lowered him in the eyes of even Funston's critics. After that Twain moved the Philippines onto a back-burner, though he surprised a *Baltimore Sun* reporter in 1907 by answering that the "funniest thing that ever happened" was the American purchase of those islands.

The *Baltimore News* version (10 May) showed clearly that he was grim in proceeding to list the imperialist coups around the globe. To many he must have come to sound like a second Tom Paine vigilant for liberty everywhere. A director of the pacifist United Nations of the World recalled "our work together" for a Pan Republic Congress soon buried in the loess of history. Much more prominently he labored to export immediate democracy with "The Czar's Soliloquy" in the *North American Review* for March 1905. Although the scouts for Russian liberals had spotted Twain as a prospect years ago, they had never managed to line up the right opening for him. Now his mock monologue, fitting the context of banner headlines, associated his name with still another tense cause. Late that summer when the Treaty of Portsmouth ended a war with Japan that was going badly for Russia and the *Boston Globe* invited comment from chief opinion-makers, only Twain soured the chorus of thanksgiving, and in November he amplified his criticism to a gaggle of Boston interviewers. Almost eccentrically violent for somebody about to scrape past seventy, he condemned the treaty as the "most conspicuous disaster known to politics" because it forestalled a revolution against "insane and intolerable slavery."

Twain could growl so militantly because Marxism had taken little hold in the United States. For most people his anticzarism recalled the Connecticut Yankee's reviling of monarchy or, more vaguely, the semi-mock excess of a Davy Crockett or some other backwoods roarer shocking the starchy cityfolk. In homelier rhetoric, Abe Lincoln of Illinois, considered by many a cousin of Twain, had gone as far. But Russian radicals saw Twain as committed to action, especially after he orated in a letter to a mass rally that he hoped a "roused nation, now rising in its strength," would forge a republic. In part this rally did advance work for a visit by Maxim Gorky, whom Twain along with other sympathetic authors planned to lionize. A *Times* story soon announced, "Gorky and Mark Twain Plead for Revolution," and a *World* cartoon had Twain overturning the czar's throne with his pen. Gorky helped his own popularity by insisting that Twain, his favorite American writer and the "best known man in Russia," had been worth the pain of being knouted for reading his work. But this build-up crumbled under the scandal that Gorky's bedmate at the hotel was not legally his wife, a moral pretext welcome to those uneasy about the serious call to arms from the left wing in Russia. At least Twain sounded poised during the general scramble to back away. Too cocky to stonewall, he placatingly admitted, "I love to be an ornament and figurehead." Too proud to desert anticzarism he had written out for reporters: "I am said to be a revolutionist in my sympathies, by birth, by breeding and by principle. I an always on the side of revolutionists, because there never was a revolution unless there were some oppressive and intolerable conditions against which to revolute."[11] The tiny American Left, charmed by such passages, staked out a place around his pedestal too. After a long strolling conversation, a young Socialist, later famous as the publisher of the Little Blue Books, pronounced him "*not* a humorist but a philosopher, a thinker, a radical, a progressive and an apostle of true democracy."

Pushed by British activists he had already sustained a more active crusade against atrocities in the Belgian Congo. No doubt grinning wryly, he accepted the most productive course of teaming up with the American Baptist Missionary Union, whose executive secretary, wearing another hat, oversaw the publication of *King Leopold's Soliloquy* in September 1905. Circulated more widely in England, it attracted some newspaper notice here and its text, backed by photographs, surely left an impression of Twain as well as its cause on anybody who saw it. However, equatorial blacks were wringing few hearts at a time when the freedman's position in the United States had sunk to its nadir. Besides pity, therefore, Twain proposed stirring up the hostility of more Protestants over the fact that the masters of the Congo were Roman Catholics. More directly, after lobbying at the White House and State Department, he tried the catchy newspaper angle of "The Deity's Thanksgiving Sentiments" and another press release stressing enormity that earned the headline "Leopold as Slayer of 10,000,000."[12]

Two days later at the lavish, jovial banquet for his seventieth birthday, he slashed at "Leopold, the pirate king of Belgium." By then most of his overlapping audiences knew about this crusade too, which lengthened his imposing, fascinatingly mixed list of vice-presidencies—from other anti-imperialist causes to a committee for a local election, from the Anti Child-Slavery League to a oneshot appeal for giving the children of the poor a relief at summer camp.

The crusade proved complicated, almost dangerous as Leopold fought back through well-financed agents and perhaps some deals giving American bankers a share of the rubber and metals from the Congo. When the Hearst papers mounted what they considered an exposé, one of their reporters muffed a chance to quiz a willing Twain about the charge that the British Foreign Office had him on its payroll and a conflicting charge that H. H. Rogers, now getting a cut of African booty, would silence him. Although more wearily than apologetically resisting plans for a speaking tour, he reaffirmed his horror over the Congo when he was interviewed in May 1907 and then when he made his last, showy visit to England. Since at least 1897 he had sporadically worked at manuscripts that turn away from the burdens of the historical present and that imply the futility of trying to help the human race overcome its vanity and meanness.[13] These manuscripts later proved a shock partly because he had accumulated such an image of engaged concern, of conviction that a mutual effort could soften man's inhumanity to man.

$$* \quad * \quad * \quad *$$

In fact no cause or occasion had seemed too small for Twain, including elections wherever he happened to be. In late October 1900 when a funeral called him to Hartford, he had quizzed reporters in turn about the political weather in Connecticut (and sneaked in a plug for a health food he had invested in but also saw as a benefit to digestion). Readers of the New York City papers soon got splashy notice that he could cast down his bucket where he lived, not just fume about problems made exotic by distance. Likewise his disdain for "politics" expressed not anti-civic privatism but disgust at graft and cynical logrolling. If such politics confirmed his inner despairs he nevertheless tried to improve it. His speeches restlessly offered biting yet practical advice, and on 4 January 1901, already looking toward the city election in the fall, one dwelt on "The Causes of Our Present Municipal Corruption." The campaign of 1884 had ratified his credentials as an independent, a label that even the straight-ticket majority admired over the long haul because they suspected that the party regular

The Brave Sir Mark

A Yankee Writer at King Arthur's Court

Life 42 (24 December 1903): 647

has to compromise more often than not. But even Twain's allies probably underrated the toughness and practicality beneath the integrity he flaunted. In late January he explained confidentially to a British friend that the reformers had just a "bare possibility" of beating the machine but also that they might lose some leverage if they toppled the colorful boss of Tammany Hall only to get a "flat man" in his place(†).

After a Fusion ticket got rolling, Twain loudly joined the Order of Acorns, which had a journalistic cadre to marshal the ways and means of publicity. In early October 1901 he granted at least two bull's-eye interviews and doubtlessly welcomed two cartoons that pitted him against the Tammany tiger. Going beyond his pledged help he delivered a carefully wrought oration that was hurried out as a supplement to *Harper's Weekly* and reprinted as an Acorn pamphlet. Then, as the voting came closer, he twice perked up a noonday rally with rough-and-tumble metaphors. At Fusion headquarters, for reporters from the *Tribune* and *Sun*, he pretended eagerness to trudge around pasting up its posters. He exultantly presided at a victory rally, led its parade of three thousand in a carriage, and then reviewed it at Times Square. After straggling back downtown it burned an effigy of Tammany's boss, and when the police moved to stamp out a fire hazard, a riot was brewing until somebody "started a cheer" for Twain that broke the tension.[14] This campaign marked his most lively and visible splashing in the mire of "politics." As Tammany had learned to expect, the "goo-goos" or good-government forces lost their emotional drive. Although they were already disorganized by the time of the 1903 election, Twain, before taking his ailing wife to Italy, contributed one public letter accusing Tammany of "wholesale robbery and murder" and another endorsing the Acorns again.

All along he was expounding the ideal of "citizenship" in interviews and speeches, one of which implored colleges to establish a "chair" for teaching it. Understandably enough, somebody proposed naming a party after him, and other amateurs dreamed of seeing him in power. Yet saturnine and hardened Ambrose Bierce was also evidently serious in suggesting an appointment to the Roosevelt cabinet, and another columnist fantasized that if the country wanted candidates without party fetters it should turn to Twain as its "ablest and most conspicuous private citizen." A creative reporter faked a boomlet for U.S. Senator though a competitor reaped the benefit of getting Twain's reaction. In pajamas and with his face lathered he managed to decline with pleasant gravity, ending in a casual yet sound restatement of his late persona: "It's a humorist's business to laugh at other folks, not inspire other folks to laugh at him."[15] A reader of the *New York Herald* nevertheless insisted that "Uncle Mark . . . altogether

too modest . . . would make a good all round representative of the people."
More plausibly he got an offer in 1905 for a syndicated column on "public
men and measures." That must have stirred his nostalgia for the 1860s.

With a typical dash of the unexpected his long-range answer to machine politics called for a pyramid of clubs or "cells," each with ten members pledged to support the result of the filtering process. They would
hold the balance of power between the major parties. The swing vote of
the morally oriented Mugwumps had endured as a lesson to him. After
the New York City election of 1905, in retrospect another "What if?" sce-
nario, a grateful reporter got his outline for a "casting-vote party" to back
the best candidate for each slot, regardless of labels. Until somebody built
from this sketch, Twain lent tone to a People's Lobby, much like Common
Cause today. The biggest surprise brought his active encouragement of
the suffragists, said to have convinced him to join one of their parades
along Fifth Avenue. Looking feeble four months before his death, he startled
an interviewer by firmly supporting "any methods" that women chose "to
attain the big results they are striving for." In the meantime he had never
stopped counseling male voters, shuffling out as late as 1909 for a political
dinner that introduced him as the "last word on all public questions and

OUR ARTIST MAKES TWO FAREWELL SKETCHES OF MARK TWAIN.

Mr. Clemens has announced his intention of leaving America and making his permanent home in Italy.

public men." To greet 1907 at a New Year's Eve party he came up with, "For New York for the New Year, my best wishes are for a good government."

*　　*　　*　　*

Skeptics judging the substance of his politics looked hard at his friendship with Rogers. Some knew enough to wonder also about George Harvey, who had mounted a portrait of J. P. Morgan in his *Harper's* office. Forging a social as well as business link with Twain he regularly introduced him to the leaders in business and finance. In 1902 Harvey held a birthday banquet for him at which a guest joked about their "coming to a millionaire's club and dining at the expense of a millionaire."[16] As toastmaster, Harvey kidded Rogers about his yacht and coups on Wall Street, but Twain orated respectfully to those captains of "all the great illustrious industries." At other banquets Twain himself kidded Andrew Carnegie, a retired captain already famous for his charities and especially those library buildings; their well-known camaraderie did credit to both except among leftists and utter cynics. Although a range of criticism from leftover Populism to the new Progressivism was clouding the status of the wealthy, Twain's intimacy with them waved a sign of his success as a self-made man whose own money was not tainted. Furthermore, he so radiated autonomy while invoking so feelingly the mottos of romantic democracy that it was easy to believe that his sympathies transcended his investments or any classbound anxieties. Only a few naysayers dared notice, much less draw linkages to, a habit of liking deferential treatment from clerks or waiters that visibly stretched back to the early 1890s.

Rogers projected a model of family life backed up with munificent gifts of buildings to his small hometown. Far ahead of his business associates in alertness to public relations he never got tagged with damning quotes even after the muckrakers brought him to the attention of several courts and the press corps. Front-page intimacy with so beloved a character as Twain paid Rogers well for overseeing his finances.[17] Yet, whatever the furtive sneers at the motives of either member of this unusual partnership, they genuinely enjoyed each other's company, as the covey of reporters and photographers made clear when they sailed for Bermuda in February or came back in April 1908 to josh again that Rogers was cadging small change from Twain. Fully aware of the darkening clouds over Standard Oil, Twain never worried that parading Rogers as his best friend devalued his own stock. Considering the politics of the *New York World*, its cartoon (26 December 1908) that showed him joining the Malefactors of Great

THE NEW MEMBER.

New York World, 26 December 1908, p. 8

Wealth Club by forming the Mark Twain Company might be taken as hostile, but it looks just amused or even impressed. Anyway, to the despair of radicals, many commoners revel vicariously in the luxury of their kings.

Eventually Twain grumbled that "the woes of the wronged & the unfortunate poison my life & make it so undesirable that pretty often I wish I were 90 instead of 70." He was finally feeling old age while the appeals for action grew faster than the population. By any reasonable standard he still responded to an impressive array—on behalf of the blind, the Tuskegee Institute, Russian Jews fleeing pogroms, victims of the San Francisco earthquake, the Children's Hospital Branch of the Anti-Noise

League. While his speechmaking continued to play ironically with his image as a reformer, his good deeds enriched an impression of repaying some of the largess showered on him and also of doing so because his social conscience twined around his heart. Until at least January 1909 he endured not just routine meetings but also clerical drudgery to promote a children's theater for immigrants on the Lower East Side, exaggerating to the press, "It is the most important work of my life."[18] That sounded goody-goody, but he customarily kept his bristles up, confiding to a daughter that he had given a "vicious half-political, half-theological speech" merely "sugared" at the end(†). To a young girl he explained that the "sure proof" a public official has fulfilled his duty is that the "best people . . . every now and then dislike him." The rule applied to volunteer statesmen too. To another girl he sent in 1910 a mixture of posturing and implied exhortation: "If I were to start over again I would *be* a Reformer" because the "increasing interest in it . . . would pay handsomely for all the hostilities I should raise." "Interest" meant he would enjoy himself, as his public had recognized decades ago. But it also believed that Twain, short on systematic radicalism but long on a winningly humorous concern for its political conscience, was making a practical difference.

CHAPTER 10

The White Peacock

IN MAKING AN EVENT of Twain's seventieth birthday in 1905, George Harvey decided to accentuate the literary. Of the more than one hundred and sixty guests who feasted sumptuously, all but seven or eight had professional standing as writers or else editors or illustrators. For that matter Andrew Carnegie thought he rated better than amateur seeding, and President Theodore Roosevelt, who sent a warm letter of regrets, admired himself as a belletrist. If nobody except a researcher can now identify all the guests, the reason is that the winnowing of time had a lean crop to start with though Harvey had tried to gather its best. The five-hour banquet inevitably cascaded words, with fifteen or so speeches and nine or so poems that filled a supplement of *Harper's Weekly*. Whatever the genre, their overall content hailed Twain as a classic author, and each diner left with a foot-high plaster bust of him as tangible proof.

A few limped to bed with worse emotional than physical heartburn but had to hide their jealousy because the consensus rated the affair as a cultural Everest. In 1917 A. B. Paine claimed that it was "remembered today as the most notable festive occasion in New York literary history." On the centenary of Twain's birth the cartoonist John McCutcheon still boggled at the "most distinguished" parade of speakers "ever heard at an American banquet." A minor humorist, closer to Twain's cast of mind and idiom, looked back on the dinner as the height of Harvey's genius at blending "gracious hospitality and the main chance" as publisher: "Not since round-eyed wonder-seekers looked through the cage-bars at Barnum's 'Happy Family' had such a varied assembly been seen in perfect amity."[1] Fully alerted, most New York dailies had decided on a front-page display. The *American* went furthest, with five drawings and a large photograph decorating a story that brimmed over to page two. Bracketing the continent the *Spokane Spokesman-Review* had much detail and a cartoon, and the *Spokane Press*, an editorial. Many accounts played up the theme of literary canonization, and the *Nation* began with, "The most significant thing . . . was the greeting from forty of the leading men of letters in England." But the press insisted even more that Twain towered beyond the realm of literature as an oracle on the human race and as a personality. His prestige was in fact outdistancing the fame of his few great books.

His own speech scored a hit that multiplied as the papers featured long swatches of it. In 1910 the *New York World* judged it one of his "widest quoted" texts while the *Tribune* encored that "most remarkable effort" by reprinting most of it and the *Boston Post* made it almost a full-page spread. The *Manchester* (N.H.) *Union* recalled that it had "revealed his true personality," the "sobs beneath the seeming carelessness of revelry." Although his touches of poetic evocativeness ("music," according to *Collier's*) had surprised more readers than it should have, "sobs" indicates rather what the public wanted to end up with. Seven years later a novelist specializing in the wisdom of plain folks would attest: "Only those who knew him as an orator, and one of the greatest of modern times—knew how serious he could be. The most masterful bit of pathos I know is at the close of the speech he made on his seventieth birthday." Evidently, Twain did not have the only selective memory in his circle. Facing up to old age with a dominant tone of serenity, he had disciplined himself with two rehearsals in front of his secretary. In spite of dropping several times into his pose as a teacher of morals and jabbing at social sins here and abroad, he kept the speech lighthearted, even puckish. By any standards and especially the reigning ones, he steered refreshingly wide of pomposity while once more professing his gusto for the art of profanity and other pungent vices. Most remarkable of all given his live audience, he paid no homage to high literature.

The banquet can now be looked at from two angles, like a trick painting: Twain's knighting as a classic artist which clinched the Uniform Edition or the take-off for his climactic sequence of triumphs as a hero of American society. Academic critics had been discussing his reputation ever more solemnly in the quality magazines, and Yale awarded a Litt.D. in 1901, emboldening the University of Missouri to follow suit, especially since "ten thousand men rose to their feet when he entered the open-air auditorium" in New Haven. His election in 1904 as one of the first seven members of the American Academy within the National Institute of Arts and Letters even gave him a large say in who got canonized next. Although never tense over his ranking like some later poets—as conscious of bulling through to "No. 1" as the hottest football fan—he got reassurance from all directions. Leading portrait artists negotiated for a date to set up their easel or lights. The hundreds of preserved images differ so widely in their effect that it is fair to analyze the motives behind each choice for reproducing them today. Pictures can be found to support any theory about his character, and if he had foreseen that, he might have called the camera a greater liar than himself.

New York World, 6 December 1905, p. 3

Selective viewing in Twain's day had the help of mainline critics, who consciously filtered the facts of life on principle—the uplifting "idealism" that detested the "cynicism" of the realistic novel. He helped too, supplying "Pudd'nhead Wilson's New Calendar" with, for instance, "Wrinkles should merely indicate where smiles have been." That advice could be impressed on the dour by way of a Mark Twain Postcard and could support the growing tendency to emphasize his sentiment more than his humor. A "little girl," who composed mighty precocious letters, gushed that her reading in Twain had identified him as "a great, bright spirit of kindness and tenderness." An adult observer stated the "crowning paradox" that while Twain "has jested more tremendously than any of his contemporaries, he is perhaps the sincerest writer in America." Although we infer that Sam Clemens felt angers and fears in Nevada that must have colored

Roughing It, Thomas M. Parrott looked back in 1904 to its "unquenchable good humor even in the most trying situations" and its "unfailing kindness toward one's fellow man." Evidently most critics found the 24-carat Twain in the sentimental "Death-Disk" rather than the elegantly pessimistic "Five Boons of Life" and registered the joke-plot of "The Belated Russian Passport" more deeply than the snobbery of "The $30,000 Bequest," which tortures a workaday couple for crowding in on the dream of getting rich. A few stories do excuse the little girl's faith, but Twain's new writing was often being judged through an image wreathed in legends out of the village past and ennobled by his tireless social conscience. While punctuated with applause or laughter, the record of the banquet failed to indicate amused whispers when Brander Matthews certified Twain's humor as "never irreverent," and perhaps there were none.

∗   ∗   ∗   ∗

At some unfixable point too many of Twain's contemporaries surely passed from interaction with his public drama—and the suspense of what would happen next—into a ritualistic trance. At the simplest level they believed that—as a waspish naysayer put it—"everything he says must be amusing and delightful. If they do not feel the fun of it themselves they think they ought to." His most determined worshippers screened out whatever bothered them rather than readjusting the image they held; others, eager to join in mass ceremony, snatched up whatever reason suited them even if it clashed with the vivid realities of the personality of Twain, who more than most heroes railed against just such self-deception. Doubtlessly he suffered moods of schizophrenia, of not recognizing himself in the eyes of some devotees or even of realizing that what they heard differed radically from what he said, of feeling like a "Mysterious Stranger" himself despite his fame, of floating blindly in a white glare like the family of his "Great Dark" fantasy. It was a temptation, not always resistible, to flow with the adulating tide—to play out what the ritualists wanted or needed and to embody the least subversive of the personae they perceived. But to a vitally irreducible degree any such compromise, which his dominant persona had always detested, was upset by his bursts of autonomous individuality—forthright, unpredictable, distinctive, and ever vibrant with iconoclasm.

While Twain's irreverence flared up until the end, his persona did mellow toward that of a venerable sage, pungent in language but too educated for vernacular, who merged more easily with the visible master of Stormfield—the showy villa built in 1908. From there a privately troubled

Samuel Clemens would give his wheel of images one last turn. Now seldom misled by naive expectations, the managing persona was ironic with a tilt toward geniality, insightful with touches of profundity and book learning too heavy for his forerunners, cosmopolitan about the present and the future, rather positive on moral and social values yet free of religious doctrine, and self-important in likably modest ways. An essay on petty deference and vanity ("Does the Race of Man Love a Lord?") projected this sage at his silvery best, but "Two Little Tales," an improbable lesson in how to outwit bureaucracy, let his complacency show, and the latest Maxims avoided hollow wordplay only to lumber into preachment. Some readers must have spotted Twain's closest approach to a portrait of how he would like to come across in the flesh—the physician of "Was It Heaven? Or Hell?" in the Christmas issue of *Harper's Monthly* for 1902. An authority figure with traces of the curmudgeon, he dominates any situation. Yet he is "impressionable, impulsive" with "no gift at hiding his feelings; or if he had it he took no trouble to exercise it." Highly sensitive to anybody around him, those "whom he loved he loved and manifested it," but "whom he didn't love he hated, and published it from the housetops." Naturally he held "opinions on all subjects; they were always on tap and ready for delivery" though not just palaver: "Whatever the doctor believed" he "would fight for it whenever he got the chance; and if the intervals between chances grew to be irksomely wide, he would invent ways of shortening them himself. He was severely conscientious, according to his rather independent lights, and whatever he took to be a duty he performed, no matter whether the judgment of the professional moralists agreed with his own or not." The action of the story centers on the point that the physician detests literal principles that violate humaneness or right reason. But the tone catches that mockery with which Twain undercut his own irascible heatedness of opinion. Elsewhere, usually in reformist contexts, he developed a fine touch for mock-megalomania that exaggerated the achievements of his do-gooder side while insisting on its strength.

James M. Cox, as his own party of one, has argued that Twain's "public personality and art were his forms of genuine expression," less censored and more revealing than even the now notorious manuscripts held back from print. Generally, intellectuals assume the total superiority of written over visceral communication and undervalue the social utility of a model for active self-integration. Twain's own era grasped better than ours that humor is a shared experience, that driving him inward toward communion with his psyche would pull him away from his genius for empathy, and that his magnetic presence encouraged vitalism. At the banquet of 1905, Richard Watson Gilder—whose assistant on the *Century* marveled at

Life 46 (13 July 1905), insert following p. 54

Twain as the "intensest personality" he had ever known—pushed Cox's point further, putting aside the "philosopher, moralist, satirist, historian, poet, preacher, patriot, pilot . . . traveller, lecturer, general kicker, and sham-smasher" to pronounce Twain "chiefly remarkable" for his "dynamic force; for the strength of his convictions, the energy and spontaneity of his expression; for his strenuous and scornful hates and intense affections; and for his lightninglike vision." This aptly caught his kinetic quality, which had impelled the editor of the *Brooklyn Eagle* to estimate at the 1902 dinner that he held "more in reserve than he has ever been called on to put forth." Earlier that year a reporter who caught him on the wing in Charleston, South Carolina, emphasized his "strong and rugged aspect indicative of power and an abundance of repressed energy" and gloated, "It is a joy to know that there is still an abundance of good copy in Twain." Instead of nursing a grand old man, Twain's fandom luxuriated in wonder about what he would do or say next to reveal what new dimensions of this growing septuagenarian. An editorial in the *New York Times* marveled: "No one is so familiar and so uniformly surprising" (7 June 1902). He made the usual stagnation, not to mention death, seem easier to hold off.

Some dimensions were now essentially worn out or as thin as ever, particularly those given a few final touches by journeyman wits, such as a story that he proposed cutting off his feet to cure the gout. The report that he preached on "The Gospel of Good Cheer" during his return to Hannibal had more credibility because of his talk a few months earlier to the adult Sunday school class shepherded by John D. Rockefeller, Jr. Biographers disposed to enshrine privatism may see him as compulsively unable or else too insecure to stop courting favor. In 1903 he jotted: "The people will shout for a person climbing to the top" but when he "starts on the downward track they'll shout too & help to butter the ways."[2] His fable "The Five Boons of Life" warned that fame attracts envy, then calumny and derision sinking toward "contempt and compassion in its decay." However, any anxiety got covered by his effect of bubbling energy and an untamable urge to invigorate others, if only at such an obscure occasion as the banquet for the New York City alumni of a business college in Poughkeepsie. He so obviously kept on the move, physically as much as mentally, that his joking about his laziness seemed funnier than ever. By now his amassed production of words proved by itself that he belonged to, believed in the Age of Energy. Along the way he had managed to trade the image of a dancing, almost manic vitality for that of loosely coiled power. A young contemporary would recall: "It was one of the secrets of his immense personal effect that he never felt nor looked like a scholar or a thought-worn literary person, but rather like a man of affairs—erect,

M. T.

Life 47 (5 July 1906): 813. One of four portraits under the heading: "Things We See Advertised"

handsome, healthy, debonair—in his earlier years like a prosperous ranch-man, later like a financier, a retired field-marshal, an ambassador, or, as his friends would have it, like a king." After 1900 some caricaturists gave Twain an intimidating, even fierce look. Today, conditioned by a Poundian ideal of nonstop experiment in the arts, we overestimate the degree to which the elderly Twain seemed to be repeating himself, even after we allow for the fact that his publics kept demanding their favorite routines. He still furnished a running puzzle about whether his innermost spirit was stable or fluid, divinely average or quirky, finally used to its limits or bottomlessly inventive.

At a calmer level two patterns dominated, the first backed up by the still potent saga of his integrity in paying his debts, the best investment he ever made. One admirer, trying to unite two realms, informed the *Collier's* audience that Twain had been motivated by "his keen sense of the dignity of humor." Although flippant by trade about bourgeois standards, *Life* greeted his seventieth birthday "because he has lived to demonstrate that solvency is not necessarily inconsistent with good writing or virtue." This ethical glory hovered around his speeches that kept professing his diligence to "regulate the moral and political situation on this planet—put it on a sound basis." While humor hedged each performance, their frequency mounted up toward insistence on his underlying wisdom, whether ha-bitual or lately developed. Second, he tried bolder and bolder candidness about his diligence to "advertise" himself attractively. At the New York Press Club of all places, he expanded on his feeling that the "world knows you much more favorably than you know yourself." Even that waspish naysayer conceded that Twain, "with certain compunctions that we believe to have been sincere," had encouraged his devotees to "say something that should be an antidote to indiscriminate eulogy."[3]

This theme had the relaxing benefit of honesty with himself. It also eased his private bedazzlement at having soared to greater heights than megalomaniacs might fantasize about. If it lowered those heights a bit, that would bring some relief from worrying whether he could continue to meet the always rising expectations. Besides flashing fair warning to the devo-tees themselves against being conned, it focused telltale light on the hero worship that degenerated into mindless awe toward persons whose rank or conspicuousness built not on achievement but on the power or wealth of their parents. "Does the Race of Man Love a Lord?" ridiculed such stupidity in part by subtly confessing his own name-dropping. More coldly he observed, "If everybody was satisfied with himself, there would be no heroes." Most dangerously of all he toyed with putting his authenticity in doubt, confiding publicly in late 1900 that "when you have talked a lot the

The Press Club Will Send a Wheelbarrow for Mark Twain.

New York World, 4 February 1906, Magazine Section, p. 1

emptier you get." He plunged on: "When I am situated like that, with nothing to say, I feel as though I were a sort of fraud; I seem to be playing a part, and please consider I am playing a part for want of something better, and this is not unfamiliar to me; I have often done this before." A wry anecdote about being mistaken on the streetcar for Mark Twain led back to, "I have been playing a part." After all he had warned long ago that he had a talent for posturing.

*   *   *   *

The banquet of 1905 officially opened the climactic phase of his role-playing, sometimes as a bereaved survivor with two daughters depending on him. It swept on with a rougher éclat though his loyally patient, shrewd wife had seldom toned him down hard. Since returning from Italy with her coffin in July 1904, he had stayed secluded, answering the many letters of sympathy and convincing the press that his grief sincerely wanted privacy. But in the fall of 1905 two semiprivate speeches had tapered off his period of mourning, and he helped Harvey's build-up with interviews, including a pell-mell monologue for a syndicate of sixty-two Western papers. Soon afterward he tapped his official biographer, whose recent book on cartoonist Thomas Nast had stressed his self-tutored genius, popularity with the common folk, and combatively firm moralism in politics.[4] While Paine was gathering materials on the spot, Twain decided to publish parts of his autobiography but—freed from the alleged tyranny of his wife— gave his older daughter, as she reminded a magazine editor, "permission to correct" his text. The installments ran in 1906–7 with much comment and some reprinting by the daily press, and the barings of Twain's breast amplified his image for free-flowing, intimate, and comic yet gritty self-dramatization based on a gold mine of experiences. Still he did not really produce the shocking, repulsive candidness sometimes promised. His flights had one eye on the compass while the other watched out for thunderheads. Since the tumult was still rising his career needed alert navigation.

With his helping to generate copy again, the winds quickened. The fund of old and new anecdotes revolved more briskly, and the gallery of photographs expanded with a premium on fresh angles and settings. As reporters found it harder to get past his retinue, they fabricated brief items more often than in the 1890s. But events helped out, as when a librarian warned that the drawings in "Eve's Diary" were sexy if looked at closely and Twain could not resist a sly comeback or when a prominent minister thundered that anybody who swears is "no gentleman." Always fascinated by inventions, Twain got photographed in motorcars, but when he joked that a wheelbarrow would be safer for traveling to a Press Club dinner, its organizers grabbed the chance for a bright story garnished with a cartoon. (When a sneak thief took his gold watch in 1907 he marched to police headquarters, the commissioner ordered the force to put on the heat, and a pawnbroker turned it in—all to the glee of reporters.) Unsurprisingly the rejuvenated Twain would get two offers for some kind of vaudeville act.

The spring of 1906 heaved up toward a new peak of celebrity. On 15 March the *Times* sedately reported, "Police Hustle Crowd Awaiting Mark Twain"; Hearst's *American* had "5,000 Rip Off Theatre Doors," and another competitor featured a "stampede" of ten thousand, while the *World* gave this "panic" or "riot" the most space. The story had national appeal; for example, the *Atlanta Tri-Weekly Constitution* played up the police "reserves" who were called out as "Crowd Fought To Hear Mark Twain." More decorously, on 2 April he held the center of attention at a Vassar alumnae affair, the next day five hundred "girls" of the Women's University Club were "all blushes and delight in the presence of their universal sweetheart," and on 7 April his talk at a Smith College luncheon revived his soubriquet as "The Belle of New York," though another "girl" had pronounced him "Simply a Dear." The educated woman had joined his procession even if he was known as a man's humorist, fully enjoyed by stag diners, London dockworkers, and sports fans. On the ninth, applause for his unannounced presence interrupted an international billiards match in Madison Square Garden. And so the month went, helped by accounts of at least seven speeches and by stories about his plans to build another house or the auction at which his letters easily outsold those of Ulysses Grant and all others, live or dead, bringing in fact "extraordinary" prices. Anybody who has noticed how some event pushed a color story on Twain out of a daily's late edition will avoid quantifying his newsworthiness, but that auction had measured him in dollars against illustrious names.

The fifteenth of April, a Sunday, marked the immediate summit with his part in the Gorky debacle splashed across the rival New York dailies. If Twain needed another lesson in the volatility of opinion as brewed by journalists, Gorky's overnight crash taught it. But the *Times* magazine section had the bad luck to carry also a background spread on Gorky in which Twain figured manfully. Elsewhere, continuing the build-up toward a fund raiser for a monument to Robert Fulton, the *Times* puffed Twain's next "farewell" performance. Apropos of nothing, the *Herald's* magazine lavishly illustrated his yarn about a speech canceled (supposedly) by a ludicrous mishap in 1895. Devoting a full page to "Playing the Rubber in the Game of Life," the *Press*, with Twain's photograph as the centerpiece, made his career the longest example of how to overcome setbacks. A visitor from space would have taken Twain as the single most active fact about the United States or else have wondered at the custom of giving so many persons the same name. It was anticlimactic for the *Tribune* to close out April with a half-page photograph of Twain "thinking for a word while he writes and smokes in bed." But his exertions were recalled by the subcaption that a "body" of Russian authors had "denounced" him for deserting Gorky.

The *Times* had printed a similar photograph six weeks earlier, and its mates were floating around. Its genesis stretched back to the tour with Cable when Twain granted several interviews while in bed or getting dressed. Once the technology of newsphotos arrived, he allowed candid shots of himself in clearly wrinkled pajamas, a detail still rare on movie or television screens. The pose seemed peculiarly appropriate, and a lithograph of it in 1906 "immediately attracted attention" to the artist. For years Twain had mentioned his practice of loafing in bed or even working there; in a newspaper piece Clara would soon comment that "the bed habit is the recipe of father's success." The photographs probably recalled his Bohemian days for some, while they stamped him as wearing his present importance carelessly. The *Times* had grouped its version with what might pass as unposed shots of Grover Cleveland reading in his "library" and Carnegie at the desk

Photographed during the late winter of 1905 or early spring of 1906 (Underwood & Underwood Stereotype)

in his "den"; both were dressed formally enough to undergo a visit from Emily Post. For those who believed that modern publicity was cutting through and dispelling the mystery around figures of authority, Twain's openness to the camera could appear as another subversive flouting of the establishment. But it more generally fitted his reputation for naturalness and approachability. With obvious relish, the *Omaha World-Herald* would recall that "rakish shock of white hair, that face beaming with good nature, that pajama-clad figure." In fact he had by 1906 come to prefer a nightshirt—according to the *Woman's Home Companion*, an "old yellow nightgown," but color prints had not arrived, fortunately. The vogue of Twain-in-bed pictures helped to encourage, then lost out to the other extreme that has lasted as the chief symbol of his daring whims and tastes.

The white suit went back still further—as early as the summers at the Hartford house in the 1870s, if not his onshore days in the South as a licensed pilot. Around Elmira his light gray for June but white duck or linen for the hottest months was considered a distinctive yet not eccentric touch. For the summer of 1890 in the Adirondacks, he ordered and wore, much wrinkled, a suit of white flannel casually styled. His daughter remembered his pleasure because white clothes got by as ordinary in India and his delight when he performed in "snow-white full dress . . . and dined

WHY NOT A BED FOR BILL HOWELLS?
SURELY, HE IS ENTITLED TO AS MUCH ADVERTISING AS MARK TWAIN.

Puck 61 (27 March 1907).

.n the same," calling it "my dontcareadam suit." Ever since bursting on the national scene he had been variously described as defiant toward eastern patterns, as cheerfully careless or just rumpled, and as almost dandified. None of these attitudes fitted into the trend toward conservative standards for men, with black the unimpeachably safe color in winter or summer; clothing no longer served as the flag for the top degrees of social or economic rank while restraint promised self-discipline and sober conduct of the business at hand.[5] Waveringly, Twain himself had inched along toward conformity since the 1880s and had often dressed quite formally after rebounding from bankruptcy.

The date of his rebellion is definite. On 8 October 1906 his secretary recorded that he was "filled with the idea of defying conventionalities and wearing his suitable white clothes all winter." He told her to order five suits to be ready at the shop of his New York City tailor. Still enjoying his summer whites in the frosty New Hampshire autumn, he had determined not to give them up completely until next year. Beyond those simple facts the details vary widely. His official biographer starts out with six suits, his housekeeper with a tidy fourteen—one for each day of the week besides seven at the dry cleaner's.[6] The fabric is given as serge, cream-colored flannel, "putty-colored, almost white" broadcloth, or doeskin, with Paine almost visibly redonning a silk waistcoat that matched Twain's before they swept down Peacock Alley at the Willard Hotel. In other words, "the" suit had several incarnations, usually in multiple copies, and reporters thereafter counted in the summer outfits that went to the washtub and that numbered twenty-four according to an interview in June 1909. Although most people now imagine an ultimate whiter than white, glowing like a commercial for detergents, the technology for cloth fell short of that. Likewise, though the personal effect is imagined today as debonair, it was then much more often seen as calculated, close to theatrical—"very soigné," said an Englishwoman.

The unveiling came when Twain paraded into the nation's Capitol to lobby on a dull, freezing day that some described later as snowy. Under a dateline of 7 December the New York dailies made the event into national news. He had been fully conscious of creating a hubbub—for the immediate sake of copyright reform. But he did not even imply that he was probably making a trial run. Taking a break in the press gallery, he identified his suit as the "uniform of the American Association of Purity and Perfection," for which he was the "only man in the country eligible." Although that joke has misled the analysts searching for gloomy compulsions, he leaned much harder on the fact that dark colors make winter all the more depressing. (He was not likely to mention that white made him

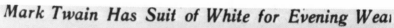

Mark Twain Has Suit of White for Evening Wear

A STUDY IN BLACK AND
WHITE

Snowy Broadcloth Cut According to
Prevailing Mode and Lined with
Silk of the Same Shade.

WILL HAVE A SPANISH CLOAK

Gray Fedora Hat and White Enamelled
Shoes Likely to Complete New
Costume of Humorist.

Mark Twain (Samuel L. Clemens) has
had made for him a suit of evening clothes

New York Herald, 15 February 1907, p. 5.

Life 49 (31 January 1907), p. 161. "M. Twain—Clemens"

feel taller than 5'8".) When quizzed on the danger of looking effeminate, he argued that garishly elegant costumes had been respected as manly centuries ago. While hardly aware that a new national monument had arisen, the *Washington Evening Star* finished a dazzled editorial with, "We need something to liven us up in these stern and strenuous days, and perhaps the immortal Mark has given us a valuable cue." A few snappy dressers would claim to have scooped him, but when the railroad magnate J. J. Hill, who had always worn black or dark gray, caused a "sensation" in St. Paul with an allegedly snow-bright get-up, the stringer for the *New York Times* labeled it a "Mark Twain costume."[7]

Twain never admitted that he took several months to screw up his nerve, which reckoned on the "stream of generous new privileges" granted him by acclamation after his charming speech on how it felt to be seventy. Today, with male rainbows everywhere, no excuses would seem necessary. Yet at first he had merely hoped to cut the gloom of a Manhattan winter now and then. Furthermore, white held out a compromise to the mores; several times he confessed his longing to display the loudest bands of the spectrum. The mystery of color preferences aside, he frankly enjoyed standing out in a crowd, and conformity had always chafed him. Extrapolating from himself, he believed that "all human beings would like to dress in loose and comfortable and highly colored and showy garments" rather than endure the "insanity" of letting practicality dictate male styles. However, since at least one model of his suit cost sixty dollars, and it was expensive to keep up to perfection in any fabric, he could not argue he was spearheading a movement against clothing as a social control. The public chose instead to marvel at another sign of his individuality, already too famous to arouse suspicions of grandstanding. As early as 1902 the *New York Times* had protested when he promised to give up making speeches: "He has borne his part with such ease and apparent spontaneity, it has seemed so much more natural for him to talk in his own way than to keep silent, that one can imagine his self-repression only as an act of self-denial."

Having made a hit out of town, Twain mounted it soon for a New Year's Eve party on Fifth Avenue. Next he let out the details of ordering a set of evening clothes, broadcloth with silk lapels and lining, fabric-covered buttons, braid down the seams, and zigzag embroidery—accentuating the flowing cut that had added to the panache of his prototypal version. The awkward, dulling effect of a black overcoat led to experiments with a cape or "Spanish cloak." Although he had never lost a boyish delight in unusual caps and hats, they would remain a problem here because a silk topper carried a touch of the minstrel show; and a soft fedora, that of the Southern planter who was becoming a comic stereotype. For an effective con-

THE MOST REMARKABLE
SUIT SEEN IN NEW
YORK THIS SEASON.

This is the wondrous white flannel suit worn by Mark Twain. He affected the peculiar style a year ago, first appearing in public dressed this way at a White House reception.
Since then he has worn nothing else on state occasions.
Last week he appeared at the Engineers' Club's dinner wearing his white flannel suit and created a sensation, where Cesare, the Metropolitan Section artist, saw him and sketched him.
Mark Twain claims that his white flannel rig is more sanitary than black. The reason he wears it, though, is just because he wants to, he says.
His white suit cost him $60. It's made of the best French flannel.
But who else but Mark Twain could appear at a fashionable dinner dressed like this without being called eccentric?

New York World, 15 December 1907,
Metropolitan Section, p. 1

trast he also tried out a black bow tie. As he wondered about going too far, the cordially grateful press corps turned his suits into a white badge of courage. With fanciful, expensive drawings in three colors, the *Herald* (28 April 1907) embellished the idea that he intended to liberate all males. For his trip to England, Clara uneasily extracted his promise not to break out into white, but he took some suits along. When British papers started begging to see the "costume that set two continents talking," he obliged after the hightoned events on his schedule were over. Steadily encouraged he again stood out the following winter so that the *World* (15 December 1907) felt a demand for a page-length drawing. By the next spring, when he sailed for Bermuda, a longshoreman asked, "Where's his white suit?" Legitimizing his deviance the public demanded steady encores of his still expanding roles, as many as possible at one time. Several late cartoons would show him wearing a white suit in an old-times pilothouse, which had kept its magic. A model labeled the *Alonzo Child* was built over the speaker's table at a banquet.

The late physical image was enhanced by accessories—as the fashion magazines used to say. Photographs of him in a rocking chair, preferably stroking a cat, caught on with magazine editors. To a painter who started to pose him as reading he objected, "I suppose the book looks better, but a cigar would be more like me." In November 1907 the Office of Patents registered Mark Twain Whiskey and Mark Twain Tobacco; his "eternal" stogies or corncob pipe reeked of masculinity, balanced for the women by his rhapsodies on down-home cooking. Editors of newspapers had a weakness for shots of him engrossed in the middle pages, giving the public still another prop for identifying with him on the level of everyday consumption. He compromised a medley of the oddly familiar and the unexpected in externals as well as ideas. The once distinctive brick color now a standard white, his curly thatch ruffled grandly in the breezes, though the painter understood that Twain's "greatest concern" was that "I should get it right." "His principal recreation," said *Life*, "is not parting his hair." Women angled for a lock of it as a keepsake, but he showed far more caution than Samson. (Almost nobody cared to mention that his yellow mustache, stained presumably from tobacco, clashed with the ensemble.) The "chrysanthemum of white hair" earned sales for cartoonists, who exaggerated it beyond their customary degree. Generally, their heavy hand did much toward flattening out his image and reducing it toward an easily graspable iconography. Therefore as he strode through a railway station one reporter saw the "mane of a literary lion." The *Grand Forks* (N.D.) *Times* would memorialize "his shock—no, his crown of hair" as his "trademark of recognition," while others treasured the drawl or the shuffling

CLOUD EFFECTS

If a hoary head were always a crown of glory, Mark Twain would have glory enough here to dazzle a world

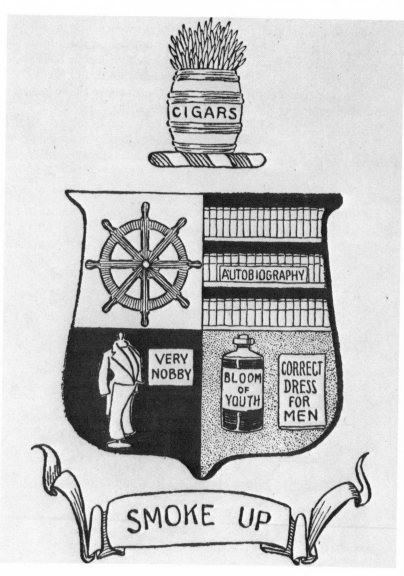

Life 49 (27 June 1907): 870. In a grouping headed: "Who's What/ In and Out of America"

walk. Just as the image had at last looked complete, however, a Litt.D. from Oxford University wrapped it in a scarlet robe.

Able "to command all the vehicles of publicity, including the King of England," Twain blazed for a while as the "most advertised man in the world," extending his record for trumping himself. When the hullaballoo stretched to three weeks, a few British editors grumbled, and *Vanity Fair*, as convinced as ever that the United States "needs above all the lesson of veneration," demurred that Twain was "quite the most pernicious influence" there. But major opinion breeders on both sides of the Atlantic did all they could for Anglo-American unity in a world of menacing political alliances. Gratified even more with royal British than Austrian recogni-

Washington (D.C.) *Evening Star*, 29 June 1907, p. 1

tion, his countrymen believed that he handled it still better, behaving reasonably at posh affairs and rising to an eloquent speech of farewell. Yet he had stayed loose, playing along with gags about the stolen Ascot Cup—a perfect lead into his ironies about his reputation for honesty. His publishers, eager to seize the day, lined up Yale's William Lyon Phelps for an essay on "our great Democrat" that was mapped as another milestone of acceptance by the critics. Disbelievers had grown so scarce as to make the crotchety *Bookman* warn that "these journalistic public 'ovations' always look the week after like public funerals of common sense"—just the kind of skepticism Twain had often sounded more effectively.

Nothing braked the self-feeding momentum. Any qualms about his fondness for making friends with prepubescent girls were smothered under the stories about his gallantry toward the ladies or a "let-the-little-children-come-unto-me" benignity. The anonymous woman who pleaded just to see him, kissed his hand when she left. If the white suit reminded some of a Southern colonel, it radiated an angelic sweetness to others. Until his certain ascent to heaven he collected the bonus from mere survival, the pride a family takes in the longevity of a grandparent, especially one continually able to "impart such vitality to a pleasantry of ripe age." But instead of saving up strength for the annual reunion, Twain kept on the move—Known To Everyone and Liked By All, cried the slogan for the Mark Twain Cigar. The public felt as much ownership as deference. On an ocean trip a stranger asserted that "it is the duty and privilege of every American to shake hands with Mark Twain." In worshipping him the country was in fact more and more doing homage to its warmest image of itself. He was almost a living statue. Inevitably someone whose rational side realized that it actually beheld the famed presence blurted, "Did you know that you look like Mark Twain?"

*   *   *   *

Within that presence crouched an alert master of the show. Public drama is trickier than the legitimate theater, and Twain hardly dared to count on a ritualistic sanctity safe from nitpickers and wiseacres. Unexpectedly faced with a touchy issue, he "looked wise" and decided not to comment before he had "consulted his files, as otherwise he might contradict some of his published interviews and get himself into hot water with the newspapers, whom he always liked to keep on the good side of." He stayed clear on just who were the reigning powers in the magazine world, noting in his guest book that the "Big Four" had come out to the country for lunch. Whether from decency or caution he avoided the slough of

Life 50 (29 August 1907): [249].
"Hello, Mark! Where Did You Get
That Hat?"

Life 50 (28 November 1907): [633–
39]. In a grouping headed: "For
These Things We Are Thankful"

arrogance. A young house guest who expressed surprise at the fuss over a visit by a mere reporter was admonished: "Always remember that in America there is nothing so important to a person in the public's eye as the Press." Of the three recurrent dreams confided to Twain's biographer, one thrust him into a "brilliant gathering" while dressed in "night-garments" or else plain rags; then when he announced his name, nobody believed him. It is plausible to infer anxiety over performing up to the level of the introduction at banquets like the one that transferred the triple George Washington

Mark Twain at Stormfield; after June 1908

"first in's" to him. But whatever the self-contempt behind some of his unfinished manuscripts, the homage kept flooding in, even as spontaneous applause when he entered a restaurant. We can see now that it would have taken some scandal too flagrant and too willfully defiant to overlook before he could hit the skids like Gorky.

His flanks were protected by both numbers and influence. All classes wanted to be his friend; on the strength of his invitations the grubby Children's Theater played to a who's who of the Northeast. Guided by Harvey, the British newspaper tycoon who had acquired the London *Times* went out to Connecticut for a social visit. When the Union Club, the lair of financiers, entertained a British nobleman, Twain mentioned to his daughter Jean that he had already met everyone at the dinner for "only a hundred"(†). But he had bottom-rung strength too, voiced in a shout from a bootblack who had enjoyed his talk at a settlement house. At Grand Central Station, to Howells' bemusement, the gatemen and conductors held up trains for his convenience, "proud" to have chatted with him. His submerged audience was just as proud of his popularity in high places and took pleasure in realizing that he knew that it knew that he knew anybody who counted. In one vignette the two worlds touched: as he left after visiting his old friend the commissioner of police, a "tattered man" yelled "Hello, Mark." City editors, both obliging and deepening his importance to the character type that vicariously shares any turn in the life of a celebrity, sent a scout to the house if Twain's bronchitis dropped him from sight for a few days.

Although the comforts of popularity also tugged at him to lie low at times, pained by the gap between what he dared and what he burned to say, that recurrent dream about being denied his identity does not translate necessarily into guilt for having repressed his pessimistic self. He had in fact responded all too quickly to the intellectuals and their popularizers who brought word during the 1890s that the hopeful vision of history had suffered derisive challenges in Europe. Increasingly chiming in, Twain directly expressed deterministic ideas from the time of "A Defence of General Funston" up through "The Turning Point of My Life" (February 1910). His personalized gloom exposed itself too, as in the Maxims that composed variations on "Pity is for the living, envy is for the dead." After 1900 his praises for death surfaced during major speeches, and to a reporter who dangled the news of a friend's funeral he exclaimed, "No good fortune of that kind comes to me!" Somewhat less gloomily, his highly visible speech to the Society of Illustrators climaxed, after running the "gamut from gay to grave," with: "the illusions are the only things that are valuable, and God help the man who reaches the time when he meets only the realities."[8] More positively, his accelerating claims on profundity implied that the human predicament was so dire that first aid took precedence over laughter. Caught in such a mood he misinformed a reporter in May 1907: "Everything I have ever written has had a serious philosophy or truth as its basis." The solemn tone of an interview set up to boost the Children's Theater outdid his effort to help Rutherford B. Hayes in 1876, but surely some reflective oldsters noticed the underlying continuity.

The highly educated count as part of public opinion even when they do not want to. While still cautious toward Twain's comic side, they too had mostly seen the glaring light and, in the process loosening the stereotype itself, were accepting him as a conventional author. A symbolic assessment came from Henry Dwight Sedgwick, an oldstock New Englander and Harvard cum Manhattan attorney turned fulltime writer of, ultimately, three volumes of essays, five histories, and sixteen biographies. Cosmopolitan and learned, his essay arrived at Twain's typifying Americans at their sprawling best with "his high character, his courage, his public spirit, his sense of duty, his energy, his patience, his kindliness, his chivalry, his adventurous temperament, and his morality."[9] For Twain alone the essay added a "long life" of "high ethical influence," thus recognizing that his irreverence had essentially held to a core of purpose and points of direction rather than lashing at the handiest target. But then Sedgwick asked just how all these qualities could emanate from his books and answered: through the "free play of his personality" in them. Unsatisfied, Sedgwick closed by speculating whether a crucial stimulus did not spring from extraliterary powers. Looking through the wrong end of the telescope, Clara Clemens warned that her father's popularity made it "difficult to realize that he was only a man of letters." Actually, not difficult but wrong.

Besides basically ignoring humor, Sedgwick underrated Twain's ingrained combative twist. *Is Shakespeare Dead?* (1909) offended the intelligentsia more keenly than anything he had published for years; to argue that Bacon wrote the immortal plays, some grieved, was to disgrace the Litt.D. from Oxford.[10] Twain's renewed attack on Mary Baker Eddy offended the Christian Scientists without pleasing the other sects because it implied an antiorthodoxy confirmed soon by *Extract from Captain Stormfield's Visit to Heaven*. In impressive proof of his own near-sanctity, critics nevertheless treated his Baedeker for paradise gently although it mocked fundamentalism much more bitingly than Will Rogers would have dared to do in a freer time. One reviewer who sounded both sincere and conventional explicitly denied that it was "profane or irreverent." For many, Twain evidently functioned as an avuncular, indeed a paternalistic figure who helped fill the void left by the weakening of the old pattern of authority. Taking comfort from his less disturbing sides or merely riding the bandwagon, they ignored his subversiveness—reaffirmed in the chapter of *Is Shakespeare Dead?* entitled "Irreverence," which lithely ridiculed the impulse to cry sacrilege on every touchy issue. Not that he felt threatened: "I cannot call to mind a single instance where I have ever been irreverent, except toward the things which were sacred to other people."

Captain Stormfield's Visit stirred up incongruities so deftly that many readers tumbled in the surface humor without resenting its erosion of their confidence that Sunday schools expound the Bible sensibly. But on reflection, fairly advanced thinkers could writhe under his satire of Christians stunned by an eternity teeming with different species of hominoids. Having toyed with the manuscript for decades, Twain was sardonically aware of its barbs and of the sporadic rumors that he was hostile toward God. In May 1908, on the reviewing stand for the police parade in Manhattan, he rubbed shoulders with a cardinal renowned for his Irish wit but tight lipped when reporters fished for his opinion of Twain. Dressed in "solemn black by way of novelty" Twain was talkative yet sly: the cardinal "told me he had read my books. He didn't say that he approved of them, but I didn't need to have him tell me that. He looks like an intelligent man, so I take it for granted he approves of high class literature."[11] A year later at a railroad station, after weighing himself (150 pounds), Twain rattled off impious humor: "though I am supposed to be an infidel, I brought a great downfall of rain with me that neither prayer or explosives had been able to bring." Another reporter caught this in more provocative detail. Doubtless, parents skipped reading some Twain tidbits aloud to the family circle.

His humanistic impulses could also still fibrillate into nonsense or his stalest Philistinism, refining on his yarn about the poet who improved his art by blowing out his brains. Twain had established the right to pose as either a sage or a low-brow comic. Unpredictably the public allows some of its favorites to embody loud contradictions and then admires them all the more for having life both ways, even several ways in defiance of the lessons drummed into children. For a medical audience Twain again raked up the physicalities as jocosely as a mining-town journalist. Past the age of seventy-three he gave elsewhere a reprise of the errant-male routine shelved after his marriage: "Once when my wife could not go with me (she always went with me when she could—I always had that kind of luck)." At the other extreme the panderers to sentimentality coaxed all the cuteness they could out of his relations with women and especially girls. There are grounds for charging that he "had long since become a generally

MARK TWAIN'S HOME, THE TWO BURGLARS, THEIR CAPTOR, AND THE TWAIN KITTENS.

New York World, 19 September 1908, p. 3

prudent, only fitfully unruly middle-class Eastern gentleman."[12] But if nothing else the past record stood, included in any collected edition. In January 1909 the *New York Herald*, getting to Twain second, after Edison, in its series on "Ten Greatest Living Americans (Excluding Politicians)," reprinted the lament over the tomb of Adam. Edison could indeed surpass Twain in appealing to the devotees of technology who gave the credit for its magic to lonewolf entrepreneurs bred in a simpler era.

More often than fitfully, Twain stayed convincingly natural, openly taking his fame for granted and basking in ovations without faking the humble bit. While capable of eloquent gratitude, he managed or perhaps just accepted the effect that his career did a favor to the world. While pontificating enough to prove his mastery of those octaves too, he upheld his reputation for detesting stuffiness. His quickness to intimate his depravity spun clear of masochism by his genial assumption that in so many ways he merely exhibited humankind on a premium scale. Still the composite was transfigured now into a model for old age—asserting a fully earned wisdom but too experienced to harden into dogmatism, facing up to the decline of vitality but not hurrying to surrender to it. At a late banquet he apologized that his powers were ebbing, then the next day roared back with his zest for life. At 2 A.M. he felt "as old as any man. . . . But the rest of the time I feel as though I were not over twenty-five years old."[13] Bronchitis capped that dizzying April in 1906; but when he improved, his secretary informed the *New York Times* that he had "thoroughly enjoyed his labors." His élan irrepressibly tempted him toward the limits of his stamina. In November 1909 he sighed: "I wish I could go on the platform and read. And I could, if it could be kept out of the papers. There's a charity school of 400 young girls in Boston that I would give my ears to talk to, if I had some more." The passage is as quintessential as any in *Huckleberry Finn*.

He never tamed his instinct for reacting near the visceral level, well above the dungeon of the id but just as far short of cold-eyed existentialism. Only an unprogrammatic analysis does justice to his impulsive commitments to a thought or mood. Yet the public perceived him as neither ideologue nor weathervane and admired instead his willingness to risk mistakes with an exuberance that suggests the Lord of Misrule. He burst the bonds of that archetype, however, through his concern for the common good. More grandly, Americans enjoyed through him a sense of triumph, both as individual success and as a collective, genial dominance over the course of history. For western society he exemplified resistance to the rigid and automatic behavior demanded by industrialism or else, for any society, defiance of the repetitiveness that always threatens vitality. In 1909 he startled an Italian visitor with his parting thought: "I am the king of buffoons; I am a dangerous person." Because of his complexity many different sorts among his contemporaries could satisfyingly join hands around him without confronting their basic disagreement. Some of the keenest minds or freest spirits prized the enigma itself, a determinist who cross-examined the logic of his convictions and who also did breathtakingly unique stunts. At his finest Twain created the role of court jester to self-esteem, blending argument and ridicule to make man humbler before himself without realizing he had been insulted.

That sounds pharisaical to those who boggle at Twain's own ego. But they should make allowances for the emotional strength that enabled him to conduct so long the taxing, intense transaction of a public drama. Sherwood Anderson's *Winesburg, Ohio* idealizes a brusque schoolteacher as "in

reality"—that is, in her hidden feelings—the "most eagerly passionate soul"
in town. But a theory of social psychology currently out of fashion holds
that we "really" are what we do in our web of relationships, that the func-
tional self inexorably forms through our traffic with the social environ-
ment. The Victorians put it more simply that character is the sum of acted
ethical choices, and their best minds doubted the later assumption of some
psychiatrists that society will mesh smoothly if everyone is made well-
adjusted. Twain had worked through to such insights while continuing to
despise the tyranny of convention and the lures of bargaining integrity
away for approval of a tin-plated front. Privately he fell short of his standards for the conduct of humanity; it is possible, as the proverb states, to
be a "joy of the streets, terror of the house." A minimal defense might
contend that he could have acted much more shabbily toward his society
(like Ernest Hemingway) without necessarily ennobling his closet life and
that accusing an individual of a failure of nerve for not indulging emotional intensity at any cost will enthrone narcissism. But, to argue positively, Twain's interpersonal self operated in ways still constructive for those
who understand it sympathetically. When the public elected him its hero
it improved its often belittled record for wisdom. Furthermore, George
Ade, a younger humorist with a gift for spotting phonies, believed that it
knew exactly what it was doing, that "out of the thousand-and-one newspaper mentions and private bits of gossip and whispered words of inside
information" it had arrived at a "surprisingly accurate" knowledge of Twain.[14]

*　　*　　*　　*

The public had also begun to nominate him for immortality, first for
great passages, then favorite books, and eventually the man himself. An
endless chain of newspaper and magazine articles got closer and closer to
the judgments of the obituaries soon to come. After reciting a litany of
the evils he had cast into "outer darkness," *Life*—still a humor magazine—
gave solemn thanks that even "Death . . . loves and leaves this shining
Mark" (31 January 1907). Despite Twain's deflating quip about a "classic"
as a "book which people praise but don't read," his writings were being
shored up against oblivion. Two teachers prepared high school texts, *Travels at Home* and *Travels in History by Mark Twain*, with hortatory introductions; but a report from the classroom informed him that the rising
generation was already converted. Likewise, when *St. Nicholas* magazine
ran a contest for caricatures of living Americans, by far the most entries
paid homage to Twain, the "good gray humorist, whom . . . all the children as well as their parents have learned to know and love." The clichés

were tenon'd and mortis'd in granite after all. For an advertisement pushing the Author's National Edition in January 1910, an excerpt from Archibald Henderson, an enthusiast already authorized to prepare a full-length critique, was headed, "Mark Twain as an American Institution." Its closing sentence claimed a verdict from a "sort of contemporaneous posterity." Parents pointed him out with an admonition to remember the historic glimpse.

Such confidently prophetic notes had crept into most commentary about him and even to him. Guilelessly he agreed with his daughter, "I'm a 'recognized immortal genius.' " That being so, he patiently let strangers snap his picture; when asked about his "serious, almost severe expression" he explained that "there is nothing more damning to go down to posterity than a silly, foolish smile caught and fixed forever"; even in bed or getting a shoeshine, he did not grin into the lens. He cooperated with at least two recordings of his voice (both lost, evidently) and stalked around for a movie camera; naturally he helped out a rising industry with a plug for a highly mortal one-reeler based on another one of his thinnest stories. When the Mark Twain Company was registered, the *New York Evening Post*, approving a solicitude that "ensures to his family all future benefits that may accrue from the use of his pen name," assumed that sales would flourish long beyond the term of his copyrights. The *American* chuckled over this new way to perpetuate the self; somebody else surely toyed with the pun in incorporated. Twain also got more previews of his later reincarnation on the stage: a professional mimic hired to surprise him at a banquet, or a lecturer whom he thought not very good, or an elderly "major" dressed in white flannels who enjoyed being mistaken for him with the help of desk clerks, alert to "valuable advertising" for a resort area.[15]

Sonorities about fame or immortality did not blind Twain to the fact that his body must return to the common dust. His tendency to bring up the corruptions of the flesh had often upset those determined to gloss over them with "sentimentering," and ever since his Nevada years his instinct for burlesque had regularly satisfied itself at the expense of the "tears and flapdoodle" that blurred the starkest of all physical facts. The escalating putridity of "The Invalid's Story" (about the corpse and some limburger cheese) has a solemn base. Looking back we can also grant that he was resisting, in his own most effective way, the gathering agreement to mitigate the terrors of the grave by pushing it as far outside the communal consciousness as possible. The *New York World* had a right to its story that he had "Always Joked about Death," meaning especially his own. Perhaps because his newspaper days had taught him how office "morgues" work, he started as early as 1895 to speculate publicly about the final eulogies over

"A CARICATURE, MARK TWAIN." BY DENYS WORT-
MAN, JR., AGE 16. (GOLD BADGE.)

Man is the only animal that blushes--or needs to.

From "Following the Equator."
Copyright. 1897. by Olivia L. Clemens.

There isn't a Parallel of Latitude but thinks it would have been the Equator if it had had its rights.

From "Following the Equator."
Copyright. 1897. by Olivia L. Clemens.

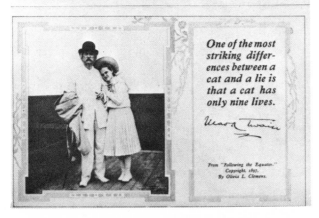

One of the most striking differences between a cat and a lie is that a cat has only nine lives.

From "Following the Equator."
Copyright. 1897.
By Olivia L. Clemens.

Postcards for sale; after July 1907. (Originals held by Mark Twain Project, Bancroft Library, University of California)

him. Fishing for speech material in 1902, he drew up an "advertisement" inviting "ante-mortem" obituaries. The idea sold to both an American and a British magazine while the Sunday *World* pirated it and arranged for fellow humorists to respond. Their rattling of fake bones filled a page wreathed with cartoons under the sly headline "Here Lies Mark Twain." Other papers got in on the gag—for instance, the *Charlotte* (N.C.) *Observer*, according to a reaction in the *Winston-Salem* (N.C.) *Business Guide.* If Twain was masking extreme anxiety about death he did so very coolly. A pre-Freudian United States must have been struck by his boldness while wondering though if it had trampled good taste again.

Perhaps because a rumor that he had been lost at sea genuinely alerted the reporters, as one told him, to his "pending obituary," he also started joking about his funeral. In May 1907 he publicly invited a "newly found friend" in Baltimore to serve as an honorary pallbearer when the time came. Like his Connecticut Yankee he "was getting up his last 'effect.' " At dockside in England he speculated gaily on the details for interviewers. The elaborate Oxford pageant, he soon announced, had inspired "ideas for my funeral procession, which I am planning on a large scale." Some British papers murmured that sticking with the subject canceled any excuse of spontaneity. However, E. A. Robinson's Captain Craig, who on his sickbed could not "think of anything to-day / That I would rather do than be myself, Primevally alive," would have laughed. That unknown "sage-errant, favored of the Cosmic Joke, / And self-reputed humorist at large" wanted a brass band at his own funeral; his dying word was "Trombones."[16] There were many failed Mark Twains in the jerkwater towns who understood the sincere impulse to impersonate him. Humorists without salary or cosmic jokers for a four-page weekly, they rose out of the same intellectual matrix and had a smattering of his range of experiences. One such kinsman joshed Twain in August 1907 because a tombstone shop had used his name as a grabber; genuinely willing to keep the humorous side of the grave uppermost, he enjoyed hearing about it. When unmistakably on his last lap he tried another of his tested angles by cabling, "While I am not ruggedly well, I am not ill enough to excite the undertaker."

In other moods he projected an air of bowing to the eternal process. Whatever his 2 A.M. tremblings, he could manifest serenity, particularly under such excellent cause as a letter from the president of Indiana University, who wondered if Twain could "pick up like a Marconi tower the streams of attention, of friendliness flowing" toward him from the "great and friendly company" he had "brought together." His draft for an answer closed, "My life is hardly real; it surely must be a dream, a fairy tale." The dream could in fact seem kindly rather than nightmarish, and he wanted to name his last mansion "Innocence at Home." That would have suited the tones of superhuman detachment Paine struck in an essay on the "House of Many Beatitudes" in May 1909; "No gentler westering sun ever illumined the afternoon of life than sheds its tranquil peace" over Twain, who lent "benediction in his very presence," which was not likely to wander from the "quiet and beautiful harbor" built in Connecticut. However, he started spending much of his time in the paradisal Bermudas where he felt so detached that, he wrote Clara, "I do not seem to be in the world or of it at all"(†). Then on his trip back for his last Christmas he had to absorb the second death of a daughter into his metaphysics. The obituaries agreed that Stormfield had proved the apter name for that harbor.

In less than four months Twain died there also, but, appropriately, his body was brought to teeming Manhattan for the funeral. He had, unlike Huck Finn, cleaved to metropolis. In 1906, asked to speculate on the wonders of the future, he had answered that New York City "suits him as it is." Perhaps he realized that his fame could not have swelled so richly anywhere outside its environs. He would have appreciated hearing that the homage of the thousands who filed past his coffin made a "most impressive spectacle." At his request he helpfully lay there in a white suit. Although always fond of the irreverent black crow, by then he seemed closer to the resplendent peacock that is wreathed in mythology, folklore, and ritual—foppish to some, magical to others with its threatening "eyes" in its almost ridiculous fan, revered but also associated with opulent worldliness. Its rarest and most striking form the white peacock, it has also served as a symbol of immortality. Although forevers are predicted too glibly, Mark Twain will live on as a personality until American character and underlying human nature have changed more than we can now imagine.

CHAPTER 11

Mark Twain Today! Tomorrow!

SO FAR, prophecies about Mark Twain's staying power are safe bets even for psychics. That power is all the more impressive because, over seventy years ago, two important sources of its strength ran down: his own manipulating of his image and the interaction between the public and his dynamic presence. Several interviews beyond the grave, with and without Ouija board, made no impact. Nevertheless he has leaped over the barrier of generations and has appealed to millions too young to consider him even a distant contemporary. He keeps bobbing up in fresh print and in the circulating fund of photographs, old and new cartoons, movies, and then television productions. The silent visual images get simplified, unfortunately, into the most graphic, composite poses—such as a mature, bushyheaded pilot or a white-suited raconteur waving a cigar at a lecture audience (as Twain never did). He stands in danger of functioning as Everybody's Mark Twain in a much less fundamental or provocative way than during his prime.

Of course the change from the live drama managed by Twain came slowly. At first Harper's pushed the Author's National Edition by trying to prolong his leading images at the time of his death. A sixteen-page flyer listed: "great boy's writer, great romancer, inexpressibly funny, sane and indignant foe of hypocrisy, master of pathos, and [a closing scattershot] philosopher, humorist, dreamer, and reformer." It was a fair though tamely stated inventory. Under the eyes of the surviving daughter, A. B. Paine also softened the contours, arranging and highlighting and omitting facts for the three-volume biography (1912) that fitted both his own cultural loyalties and his vested interest in Twain's reputation. Nevertheless, the portrait was striking because it did catch the spirit of the living man (at times conscious of his appointed Boswell)—his capacity for affection, passion for riches, élan, pettinesses, hatreds, love of justice, and vanities. Some reviewers picked up on the dark clues; one expanded them into the "pessimism of Shakespeare," and another featured the "spiritual tragedy" of Twain's longing to be taken seriously. But they admired his personality more than ever as the embodiment of American culture, even magnifying his career into an "epic of the soil, the history of a century, the growth of a nation, and the characterization of most of the great men of thought and action of that time."[1] To borrow from a Twain anecdote about an overdone eulogy, anybody who tried to add "another flower of fancy" to that was a fool. But no one snickered, and the first volume in the *Harvard Classics Shelf of Fiction* (1917) that admitted some Americans did include Twain, if only with the Jumping Frog yarn. Nobody could have expected it to choose *The Mysterious Stranger*, now so closely studied and heavily weighed. Illustrated as a "romance" for children, a text had been patched together for the Christmas trade of 1916.

While Van Wyck Brooks at once became a lion in the path for other critics, *The Ordeal of Mark Twain* (1920) did not lower the quarry's general prestige. Besides, Twain's works gave off more than enough earthy and acid humor to save him from being ignored as genteel; H. L. Mencken himself would have liked credit for, "I have traveled more than anyone else, and I have noticed that even the angels speak English with an accent." A tactician in public relations might even welcome Brooks as a counterpoint to the palling chant of praise. Furthermore, Brooks drove Bernard DeVoto into the lyrically passionate rebuttal of *Mark Twain's America* (1932). Although their confrontation left a well-visited battleground, the basic split still ran between the submerged audience Twain had always counted on and the intellectuals judging his work in the cold light of eternity. For a while, a string of posthumous books compiled from his speeches, letters, notebooks, and uncollected items kept him somewhat contemporary after all. In effect he continued to help shape his own legend—especially through the two volumes of autobiography (1924), which the unwary still trust far too much—and to give it more of the unexpectedness that had always made part of its charm. Charm, almost quaintness, may have dominated his popular image during the 1920s as a Ford-Lindbergh America waffled between nostalgia for a simpler past and delight in a technology humming with progress.

Twain's readership intent on empathy rather than analysis has occasionally produced a highly verbal admirer. The playwright George S. Kaufman liked to figure out parallels between their lives and kept an engraving of Twain mounted in a series of residences. Most obviously, Will Rogers could not help taking lessons from his career while Twain benefited from comparisons by reviewers that seldom hurt either of them. Having left behind neither a body of lasting work nor biographical enigmas, Rogers

Life 76 (9 December 1920): 1102

now arouses little controversy though the paradigms of national character built around him during the 1920s and afterward usually mention Twain as his forerunner in a tradition that fits DeVoto's principles. As put in imaginative terms that implicitly measure relative status: "at the end of *Huckleberry Finn* that all-American boy is planning to flee to the open spaces of Indian territory. He entered, and came out as Will Rogers."[3] Generally, anybody who dispenses amusing wisdom invites the risk of comparison with Twain if the humor has a core of both geniality and iconoclasm.

The centennial of Twain's birth proved again that his multi-level audiences at home stood fast, encouraged by more of those tributes to his universality that came from around the world. With Rudyard Kipling as the British counterpart, President Franklin Delano Roosevelt served as Honorary Chairman of a national committee, but Twain was jealously claimed for various places: Hannibal and St. Louis, Buffalo, Elmira, and New York City, where a program at Columbia University was directed by its president. The write-ups by the mass media favored the colorful river and Nevada years, but the magazine *Industrial Arts and Vocational Education* emphasized the "sterling honesty" of paying those debts, a lesson usable "in the classroom and in the school shop."[4] While anecdotes replayed the whole gamut, Twain's homey qualities dominated, partly because the Great Depression had inspired a discovery of Americana including the humorists of the Old Southwest. He was even classed—or declassed—as a "folk writer," and an astute but not snobbish academic went further to predict his survival "far less as a writer, at the best, than as a figure, a folk hero, a grand half-legendary personality." Too cryptic, though intended favorably, Gertrude Stein's centenary tribute also generalized him: "Mark Twain did a great many things and everything he did was all he did and he did make a dead man dead. I think he was the first man to ever do that and it was a great American thing to do." How true (or untrue!) it was safe to say. Surprisingly, Eugene O'Neill not only answered a request for a testimonal but came through unequivocally.

In his work, the living spirit of America, the essential personality and quality of the American, is expressed in more varied elements than ever before or since his time. In his books, as in [no?] others, the American, who could be born of no other soil than this America, lives with unique American gusto and color.

O'Neill added a "tribute to the memory of so finely human an American man." If the note of nationalism was obligatory, the admiration for Twain's own personality was not. But then O'Neill once had, in the first flush of success, fancied the idea of buying Stormfield for his own home.

By force of intellect, the authority won by *Mark Twain's America*, and witty skill at dueling, DeVoto had the most lasting impact on the centennial.[5] While hardly any insistence on folk qualities could go too far for him, he expounded a pluralistic approach, warning that the significances of Twain's career are "hazards of intersecting forces which war with one another so furiously that only in our minds and only years later can an illusion of simplicity develop." Overall, the later interpreters of Twain would in fact argue more tentatively or at least several decibels less accusingly than DeVoto himself. He also shrewdly pointed out that Twain was surviving the strains of the Depression because he had shown awareness of the failures as well as the humanitarian strengths of democracy. DeVoto even predicted that someday a case would be made for him as a thorough radical. Meanwhile, hot-stove agnostics, patrons of E. Haldeman-Julius's booklets, upbeat spirits for whom the mores were not loosening fast enough, and gut-level nonconformists were keeping his memory green. He also functioned occasionally during the 1930s as a felt or prescribed antidote to passivity and defeat.

The professoriate, who had yet to develop a dignifying rationale for Twain's lasting readership, found far more eccentricity than insight in Hemingway's now familiar opinion that "all modern American literature comes from" *Huckleberry Finn*. But by 1935 both the Marxist and Freudian critics had at least added fresh perspectives to the critical wars. Leftists have seldom attacked Twain's good faith, instead blaming his get-rich side or his flaws of doctrine on the blinders of capitalism; they like to chisel out usable passages. Conversely, the Freudians' severity with everyone blunted any damage to Twain, whose profaning one-liners and flights of wild comedy, furthermore, upset the diagnoses of repression, for the time being a much more disgraceful sin than aggressiveness. A highly cogent essay, "Mark Twain's Despair: An Explanation in Terms of His Humanity," gave his dark side a fixed rather than fitful quality, but the depression years could accept gloom much better than the chirping of discredited optimism.[6]

Centennial enterprise brought forth the *Mark Twain Omnibus* aimed at the schools and *The Family Mark Twain*, a fat anthology. That his writings should attract new generations of readers poses no problem except for those critics subscribing to the theory that each age recreates the classics, that is, reconceives its understanding of those to which it grants another term of favor. As yet most Americans, anyway, have opened Twain's books with similar expectations, gathered from a seamless web of clues—word-of-mouth praise, textbook judgments, and Twainisms retreaded by wits or statesmen. The great bulk of his audience has evidently ignored

THE TRAMP PRINTER

Copyright, 1952, New York Herald Tribune Inc.   5-9-

New York Herald-Tribune, 9 May 1952, p. 21

the shifts of critical opinions,[7] though no sound demography of its exists because the sociology of literature meets insoluble problems in determining even why individuals of whatever group choose to try a book and what they get out of it at what level of attention. Without the cues of reporters talking to Twain, much guessing also underlies any sketch of how the 1930s visualized his presence as a personality. It is certain, however, that a mock author encompassing the writings—especially those in which Mark Twain appears by name—and a somehow imagined person behind him appealed to widely shared, enduring attitudes. The centennial of Twain's birth brought a last big roundup of reminiscences about personal contact—with the old man, necessarily, as a genial but provocative oracle. Twain's face, if only through its use by advertisers and, more important, its photogenic qualities, remained familiar. Beyond any commercial motives the vein of affection ran steadier than a Comstock "lead." Prospectors can easily find continuing signs of hero-worship like two sonnets in the *Chicago Tribune* on his birthday in 1942.

✳   ✳   ✳   ✳

As high school and college courses in American literature leaped forward with the federal budget after World War II, Twain has increasingly been "assigned," a long-term benefit all around no matter how hard the captive student resists at the moment. Furthermore the publishing industry reinvented its wheel, the paperback sold at outlets in the path of lingering traffic. For a special countercurrent, E. L. Doctorow's *Book of Daniel* (1971) mentions the new Red scare: "and there were now people who couldn't find Mark Twain in the library because the Russians liked him and he was a best seller over there." If such popularity raised hackles they smoothed out by 1960, at least judging from *Newsweek* (22 May), which decided on a (by its standards) long article, "Mark Twain: Yearning for Yesterday." Sounding improbably buttressed by research, it tagged nostalgia as "one root of the Twain vogue," which had "producers, publishers, and editors" straining over "how to wring another profitable idea out of Twain's spectacular personality or out of his writings." With the inside warning that "as dispensed by the mass media he seems to be a bit of Americana rather than an artist," *Newsweek* did give intelligent commentary on the Brooks thesis, Twain's social criticism, and his late pessimism. Scholars could not complain they had been heard only by each other, just as today the popularized treatment of Twain rather quickly reflects their major work. Although that has never been true of movies based on his life, none of them has lasted as a monument of influential images, while the hour-long "Mark Twain: The Tears Beneath the Laughter" (1979), which used first-class consultants, has yet to establish itself as an encored piece for television. Familiar to devotees of science fiction anyway, Philip José Farmer's *The Fabulous Riverboat* (1971) builds on a detailed, balanced, and sensitive knowledge of Twain's career. It even has him complain about having to contend with impersonators in eternity too. The most graphic fact, however, is his captaincy of the grandest riverboat ever conceived (440.5 feet long).[8] Although critics find it richer to explicate a human being, Twain's admirers may care more about his Mississippi than about Huck Finn.

The strongest popularizing influence since around 1960 has been the one-man show by Hal Holbrook. A direct competitor who was a veteran of stage and screen and a later, thickening stream of imitators prove that his "Mark Twain Tonight" was bound to happen. By now a part of the Twain image, available on records and videotape, it resurrects his presence so concretely for some that the prize-winning dustjacket of Paul Fatout's *Mark Twain Speaks for Himself* (1978) features Holbrook's stage face. While experts quibble over his props, most of them approve the overall impression, on the casual level that of another great yarn spinner but defined for the reflective as "what our national character is ideally supposed to be but rarely is—independent, skeptical, rational, humorous, plagued by demons but coping." Later, Holbrook worked in a political thrust, and some of his recent competitors have let satire upstage the comedy. Yet they all present a silver-headed sage, thus evoking what Holbrook considers a "national grandfather" figure especially welcome in a society of mobile nuclear families. More specifically, an eloquent drama critic, who assumes that Holbrook got it right, registers an "Idealization of old age . . . the old man all of us aspire to be and few of us will become, a wise, crusty old gentleman who is a marvel of composure. Having lived long and tested himself and his opinions in all manners of circumstances, he knows precisely who he is, what he values, and what he despises."[9] Although Twain's contemporaries would have recognized his curmudgeon side in this portrait, it leaves out the foxy self-deprecation and makes him a shade colder than the "Uncle Mark" often invoked between 1900 and 1910.

Twain's growth as a commanding figure has, nevertheless, collided with trends in criticism and biography that widen the split between his popular and self-conscious audiences. The most influential essay, Henry Nash Smith's introduction to *Huckleberry Finn*, takes his masterpiece as pitting the two saints on the raft against the vicious, dishonest goats along the shores; student papers have echoed that view so faithfully that it must outlast their memory of the commencement oration. Smith's full analysis (1962) of Twain's artistic problems, the dynamic of his flawed solutions, the crafting of a persona, and the subversive but faltering effects of the vernacular style has colored the approaches of those students' instructors. However, Justin Kaplan's *Mr. Clemens and Mark Twain* (1966) has swayed a wider readership impressed by a National Book Award or a Pulitzer Prize. Seductively written and neo-Freudian without sounding doctrinaire, it conjures up a superbly gifted spirit betrayed by his hunger for wealth as much as for popularity and increasingly stewing in self-contempt. John Kenneth Galbraith's rave review in the photoweekly *Life* deserved its title of "Twain the Genius vs. Clemens the Flop." Only two scholars objected substantially, and only in professional quarterlies.

Mark Twain: God's Fool (1973) went further than Kaplan liked in shrinking Twain's inner stature during his final years. The vain, domineering "king" conceived by Hamlin Hill loses even the aura of family man that had still been thickening. Uneasily, most reviewers accepted the debunking in the spirit of too bad it's true and had to be done.[10] *Mark Twain in the Movies: A Meditation with Pictures* (1977) confirmed much of Hill's sternness while adding the lure of John Seelye's wit. However, his shimmering puns divert our minds from the depth of his skepticism about the "foxy grandfather to us all." Likewise, while warning that Twain had maneuvered for beguiling photographs, Seelye introduces many fresh shots whose nostalgic charms dilute any news of four-flushing that he brings. In 1974 Kaplan had already arranged a pictorial document, *Mark Twain and His World*, in which visual beauty likewise softens the harshness in the text. Twain was right, it seems, to worry so hard about the illustrations for his books.

In the neatest irony, his faults came fully on line just as a slightly masochistic mood turned hostile toward rosy perfection. A Bicentennial case for him as the avatar of national character took this keynote: "Of all our present historical favorites, Mark Twain alone seems both timeless and contemporary. His writings and stage posturings exude a sweaty odor of fallibility and vulnerability."[11] Until Washington's philandering and Jefferson's mulatto children are unarguably documented or Lincoln's bottomless patience dissolves into a cover-up for malignity, Americans feel closer to Twain. The exposé of his tantrums has encouraged them to hear his cynicism as not just a comic voice but a heartfelt cry. The tragedies of his disintegrating household have aroused sympathy for another parent unable to cope with older children and respect for his gloom as validated more by experience than amateurish determinism. An agonized Twain also makes a more convincing author for the subversive passages that the guerrilla Left mined out during the late 1960s and for the programmatic radicalism expounded as early as Philip S. Foner's *Mark Twain: Social Critic* (1958) and as late as Maxwell Geismar's *Mark Twain: An American Prophet* (1970).

*   *   *   *

Twain is surviving his biographical trial by fire though American and western society now flounders in such a flood of words, images, artifacts, and subcultures that the degree of proof is more problematic than ever. The 1980 U.S. Census, many agreed long before the process started, was badly flawed. How much, absolutely or relatively, can be made of the fact that Twain anecdotes steadily appear in all kinds of places?[12] Who can demonstrate, except through eloquence, which of Twain's images strike more poignantly on whatever level of categorizing the public she or he dares to try? What cause or effect can be tied to the Associated Press filler (7 December 1980) recalling Twain's white suit and a habit of washing his "fluffy white hair" daily with "laundry soap"? How much of an elite audience noticed among the ads, lingered over, grasped, and then accepted how much of Robert Penn Warren's poem "Last Laugh" in the *New Yorker* (12 June 1978)? Many more understood a talk-show host immediately responding "Samuel Clemens" when asked which historical personage he would choose to interview. But as much puzzlement as native pride greeted the news that Pope John Paul I had long fancied Twain's writing. Trying to explain, the *Washington* (D.C.) *Star* hoped that the pope was impressed with the "debunker" in Twain which "is, of course, an aspect of his enormous zest for life" but hoped also that the pope was taken with the "tragic old man he became when doubts and disappointments" soured that zest. Still, as during Twain's life, endorsement from popes or presidents has not driven away the rebels. Nobody is astonished when Kurt Vonnegut, who once took over a column headed "Innocents Abroad" in the campus newspaper, states that he named a son after Twain or introduces a huge paperback anthology of his work, or when Rita Mae Brown adopts him as a literary parent.

Some of the recognition is pure business—the T-shirts with a Maxim, joke books cobbled from his pages, buttons of a banking promotion, the twelve-inch bust for $47.50 featured in a Literary Statuary Series, the plastic and metal robot that gives a sales-pitch at a fee scaled to a $750,000 investment. Like Colonel Sellers, Twain would have understood these entrepreneurs. Partly because of them, his old-age face remains so familiar that Exxon's TV spots which had him recall running away from home as a boy did not have to give his name. When General Electric televised a folksy Anniversary gala for itself, the only two real-life characters invited were Will Rogers and a Twain whose happiest memories yearned for his pilot days. The tourist industry cannot afford to let him fade into a mummy, and the expensive *Delta Queen* calls at Hannibal or carries along a performing "Twain." As for houses to drive to with the family, Twain is made touchable by three, plus a cabin at Jackass Hill, a free-standing octagonal study in Elmira, and the whole town of Virginia City. The restored home in Nook Farm radiates technicolor images heightened through spreads in the glossiest magazines. Surely these reminders send some of the sightseers and browsers back to his writing or even entice a few to take a first dip.

Most airport bookstands stock some Twain, and a surprising number of passing acquaintances can talk about *Letters from the Earth*. He may end up making the transition from celebrity to fame again, that is, to being admired for his writing rather than his visibility or charm of character. In either case he can be called the Non-Disposable Twain. The steadiness with which his face and words show up on a throwaway circular or a please-take-one weekly proves how indelibly they have penetrated our collective memory.

There is no use groaning about the commercialization, a process basic to the society that could let Twain invent his career. Nor is it realistic to wish he could live on entirely in his printed works. Like classical humanism, mass taste asserts, by choices rather than doctrine, that all learning, technology, symbols, and verbiage center in and upon the individual. *People* magazine stimulates, but more fundamentally just satisfies an irresistible appetite. Rather than pointing with alarm, modern humanists can offer Twain as a fascinating yet significant personality who made as strong an impact on his society as anyone can hope for without controlling the levers of power. The offer entails aggressive vigilance for keeping Twain's core image true to its sources. Even while the media flow with the meanderings of taste, they try to channel it for better management, showing authenticity no mercy, and they insist on simplifications that blaze for the moment but leave hardly ashes.[13]

Even at their finest, movie and television versions cannot do justice to Twain's texts and the authorial presence behind them. The complexity of his most engaging personae, who change shape faster than the mind's eye, is flattened by the visual media and is hobbled by any coherent linearity of a script. The recent dramatization (1980) of the "Old Times" chapters from *Life on the Mississippi*, a pleasant two hours of TV, had to enforce some drastic decisions about the cub pilot, who for the sake of believability sheds much of his naiveté but then also much of his comic magic. More fundamentally, the Twainian tone almost disappears under the demands of convincing dialogue. Holbrook took the right decision by stepping into the Twain persona speaking for himself and, so often, about himself. For 1981 the University of Alabama Symposium shrewdly decided on the theme of "The Mythologizing of Mark Twain." Its collective effect should increase the respect for his genius at dramatizing his celebrity into a memorable personality, taken most hearteningly on his own terms and in his unique ways. We also need to get beyond the classic boyhood novels. Making *Huckleberry Finn* carry so much of Twain's essence has put it under inhuman pressure and isolated it with a now deadening reverence that prejudices his other writings. *The Innocents Abroad* is a fine place to start a rebound of acquaintance with his millions of printed words.

More recklessly than ever, western society is frittering away the strengths and pleasures of a shared tradition. Although Twain foments revolt against dead values, his image can help us hold on to a viable past that will add resonance to the future. To protect that image the ersatz must be counteracted by the facts about his interpersonal self and by informed delight in the heart of his writings and personality—that humor which at its most electric sprang from his anti-elitist irreverence. We will do ourselves a crucial service as well as a favor. A strictly amateur humorist, John Kenneth Galbraith, identifies Twain's best target as "pompous absurdity." That is an invincible enemy, and we need as much support from the true Twain as we can get just to hold on. Perhaps the current generations have little to learn from his more visceral attack on prim nineteenth-century taboos. But hypocrisy, vapid routine, insincerity, and official deceit always make a comeback, and we must keep Mark Twain alive to help us, even against ourselves.

A Note on Bibliography

THIS BOOK USES notes sparingly for two reasons. First, Thomas A. Tenney's *Reference Guide to Mark Twain* (1977), carefully annotated and indexed and backed up by annual supplements, records all major and middling items and also many that were, as Twain once jeered, hardly "suspected of being in the world at all"; my project was not soundly conceivable before his work. A little patience in using the *Reference Guide* will lead to most of the secondary material I quote, along with much else of interest. Paul Fatout's *Mark Twain Speaking* (1976) is another storehouse too rich to acknowledge at every step. Finally, it is a pleasure to mention the lately heightened flow of volumes in the Mark Twain Papers series (notebooks, manuscripts, letters) and in the Iowa/California Edition with its historical introductions and authoritative texts for writings published during Twain's lifetime. These three sources underlie my book throughout. My collection *Critical Essays on Mark Twain, 1867–1910* (Boston: G. K. Hall, 1982) reprints some of the background pieces I draw on here.

The second reason for the sparse notes is that the more I pondered the world of newspapers and magazines, the more I became aware of conducting an interpretation. Even if the problem of who really is the "public" gets crammed into the distorting limits of what was printed, there are major flaws in the evidence on hand. To leaf through Madeleine B. Stern, ed., *Publishers for Mass Entertainment in Nineteenth Century America* (1980)— with articles on forty-five firms that churned out "cheap books for the millions"—is to realize there were audiences much vaster than those that read Twain. Furthermore, on the level of literacy where his image flourished, the indexed newspapers and magazines inevitably get too much weight; his friendships or, in the case of *Harper's Weekly*, the self-interest of a publisher also distorted the equation. For most newspapers I had to depend on hit-and-miss scrapbooks, stray clippings, incidental leads, and plain luck. Only the fascination that Twain's personality exerts justified going on.

Eventually I hoped I had a grasp of the pattern running under Twain's many, sometimes competing images. Still, it is impossible to measure which ones really counted how much. Communication theory has recently developed the formidable concept of "flow," which emphasizes not an individual book, essay, or picture but the "rhythms of repeated deliveries of similar yet varying messages." Beyond that, anybody who ponders the first two articles in the Bibliography Issue for 1980 of the *American Quarterly* will see the intractability of genuinely proving that a particular idea was transmitted by a piece of print to an identifiable audience. Or, to take Twain historically, his fame coincided with, indeed grew out of the losing but desperate struggle of journalism to generate enough lively material to make the paid advertising look incidental. The "news" became a noisy industry whose impact on the slowly deafening consumer's life at the bone is probably overrated, certainly so by the press itself. Therefore, I have basically presumed to demonstrate not how important one special personality was but how interesting, stimulating, and educative he became to his society.

Ordinarily notes show good faith; they let the skeptic check for accuracy. But heavy use of them in rich areas, such as the career of "reverence," could have intimated "proof" for a paper-thin case elsewhere. Paradoxically the wealth of material at some points warned me that the tenth piece of evidence can destroy the inferences drawn from the first nine. I now appreciate the risks run by a biographer of Christopher Marlowe or Edgar Allan Poe. Not even a computer utopia will dredge out detailed indexes for the newspapers and magazines of the last hundred years. In fact, there is no complete file of all editions of the New York City dailies published by Pulitzer or Hearst between 1900 and 1910. Although spared a calamity like the San Francisco fire, they used cheap paper, an added reason for wellbred librarians to refuse to collect them. We have enough material on Twain's image for a lively debate, but the record will never be so clear as to justify an inquisition against minority views.

To be sure, I claim both honesty and diligence in the use of sources. Beyond the world of Twain scholarship I have especially learned from studies of the reputation of Andrew Jackson, Davy Crockett, P. T. Barnum, Robert E. Lee, Thomas A. Edison, Charles Lindbergh, and Will Rogers, though my approach differs in one or sometimes two ways. I concentrate on Twain's herohood during his lifetime, and I contend with the fact that he was— primarily or equally or whatever—a publishing author with an implicit persona that often pretended to display itself explicitly. Even so, many capable women and men have already contributed to a mountainous body of commentary relevant to my subject. Therefore, as a rule my notes indicate only (1) unpublished materials whose copyright resides with the Mark Twain Estate, (2) direct borrowing from scholars and critics, and (3) out-of-the-way items. The next criterion would have required at least ten times as many notes.

Notes

INTRODUCTION

1. Roy Meador, "Mark Twain Takes on Classical Music," *Ovation* 2 (Aug. 1981): 8.
2. I am quoting the paraphrase in J. G. Riewald and J. Bakker, *The Critical Reception of American Literature in the Netherlands 1824–1900: A Documentary Conspectus from Contemporary Periodicals* (1982), pp. 68–69.
3. Don Marquis, *Chapters for the Orthodox* (1934), pp. 138–39.
4. "Introduction," *Forms of Talk* (1981), p. 4.
5. See especially Robert M. Rodney, *Mark Twain International: A Bibliography and Interpretation of His Worldwide Popularity* (1982).

CHAPTER I
"This Shining Mark"

1. For primary texts I am heavily indebted to Thomas A. Tenney, "Mark Twain in 1910: A Survey of His Popular and Critical Standing at the End of His Career," M.A. thesis, Columbia University, 1964. Also, Tenney loaned me his three volumes of photostats from newspapers of late Apr. 1910. Reaction to Twain's death has many suggestive parallels to that evoked in Nov. 1910 by Leo Tolstoy, whose mourners disagreed startlingly about what he represented.
2. Paul Fatout, ed., *Mark Twain Speaking* (1976), pp. 606–7. See also A. B. Paine, ed., *Mark Twain's Autobiography* (1924), 1:248–50. The meeting occurred in Apr. 1888.
3. "Topics of the Week," 7 May 1910, p. 253.
4. Archibald Henderson, *Mark Twain* (1911), p. 15. I do not go on to A. B. Paine's biography because his livelihood was staked on Twain's reputation.
5. George Ade, "Mark Twain as Our Emissary," *Century* 81 (Dec. 1910): 204.

6. Henry Mills Alden, "Mark Twain: Personal Impressions," *Book News Monthly* 28 (Apr. 1910): 581. This essay was published before Twain's death.

7. Henderson, *Mark Twain*, p. 164.

8. An essay that should be better known is Sholom J. Kahn, "Mark Twain as American Rabelais," *Hebrew University Studies in Literature* 1 (Spring 1973): 47–75.

9. *Midstream* (1929), p. 56.

CHAPTER 2
Live Drama

1. Anon., *Facts/By a Woman* (Pacific Press, 1881), pp. 45–46. Copy in the Library of Congress.

2. Bruce Kuklick, "Myth and Symbol in American Studies," *American Quarterly* 24 (Oct. 1972): 444–46. Karl R. Popper, *Conjectures and Refutations* (1962), p. 341, warns against "naive collectivism" that easily assumes the existence of "social wholes."

3. John G. Cawelti, *Adventure, Mystery, and Romance: Formula Stories as Art and Popular Culture* (1976), pp. 30, 36. This strikes me as more workable than the thesis in Wyn Wachhorst's excellent *Thomas Alva Edison: An American Myth* (1981) that the culture hero always "functions to resolve mechanically contradictory" values.

4. Edwin H. Cady, *The Big Game: College Sports and American Life* (1978), pp. 46–57, expounds these archetypes extremely well.

5. I have benefited especially from the ideas of Orrin E. Klapp in *Symbolic Leaders: Public Dramas and Public Men* (1964); also "The Creation of Popular Heroes," *American Journal of Sociology* 54 (Sept. 1948): 135–41; "The Clever Hero," *Journal of American Folklore* 67 (Jan.–March 1954): 21–34; *Heroes, Villains, and Fools: The Changing American Character* (1962).

6. Neil Harris, *Humbug: The Art of P. T. Barnum* (1973), pp. 56, 61–62. The best statement of this point with reference to Twain is in Martin Green, *Re-Appraisals: Some Commonsense Readings in American Literature* (1965), pp. 113–18. W. D. Howells commented in "The Country Printer," *Scribner's Monthly* 13 (May 1893): 548–49, that the "printing-office of former days had so much affinity with the theatre, that compositors and comedians were easily convertible."

7. Quoted in the introduction to Franklin J. Meine's edition of *1601* (Chicago, 1939). As late as Apr. 1920 (*Atlantic Monthly*) Gamaliel Bradford fretted at length that Twain's "irreverence" might sway the "average ignorant reader of democracy." Morton Gurewitch, *Comedy: The Irrational Vision* (1975), pp. 56–59, capably praises "cynical wit" as an enemy of social and economic oppression.

8. L. W. Kline, *American Journal of Psychology* 18 (1907): 421–41. D. H. Munro's balanced *Argument of Laughter* (1951), pp. 177–81, regards Kline as still quite cogent. Kline named as his main forerunner a French essay of 1893.

9. See Anthony Caputi, *Buffo: The Genius of Vulgar Comedy*; Maurice Charney, *Comedy High and Low*; and Robert M. Torrance, *The Comic Hero*—all three published in 1978.

10. Henry Nash Smith, in *Mark Twain: The Development of a Writer* (1962),

p. 107, suggests that "both the best and the worst of his work derived from the popular culture." In *Harvests of Change* (1967) Jay Martin begins by declaring Twain was "incredibly sensitive to the shifting, unpredictable mass mind" (p. 166).

11. See Oscar Handlin, "Comments on Mass and Popular Culture," pp. 63–70, in Norman Jacobs, ed., *Culture for the Millions?* (1961). Herbert Gans, *Popular Culture and High Culture* (1974), is particularly good at challenging arguments for the prima-facie superiority of elite tastes and the harmful effect of low-brow ones. John G. Cawelti, "Recent Trends in the Study of Popular Culture," *American Studies: An International Newsletter* 10, no. 2 (Winter 1971), is still cogent, especially for his sensitivity to basic definitions.

12. Quoted approvingly in Erving Goffman, *The Presentation of Self in Everyday Life* (1969), p. 57.

CHAPTER 3
A Blood Relative

1. Edgar M. Branch and Robert H. Hirst, "Introduction" for *Early Tales & Sketches: Vol. 1, 1851–1864*, in *The Works of Mark Twain* (1979), 15:24. For the broader pattern see Green, *Re-Appraisals*, pp. 125, 130–31.

2. John C. Gerber, "Mark Twain's Use of the Comic Pose," *PMLA* 77 (June 1962): 297–304, convincingly lays out a pattern of seven personae for his entire career.

3. Hamlin Hill, *Mark Twain and Elisha Bliss* (1964), is the most informed source on the subscription trade; still more relevant here is his essay, "Mark Twain: Audience and Artistry," *American Quarterly* 15 (Spring 1963): 25–40.

4. Leon T. Dickinson, "Mark Twain's Revisions in Writing *The Innocents Abroad*," *American Literature* 19 (May 1947): 143–44.

5. Teona Tone Gneiting, in pp. 89–91, 190–91, of her excellent "Picture and Text: A Theory of Illustrated Fiction in the Nineteenth Century," Ph.D. diss., University of California (Los Angeles), 1977, is much more certain that a recognizable likeness of Twain appears throughout the illustrations of *Innocents Abroad* and that they helped to make the public familiar with his face.

6. I am indebted to chap. 2 of Eileen Nixon Meredith, "Mark Twain and the Audience: A Rhetorical Study," Ph.D. diss., Duke University, 1976. The comments of Warwick Wadlington, pp. 196–201 in *The Confidence Game in American Literature* (1975), are especially provocative.

7. *St. Louis Republic*, 1 June 1902, p. 9. In 1901 Howells hoped the day would never come when the passage was "declaimed" as a "mystical appeal for human solidarity." Martin, in *Harvests of Change*, p. 170, reads the passage, reasonably, as Edenic myth. According to the St. Louis papers of June 1902, *The Innocents Abroad* had been banned in Russia because Twain wept at the wrong locality and therefore weakened the faith of the devout. If the story was a hoax, the domestic fame of the passage benefited anyway; up until 1910, reporters could depend on casual allusions to it.

8. Robert H. Hirst, "The Making of *The Innocents Abroad*: 1867–1872," Ph.D. diss., University of California (Berkeley), 1975, p. 383. I have learned much from this outstanding study. As late as 1912 W. B. Cairns, *A History of American Litera-*

ture, p. 449, fretted: "The much quoted meditation at the tomb of Adam is not irreverent in the sense that it shocks anyone's religious faith; but it shows a disposition to force mirth on any subject."

9. 31 Aug. 1869, p. 8. More generally see Hirst, "Making of *The Innocents Abroad*," pp. 143–45, 301–7. Twain was content even with the *New York Tribune* review, which noted an "abominable irreverence for tradition and authority." The *New York Times* was calmer: "Pleasant but rather irreverent."

10. Richard Taylor Stith, "A Theory of Respect," Ph.D. diss., Yale University, 1973, is helpful. The best single article is the entry in James Hastings, *Encyclopedia of Religion and Ethics* (1908–26). The sermon "Reverence" by the well-known British minister H. P. Liddon contended that the "gravest anxiety" of "thoughtful Americans" was caused by the absence of reverence among all classes of her people"— *Easter in St. Paul's* (1885), p. 327. Of course Twain's subtitle trifled with John Bunyan's devout classic. Incidentally, nobody commented that the spelling on the spine (Pilgrim's Progress) and the spelling on the title page (Pilgrims') pointed in different thematic directions.

11. Paul Boyer, *Urban Masses and Moral Order in America 1820–1920* (1978), brilliantly fixes the dimensions of the campaign for social discipline. Reading Boyer reminds us of the error in talking about "everybody" in relation to the downward reach of Twain's audience or even of the newspapers. Boyer also makes us realize that the appeal for reverence seldom reached those judged most in need of controls, that the raptest listeners were already converts, as usual. Gurewitch, *Comedy: The Irrational Vision*, pp. 21–24, dissects Matthew Arnold's antagonism to humor that flouts moral seriousness and undermines social norms.

12. Charles W. Bardeen, *Authors' Birthday*, ser. 3 (1899), p. 329.

13. The original review is from the *Chicago Tribune* of 8 Jan. 1869; the reprinting is an unidentified clipping in the Yale Collection of American Literature. Paul Fatout, *Mark Twain on the Lecture Circuit* (1960), pp. 134–35, has a good sampling of other comic descriptions.

14. Dixon Wecter, ed., *The Love Letters of Mark Twain* (1949), p. 65.

15. See the three items quoted in Ernest Jerome Hopkins, ed., *The Ambrose Bierce Satanic Reader* (1968), pp. 192–93.

16. In 1873 J. C. Hotten asserted in London that he had seen a "comic paper" from Trinidad that was "illuminated by two of Mark Twain's jokes." Hotten also quoted some newspaper fillers about Twain too slight, one would expect, to have gone beyond the American press.

17. Wadlington, *Confidence Game*, p. 189.

CHAPTER 4
"The Mark Twain Mazurka"

1. Stow Persons, *The Decline of American Gentility* (1973), is especially helpful. More particularly, scholars still value Kenneth R. Andrews, *Nook Farm: Mark Twain's Hartford Circle* (1950).

2. The *Twainian* 16 (Jan.–Feb. 1957): 4, prints the correspondence.

3. The piece first ran in the *London World* in late 1877 or early Jan. 1878, and then in Edmund H. Yates, *Celebrities at Home*, ser. 3 (1879).

4. See especially item 3366 of the Clemens section in Jacob Blanck, *A Bibli-*

ography of American Literature (1957), and Albert Bigelow Paine, *Mark Twain: A Biography* (1912), pp. 555–57; also William M. Clemens, *Mark Twain: His Life and Work* (1892; 1894), pp. 123–24, and the surprising length of detail in an interview in *St. Louis Post-Dispatch*, 29 May 1902. This last item may explain why the jingle came up a few days later in Hannibal, where Twain responded by stating its "moral."

5. This is an enlargement of an illustration ("Return in War-Paint") on p. 124 of *Innocents Abroad*. Twain may have resurrected it himself; he had praised it to his fiancée in 1869 because, says Teona Gneiting, it captured the "spirit of swashbuckling exaggeration."

6. Detailed analysis of Twain's lecturing depends on two solid, complementary books: Fatout, *Mark Twain on the Lecture Circuit*, and Fred W. Lorch, *The Trouble Begins at Eight: Mark Twain's Lecture Tours* (1968).

7. "Mark Twain Tonight," 19 Dec. 1871, p. [4]. For the Lyceum Circular see Lorch, *Trouble Begins at Eight*, p. 120. The author can be identified because his autobiography retreaded his review as his memories—William A. Croffut, *An American Procession* (1931), pp. 169–71.

8. The richly basic text is Fatout's *Mark Twain Speaking*.

9. The center for discussion is still Henry Nash Smith, "'That Hideous Mistake of Poor Clemens's,'" *Harvard Library Bulletin* 9 (Spring 1955): 145–80. Nobody has yet gone so far as to take the speech as ritualized insult, but those who propose to diagram the social dynamics of the affair ought to consider "The Nature of Deference and Demeanor" in Erving Goffman, *Interaction Ritual: Essays in Face-to-Face Behavior* (1969).

10. In the Lilly Library at Indiana University. Franklin J. Meine's notes on the copy in his collection (University of Illinois, Urbana-Champaign) identify the composer as Felix Kraemer, "otherwise unknown to fame." Meine also found a handout for Mark Twain Cigars that uses a picture of Twain probably taken in the late 1870s. The *Twainian* 2 (Feb., 1940): 7–8, reports a "Mark Twain Waltz" (1880) with otherwise identical details about its publisher.

11. Twain clipped another jocular review (Scrapbook #8, item 23, Mark Twain Papers; cited hereafter as MTP) that found "not an objectionable line" while recalling that "some people, even those who have not the bump of reverence developed like a goose egg," had resented the "trifling with sacred traditions" in *Innocents Abroad*. His promotional letter appeared in *New York Herald*, 11 Dec. 1876.

12. The first of these items may have been a reproof of Twain for a speech on 30 Sept. supporting Hayes for president. The author of the third item, if not the first two also, was probably Edward P. Mitchell—Frank O'Brien, *The Story of the "Sun"* (1918), p. 406.

13. James M. Cox, *Mark Twain: The Fate of Humor* (1966), is especially good on its tall tales; William M. Gibson, *The Art of Mark Twain* (1976), pp. 36–39, best sums up the "sustained motif of violence and adventure." Edgar M. Branch and Robert H. Hirst comment about the Nevada years: "The impulse to embroider the facts was, even at this early date, recognized as Clemens' distinguishing idiosyncrasy"—"Introduction," *Early Tales & Sketches*, 1: 26.

14. See pp. 216–18 of Cawelti's consistently brilliant *Adventure, Mystery, and Romance*.

15. See particularly pp. 60–65 of Robert Regan, *Unpromising Heroes: Mark Twain and His Characters* (1966). Regan enriches his analysis by contrasting the *Roughing It* persona with that assumed by Twain during his Nevada years.

16. Theodore Bolton, "Introduction to Reading: Recollections of Princeton," *Princeton Library Chronicle* 25 (Winter 1964): 121–28. He recalls that, as a nine-year-old in an educated family, he had to look up only two words in a dictionary. As early as 1877 Twain composed a form letter to answer inquiries about whether he planned to continue Tom Sawyer's "history."

17. Cox, *Fate of Humor*, p. 135, is particularly cogent on this point and my following one; see also E. N. Meredith, "Mark Twain and His Audience," chap. 4.

18. [John Henton Carter], "A Day with Mark Twain," *Rollinpin's Humorous Illustrated Annual* (1883); perhaps this appeared first in the *St. Louis Times* in May 1882. Walter Blair has kindly furnished me with a typescript of this now rare item.

19. Both the facts of his reading and the larger implications have been examined painstakingly by Alan Gribben, especially in *Mark Twain's Library: A Reconstruction*, 2 vols. (1980).

20. Regan, *Unpromising Heroes*, pp. 162–63.

21. Typescript of Morse diary in MTP.

CHAPTER 5
The Year of Jubilee

1. *Life* 1 (22 Mar. 1883): 142, and 15 (27 Feb. 1890): 121. Orion Clemens thought that the sabots Twain is wearing in the 1890 cartoon and the black cat he is holding referred to touches in *A Connecticut Yankee* favorable to Henry George's radicalism.

2. Arthur L. Vogelback, "Mark Twain: Newspaper Contributor," *American Literature* 20 (May 1948): 128. However, posing another of the puzzles that Twain's public career created so abundantly, some authoritative scholars believe that the letter of 1859 may be genuine. Opie Read would become a cottage industry for fabricating Twain anecdotes; on 20 Dec. 1885 the *Knoxville Chronicle* credited the *Arkansaw Traveler* for a long yarn about how a country bumpkin outsmoked Twain with a malodorous pipe.

3. "Mark Twain Aggrieved," *New York Times*, 4 Dec 1883, p. 2. Any reader of Paine's biography (Appendix P) knows that the reference to a monument for Adam is factual; see also Fatout, *Mark Twain Speaking*, pp. 78–80. He signed the *Times* letter as S. L. C.; some of such decisions are intriguingly opaque.

4. See his letter to George H. Warner, 1 Dec. 1891 (MTP). In 1892 he gladly donated two sets of his books to the Workingmen's Library of Lancaster, Pa.

5. James B. Pond, *Eccentricities of Genius* (1900), p. 247.

6. "Samuel Langhorne Clemens," in the short-lived, now scarce *Literature: An Illustrated Weekly Magazine* 1 (16 June 1888). This article was followed by reprintings of four other Twain items, but it is judicious to note that the magazine was struggling for material. Nye's commentary ran in the *New York World*, 16 June 1889, p. 21.

7. Gerald W. McFarland, ed., *Moralists or Pragmatists? The Mugwumps 1884–1900* (1975); see especially Geoffrey T. Blodgett, "The Mind of the Boston Mugwump."

8. From a *New York Times* article quoted in J. Henry Harper, *The House of*

Harper (1912), p. 573. In 1878 Twain hesitated to offer his essay "Mental Telegraphy" for publication because it might be taken as a joke.

9. Arthur L. Vogelback, *"The Prince and the Pauper:* A Study in Critical Standards," *American Literature* 14 (Mar. 1942): 48–54; also, Lin Salamo, "Introduction" for *The Prince and the Pauper* (1979), in *The Works of Mark Twain,* vol. 6. The *Boston Herald* did insist on finding confirmation of his "love of truth, a hatred of humbug and a scorn for cant." Some readers could have felt that Miles Hendon is Twain himself, winning the right to sit in the presence of gentility.

10. Anon., *Harper's Weekly* 31 (2 Apr. 1887): 248.

11. My quotations mostly come from Arthur L. Vogelback, "The Publication and Reception of *Huckleberry Finn* in America," *American Literature* 11 (Nov. 1939): 269–71. However he does not cite the *New York World,* which also complained about the "irreverence which makes parents, guardians and people who are at all good and proper ridiculous."

12. Albert E. Stone, *The Innocent Eye: Childhood in Mark Twain's Imagination* (1961), p. 133.

13. Samuel C. Webster, ed., *Mark Twain: Business Man* (1946), pp. 275–78, 388–89. That 1887 woodcut was replaced by a full page engraving. Interest in the 1885 heliotype has centered on its usefulness for identifying early states of the first edition; see *Twainian* 6 (Jan.–Feb. 1947): 1–2. The *Hartford Courant* described the bust on 9 Nov. 1884. A front view of it was printed in *Harper's Monthly* 71 (Oct. 1885): 721; also in *Harper's Weekly* 31 (2 Apr. 1887): 248. Twain earlier had Karl Gerhardt do a clay medallion of Cable and him for use in publicity; fairness should add that he made unselfish efforts to advance Gerhardt's career. The bust stood in the foyer of the Hartford house, to where it has been returned. Walter Blair has suggested in passing that the bust-photo comically stressed the incongruities between Huck and his creator.

14. See Everett Carter, "The Meaning of *A Connecticut Yankee,*" *American Literature* 50 (Nov. 1978): 418–40. Regan, *Unpromising Heroes,* pp. 165–82, is particularly suggestive on its closing implications. In parts of three different books Henry Nash Smith made the most sophisticated case for a pessimistic reading; but he stays neutral in his historical "Introduction" for vol. 9 (edited by Bernard L. Stein; 1979) of *The Works of Mark Twain.* After the immediate wave of reviews, Henry C. Vedder's essay in *American Writers of To-Day* (1894) still praised ringingly its attack on the "romantic and picturesque view" of Malory and Tennyson.

15. Robert F. Horton, *Alfred Tennyson: A Saintly Life* (1900), p. 272. Twain's draft of a reply to Arnold in 1888 (DV16, MTP) specifically attacked reverence though it focused on the British concern over precedence at social gatherings. In a coherent interview by a British journalist (*New York World,* 31 May 1891, p. 26), Twain commented in detail on his novel, Tennyson, and definitions of reverence.

16. Clyde L. Grimm, *"The American Claimant:* Reclamation of a Farce," *American Quarterly* 19 (Spring 1967): 86–103, states best the weighty issue that the novel could have brought into focus.

17. *Cleveland Leader,* 30 Nov. 1884, p. 9. The sketch was reprinted, as in the *Rochester* (N.Y.) *Union Advertiser,* 8 Dec. 1884, p. 1. For the author "Carp," or Frank George Carpenter, see *Carp's Washington,* ed. Frances Carpenter (1960).

18. *Cincinnati Commercial Gazette,* 4 Jan. 1885, p. 8. The entire "report" was reprinted in the first book-length biography of Twain by Will M. Clemens in 1892.

Edgar C. Beall, the phrenologist, would claim later to have analyzed Twain in person somewhere; see Madeleine B. Stern, "Mark Twain Had His Head Examined," *American Literature* 41 (May 1969): 212–13.

19. *Critic* 6 (17 Jan. 1885): 25–26. This piece was frequently mined for excerpts. It was reprinted in full in Jeannette Gilder and Joseph Gilder, *Authors at Home* (1888); Will Clemens drew on it in 1892. Twain was especially pleased with the entry in the eleventh edition of the prestigious *Men of Our Time* (1884). In 1885 an editor of the *Columbus* (Ohio) *Dispatch* sent him a birthday poem he had published.

CHAPTER 6
"Working the Newspapers"

1. See, for example, *Hubbard's Newspaper Advertiser* 2 (Nov. 1876): 1. Among other papers the *Chicago Tribune*, 20 Dec. 1871, and the Columbus *Ohio State Journal*, 6 Jan. 1872, especially liked this passage. I have seen a reprinting as late as the 1960s under the headline "Mark Twain Enjoyed Reporting." The "Introduction" for *Early Tales & Sketches*, 1: 52–54, has a fine summary passage.

2. *Backlog Studies* (1872; 1899), pp. 133–34. For several good reasons Twain is accepted as "Our Next Door" in a series of informal conversations.

3. See especially pp. 180–81 of Dan Schiller, *Objectivity and the News: The Public and the Rise of Commercial Journalism* (1981). To my mind this keen analysis somewhat skirts the issue of sensationalism and too simply implies that objectivity was achieved—or is possible when getting out a newspaper requires a large capital investment.

4. Letter of 3 Aug. 1892 in Janet Ross, *The Fourth Generation* (1912), pp. 321–22. See also Appendix F of *A Tramp Abroad*.

5. I follow up this point more concretely in "Color Him Curious about Yellow Journalism: Mark Twain and the New York City Press," *Journal of Popular Culture* 15, 2 (1981): 25–33, with most emphasis on the *Evening Post, Sun,* and *World*.

6. Besides the standard histories of American journalism, Harry W. Baehr's history of the *Tribune*, and the official biography of Reid by Royal Cortissoz in 1921, see Arthur L. Vogelback, "Mark Twain and the Fight for the Control of the *Tribune*," *American Literature* 26 (Nov. 1954): 374–83.

7. Quoted from George Monteiro, "A Note on the Mark Twain—Whitelaw Reid Relationship," *ESQ*, no. 19 (2d quar. 1960): 20. The forthcoming edition of Twain's letters will print all of those to Reid, expertly annotated. Somewhat surprisingly, the *Tribune* of 11 Jan. 1885 carried a long excerpt from *Adventures of Huckleberry Finn*.

8. *New York Evening Post*, 16 May 1876, p. 1. Allan Nevins has written the standard history of the *Post*. William M. Armstrong's biography (1978) sums up Godkin's career without any surprises. The entry for the *Post* in Gribben, *Mark Twain's Library*, is useful, as are the entries for the other New York dailies.

9. *New York Times*, 9 Mar. 1884, p. 6. See *Mark Twain, Business Man*, pp. 216–19; Dixon Wecter, ed., *Mark Twain to Mrs. Fairbanks* (1949), p. 215; Henry Nash Smith and William M. Gibson, eds., *Mark Twain—Howells Letters* (1960), 2:866–67; R. D. Jerome and H. A. Wisbey, eds., *Mark Twain in Elmira* (1977), p. 192.

10. See especially Paul Fatout, "Mark Twain, Litigant," *American Literature* 31 (Mar. 1959): 39.

11. Quoted in George Juergens, *Joseph Pulitzer and "The New York World"* (1966), pp. 231–32. Recent provocative commentary occurs in Michael Schudson, *Discovering the News* (1978). Edwin Emery and Michael Emery, *The Press and America*, 4th ed. (1978), a middle-of-the-road textbook, speaks respectfully of the *World* as the "people's champion."

12. The letters from Dana, still unpublished, are in MTP. "Interviewing the Interviewer" will be included in a forthcoming volume of *Early Tales & Sketches*.

13. Scrapbook #23 in the MTP is an exhaustive gathering of clippings about the *Memoirs*; also helpful is Herbert Feinstein, "Mark Twain and the Pirates," *Harvard Law School Bulletin* 13 (Apr. 1962): 10–12.

14. On reading my "Who Wants to Go to Hell? An Unsigned Sketch by Mark Twain?" *Studies in American Humor*, n.s. 1 (1982): 6–16, Robert H. Hirst, editor of the Mark Twain Papers, sent me a copy of the galleys for the sketch, evidently mailed to Twain by W. M. Laffan. In 1887 he offered another item to Laffan—see Robert Pack Browning and others, eds., *Mark Twain's Notebooks and Journals: Vol. 3, 1883–1891* (1979), p. 275; see p. 58 for evidence that he considered offering the *Sun* a chance to serialize *Huckleberry Finn*. The manuscript for the slur on Wanamaker, excerpted in Smith and Gibson, eds., *Mark Twain—Howells Letters*, 2:572, is in the Barrett Collection at the University of Virginia.

15. The article in the *Dictionary of American Biography* is by Frank M. O'Brien, first historian of the *Sun*. See also Candace Stone, *Dana and the "Sun"* (1938), pp. 43–45; Charles J. Rosebault, *When Dana Was "The Sun"* (1931; repr. 1961), pp. 191, 330; Eugene Exman, *The House of Harper* (1967), pp. 172–73, 205.

16. *New York Times*, 24 Oct. 1903, p. 758. All those listed by the *Times* except one are in *Who's Who in America 1903–1905*, which used "capitalist" on a neutral par with "banker" and "litterateur."

CHAPTER 7
A Domestic Tragedy

1. John G. Cawelti, "The Writer as a Celebrity: Some Aspects of American Literature as Popular Culture," *Studies in American Fiction* 5 (Spring 1977): 166.

2. Vedder, *American Writers of To-Day*, p. 139. This was nevertheless a drastic retreat from the ill-timed concluding paragraphs of Vedder's original essay in the *New York Examiner*, 6 Apr. 1893, p. [2].

3. Quoted in William M. Clemens, "Mark Twain on the Lecture Platform," *Ainslee's Magazine* 6 (Aug. 1900): 32.

4. A. B. Paine, ed., *Mark Twain's Letters* (1917), 2:614.

5. James B. Pond, "Across the Continent with Mark Twain," *Saturday Evening Post*, 29 Sept. 1900, p. 7; Clara Clemens, *My Father Mark Twain* (1931), p. 136.

6. Regan, *Unpromising Heroes*, p. 31, is especially cogent on this point, as is Gerber, "Mark Twain's Use of the Comic Pose," *PMLA* 77 (June 1962): 299.

7. Ronald G. Walters, "Mickey and Adolf," *Johns Hopkins Magazine* 31 (June 1980): 26–29, has stimulating commentary.

8. The clipping quoted here should be dated after 25 Jan. 1897. A reprinting, it credits the London Correspondence of the *Chicago Times-Herald*. It was

probably saved by Orion Clemens. Perhaps the first clipping mentioned by Twain was actually "The Closing Days of a Great Career," *Hartford Globe*, 14 Feb. 1897.

9. Some of the key letters are in Lewis Leary, ed., *Mark Twain's Correspondence with Henry Huttleston Rogers* (1969); his notes for the lecture are in DV238, MTP.

10. For a photograph of the note see Frank Marshall White, "Mark Twain as a Newspaper Reporter," *Outlook* 96 (24 Dec. 1910): 961–67. The note is in the Barrett Collection of the University of Virginia (and a copy is in MTP); so anyone may judge whether the comma is actually a semicolon and whether the notation on the reverse side about substituting a prissy "were" for "was" applies (I think not) to this text. White's resulting interview ran in the *New York Journal*, 2 June 1897, p. 1. As early as 1863 Twain joked of somebody reported dead: "I asked him about it at church this morning. He said there was no truth in the rumor"— *Early Tales & Sketches*, 1:258.

11. *New York Herald*, 27 June 1897, p. 8. Key passages of related letters are quoted in the edition of his correspondence with Rogers, pp. 285–89. The complete originals or copies are available in MTP. Fatout, for *Mark Twain on the Lecture Circuit*, pp. 266–67, looked more closely at the *Herald's* running account than anybody else.

12. Anna Katona's paper "Success of the Entertainer: An Assessment of Mark Twain's Lecture in Budapest" was read at the 1977 meeting of the Modern Language Association.

13. For his implicit defense of his writing apart from his humor see *Mark Twain's Notebooks*, p. 245. The best-known text is the "Belly and the Members" argument carefully drafted with Andrew Lang in mind—*Mark Twain's Letters*, 2:525–28. It is also a ringing defense of popular culture, both as entertainment or relaxation and a first stage of esthetic mobility; written soon after *A Connecticut Yankee*, it assumes the political egalitarianism helpful to any such defense.

14. DV238, MTP, the notes for the aborted benefit lecture of 1897 (†). Sloane, *Mark Twain as a Literary Comedian*, pp. 180–81, comments on the vogue of the maxims; Gibson, *Art of Mark Twain*, pp. 159–76, gives by far the best literary analysis; S. J. Sackett, *Edgar Watson Howe* (1972), discusses later practitioners; Gurewitch, *Comedy: The Irrational Vision*, pp. 59–71, brilliantly discusses the corrosive potential of witticisms and epigrams.

15. Hamilton W. Mabie, "Mark Twain the Humorist," *Outlook* 87 (23 Nov. 1907): 651. The most tolerantly incisive analysis of *Joan of Arc* is in Stone, *Innocent Eye*, pp. 205–27; Cox, *Fate of Humor*, pp. 261–62, states best the disappointment of critics today.

16. Frederick Anderson, ed., *Mark Twain: The Critical Heritage* (1971), has a well-chosen selection of reviews.

17. I develop this subject in detail with "Mark Twain and the Magazine World," *Univ. of Mississippi Studies in English*, n.s. 2 (1981): 35–42.

18. Arnold Bennett later recalled hearing that the *Journal* had offered $52,000 for fifty-two articles. Twain's letter to Moffett of 7 July 1897 (MTP) indicates that a "large" deal had been discussed but also that Hearst did not approve it(†). In 1894, Twain, intriguingly, reminded his brother that he had earned as much as $1,000 "at a single sitting" writing for the press(†).

19. Charles Miner Thompson, "Mark Twain as an Interpreter of American

Character," *Atlantic Monthly* 79 (Apr. 1897): 443–50. Henry S. Canby, *The Age of Confidence* (1934), would recall that during the 1890s a "home library"—that is, the collection for a well-bred and prosperous family—gave little space to Twain, a "cheap and flippant writer."

20. In *Mr. Clemens and Mark Twain* (1966), pp. 355–57, Justin Kaplan draws striking patterns from Moffett's essay. The reader should be clear that the inferences apply to it rather than the notes Twain supplied.

21. George C. Carrington, Jr., *The Dramatic Unity of "Huckleberry Finn"* (1977), develops an interesting theory about Twain's "drama-making activity" on behalf of his characters.

CHAPTER 8
Moods and Tenses in Interviews

1. The entry in the *Oxford English Dictionary* is helpful. Raymond L. Schults, *Crusader in Babylon: W. T. Stead and the Pall Mall Gazette* (1972), pp. 61–65, 83–85, has details on British resistance. Retrospectively the enemies of N. P. Willis would accuse him as the inventor; see the *Connecticut General Advertiser*, 15 Jan. 1870, p. 1, which also noted that even flamboyant Benjamin Butler detested interviewers. As late as Mar. 1877 *Puck* had a full-page set of jeering cartoons.

2. See the preface of my *Listing of and Selection from Newspaper and Magazine Interviews with Samuel L. Clemens* (1977), also published as vol. 10, no. 1 of *American Literary Realism, 1870–1910*. The interviews cited in this chapter can be located more precisely through my listing except for one handful I have located.

3. See especially the three items reprinted in my "Mark Twain Talks Mostly About Humor and Humorists," *Studies in American Humor* 1 (Apr. 1974): 4–19. He gave highest approval to the interview in the *Portland Oregonian*, 11 Aug. 1895—reprinted in my *Listing and Selection*.

4. *Twainian* 32 (Mar.–Apr. 1973): 3. The *Brooklyn Eagle*, 23 June 1900, p. 15, had a photograph of Twain supposedly on the Picnic Platform, announcing his "self-named candidacy for the presidency of the Plutocratic Ticket."

5. For a brilliant pioneering essay see Neil Harris, "Iconography and Intellectual History: The Half-Tone Effect," pp. 196–211, in John Higham and Paul K. Conkin, eds., *New Directions in American Intellectual History* (1979).

6. Paine 136, MTP. Dating this item as 1898 depends on its reference to the fiftieth anniversary of the movement for women's rights. In 1883, intent on a parody of biblical fundamentalism, Twain's notebook recorded an impulse for a burlesque interview with the disciple John.

7. Paine 27, MTP (†). The dating of summer 1902 seems soundest. For other details see Twain's letters to Franklin G. Whitmore—who had long served as his business agent—particularly on 2 Mar. and 19 May 1902 (in MTP).

CHAPTER 9
Statesman Without Salary

1. For an early use of the phrase, hedged with humor, see Fatout, *Mark Twain Speaking*, pp. 370–71. William R. Macnaughton, *Mark Twain's Last Years as*

a Writer (1979), p. 143, judges that Twain made a fairly conscious decision to become a "moralist and reformer." Macnaughton discusses the late political essays luminuously for both method and doctrine. Also insightful is the chapter entitled "Polemical Pieces" in Gibson, *Art of Mark Twain*. Others may find more than I do in Maxwell Geismar, *Mark Twain: American Prophet* (1970).

2. *New York Times*, 19 June 1907, p. 1. A shortened version reappeared in the obituary editorial of the *New York Evening World*, 25 Apr. 1910, p. [15]. Besides suggesting that reporters often read their rivals' stories about Twain, it heightens the daring (at "some big public occasion" where he heard a "long and tiresome" paean to progress) and the gunfighter terseness—"'Yes,' drawled Twain, 'I think [the world] is better than it used to be. But I don't like to talk about my achievements.'"

3. The longest, probably most dependable inside version is Katy Leary, *My Lifetime with Mark Twain* (1925), pp. 196–200. In 1895 Owen Wister had noted that "one of the common [New York City] papers has a sort of play in which [Twain] is represented complaining about streetcars and crossing sweepers."

4. Quoted in Paine's biography, pp. 1279–80, and attributed to the *New York Evening Mail*; the date is probably 1905.

5. See especially Allison R. Ensor, "The House United: Mark Twain and Henry Watterson Celebrate Lincoln's Birthday, 1901," *South Atlantic Quarterly* 74 (Spring 1975): 259–68.

6. Hamlin Hill, *Mark Twain: God's Fool* (1973), pp. 20–25, quotes heavily from Twain's correspondence during this period.

7. Gibson, *Art of Mark Twain*, pp. 149–51. Philip S. Foner, *Mark Twain: Social Critic* (1958), pp. 277–95, has much detail on the reputation of this essay and related writings. I cite the *New York Times* and the *Tribune* most often because they had careful though understandably incomplete indexes. Still, *Current Literature* 30 (Mar. 1901): 281, noting that Twain had recently drawn "no little adverse criticism," singled out the *Times*, which "does its best to discredit him as a serious writer."

8. E. Berkeley Tompkins, *Anti-Imperialism in the United States: The Great Debate 1890–1920* (1970), p. 12. Foner, *Social Critic*, pp. 279–82, is useful on the response to Twain.

9. William W. Ellsworth, *A Golden Age of Authors* (1919), pp. 224–25; chances are good though not excellent that this detail is sound and that it concerns "To My Missionary Critics."

10. To "Dear Madam," 13 Apr. 1901, MTP (†).

11. Slightly differing versions ran in the *New York Sun, Times, Tribune*, and *World* of 15 Apr. 1906. The Gorky fiasco has been much discussed; for emphasis on Twain's part see my "Twain, Howells, and Boston Nihilists," *New England Quarterly* 32 (Sept. 1959): 365–70. More generally, see Emanuel Julius, "Mark Twain: Radical," *International Socialist Review* 11 (Aug. 1910): 83–88.

12. For his newspaper statements see the *New York World* and the *American*, 28 Nov., and the *New York World*, 3 Dec. 1905. Foner, *Social Critic*, pp. 300–301, is useful. Hunt Hawkins, "Mark Twain's Involvement with the Congo Reform Movement: 'A Fury of Generous Indignation,'" *New England Quarterly* 51 (June 1978): 147–75, is highly knowledgeable.

13. The handiest, most knowledgeable sampling of this material is John S. Tuckey, ed., *The Devil's Race-Track: Mark Twain's Great Dark Writings/The Best from*

"Which Was the Dream?" and "Fables of Man" (1980); see also William M. Gibson, ed., *Mark Twain's Mysterious Stranger Manuscripts* (1969).

14. *New York Tribune,* 7 Nov. 1901, p. 3.

15. *New York Herald,* 11 Mar. 1906, sec. 1, p. 5, and 19 Mar. 1906, p. 8. The *Tribune* had started the idea. *Collier's Weekly* 37 (31 Mar. 1906): 11, made the story a pretext for a paragraph of general praise.

16. The dinner was widely reported, and Harvey soon got out a handsome book which gave the seating chart and the speeches. See also Paine's biography, p. 1184. Somewhat cryptically, *Life* (27 June 1907) would joke that Twain's "true greatness consists in the fact that he is still regarded with pure affection, in spite of the fact he has been advertised by George Harvey."

17. Kaplan's biography, pp. 383–85, states best the case against Twain for not only hobnobbing with the plutocracy but helping Standard Oil to woo the press. See also Lewis Leary, "Mark Twain Among the Malefactors," in Brom Webber, ed., *Sense and Sensibility in Twentieth-Century Writing* (1970). Just before Ida Tarbell's history of Standard Oil began appearing, Samuel E. Moffett made a sane brief for Rogers in the "Captains of Industry" series in the *Cosmopolitan* (Sept. 1902).

18. Brooklyn *Eagle,* 24 Nov. 1907, p. 1; this was a particularly dependable interview. For an eye-catching story see *New York Herald* of the same date, p. M3. Boyer's *Urban Masses and Moral Order* would place such an activity in a searchingly critical context but still, I believe, accept its constructiveness.

CHAPTER 10
The White Peacock

1. James L. Ford, *Forty-Odd Years in the Literary Shop* (1921), pp. 149–50; the most artful description of the dinner is in Justin Kaplan, *Mark Twain and His World* (1974), pp. 185–87. *Smoker's Straight Cuts,* a giveaway pamphlet from a pipe manufacturer, reprinted the *New York Times* story. The Franklin Meine Collection at the University of Illinois (Champaign-Urbana) holds a five-page leaflet, printed privately, with the title "How To Reach the Age of Seventy." *Life* (28 Dec. 1905) put Harvey on its Christmas list "because there was never such a dinner as he gave Mark Twain."

2. In the Isabel Lyon papers for 1903 at Vassar College; perhaps the writing is that of Lyon, the secretary who often set down Twain's comments verbatim (†).

3. Attributed to Harry Thurston Peck, in "Chronicle and Comment" (New York) *Bookman* 12 (Jan. 1901): 441. Peck's criticism aroused surprise and indignation; see *Literary Digest* 22 (26 Jan. 1901): 100; *Current Literature* 30 (Mar. 1901): 281; and especially the editorial "A Little Man and a Great Subject" in *Washington* (D.C.) *Times,* 31 Jan. 1901, p. 4.

4. I borrow from Gribben's analysis in *Mark Twain's Library,* 2:523.

5. In chap. 9, "Personality in Public," Richard Sennett, *The Fall of Public Man* (1977), conducts a sophisticated analysis of dress in Twain's era. In "Twainiana," *Hobbies* 48 (Oct. 1943): 96–97, Cyril Clemens has some fresh but garbled details about the suits. John Seelye, *Mark Twain in the Movies* (1977), pp. 21–22, 54–55, speculates imaginatively about sectional reactions.

6. Hudson Strode, *The Story of Bermuda* (1932), pp. 189–90, records a late

solution for bibs to keep those suits clean. For the *London Express* (3 June 1908—reprinted in *New York Times*, 14 June) Clara Clemens suggested that Twain took to wearing white because it "soothed him and reminded him of bed." Also she offered as a case of sympathetic coloration: "His hair has gradually assumed the color of his pillow." Eventually she donated one of the suits to the Mark Twain Museum in Hannibal, Mo.

7. 23 July 1907, p. 1. *Minneapolis Journal*, 30 June 1907, edit. sect., p. 8, had details on the evening suit, which I find first described in *New York Herald*, 15 Feb. 1907, p. 5.

8. *New York Tribune*, 22 Dec. 1905, p. 7; see also Fatout, *Mark Twain Speaking*, p. 476.

9. "Mark Twain," *The New American Type and Other Essays* (1908), p. 299. Except for not hurrahing over payment of the debts, Sedgwick comes very close to the main points, as highlighted in the margins, of an anonymous booklet, *Mark Twain: Printer, Pilot, Miner, Journalist, Humorist, Traveler, Lecturer, Novelist, Publisher* (1900). The point is not plagiarism, of course, but a widening consensus.

10. Although not concerned with Twain, in "The Baconians: Madness Through Method," *South Atlantic Quarterly* 54 (July 1955): 359–68, I try to explain why some responsible minds got stuck in this groove.

11. *New York Tribune*, 10 May 1908, p. 1. The *World*, p. 8, and the *American*, p. 1W, had highly similar reports. As late as 1903 the pastor of a Roman Catholic church in Yonkers, while sermonizing on the "veneration of relics," attacked that "scurrilous buffoon, Mark Twain," and, apparently, *The Innocents Abroad*; see *New York Tribune*, 10 Nov., p. 2.

12. Guy A. Cardwell, "Mark Twain: A Self-Emasculating Hero," *ESQ* 23 (3d quar. 1977): 173–86. The cuteness grew heaviest in stories describing Twain's return from England in the company of young Dorothy Quick; see especially the *New York World* version of 23 July 1907, reprinted for instance in *Minneapolis Journal*, which credited its "Leased Wire Service."

13. The unreliable *New York American*, 25 Apr. 1910, p. 3, was alone in reporting that he said on his deathbed: "I can't travel; I can't even write. But what makes it easiest to go, is that I am so old—and there isn't anyone for me to play with any more."

14. "Mark Twain as Our Emissary," *Century Magazine* 81 (Dec. 1910): 204–5.

15. *New York Herald*, 1 Aug. 1909, mag. sec., p. 6. The encounter at the banquet is still unclear; the remarks about split identity that are attributed to Twain may have come from the mimic.

16. Incidentally, I see no reason why Robinson's sonnet "Doctor of Billiards" may not be a severe judgment on the frothiest side of the late public Twain.

CHAPTER 11
Mark Twain Today! Tomorrow!

1. *North American Review* 197 (Jan. 1913): 136. Irving Bacheller went almost as far, more effectively, in *Literary Digest* 45 (16 Nov. 1912): 909. *The Nation's* reviewer called it the "prose odyssey of the American people" (12 Nov. 1912).

2. By far the keenest yet also most factual analysis of the Brooks-DeVoto

wars is Guy A. Cardwell, "Mark Twain: The Metaphoric Hero as Battleground," *ESQ* 23 (1st quar. 1977): 52–66.

3. The conclusion of William R. Brown, *Imagemaker: Will Rogers and the American Dream* (1970). Rogers also had a fine sense for physical props, which included a blue serge suit.

4. Once again I acknowledge the rich usefulness of Tenney's *Reference Guide to Mark Twain*. For 1935 his annotations of entries made a concise survey of opinion. In *Letters of Askance*, pp. 81–82, Christopher Morley nicely sums up the image of the later 1930s.

5. I refer to the last two essays in *Forays and Rebuttals* (1936); one was delivered for Mark Twain Week in Columbia, Mo., in Dec. 1935.

6. Richard D. Altick, *South Atlantic Quarterly* 34 (Oct. 1935): 359–67.

7. Such is the conclusion of a persuasive analysis by Charles H. Compton, "Who Reads Mark Twain?" *American Mercury* 31 (Apr. 1934): 465–71, reprinted in expanded form in his *Who Reads What?* (1935).

8. Twain also appears in two other novels of the Riverworld tetralogy.

9. Richard Schickel, "Hal Holbrook Tonight," *Holiday* 40 (Aug. 1966): 103. I know of several currently performing Mark Twains in the Southeast and hear of many others elsewhere. Also, see *Newsweek*, 30 June 1980, p. 24, and *Washington Star*, 9 Apr. 1981, for presentations by William McLinn, who is close to national visibility.

10. The longest of the most approving reviews is Robert Bray, "Mark Twain Biography," *Midwest Quarterly* 15 (Spring 1974): 286–301. John Tuckey wrote two cogently quizzical evaluations—in *American Literature* 46 (Mar. 1974): 116–18, and *American Literary Realism 1870–1910* 7 (Spring 1974): 175–77.

11. Arthur G. Pettit, "Mark Twain and His Times: A Bicentennial Appreciation," *South Atlantic Quarterly* 76 (Spring 1977): 133–46.

12. Polls are very loose indicators, though once publicized they can have a self-validating influence. A Gallup poll among teenagers in 1979 shows the following rates of recognition: Hawthorne, 14% for *The Scarlet Letter*, Hemingway, 15% for *The Old Man and the Sea*, Twain 52% for *Tom Sawyer*, and (in a reflection of recent popularity not yet tested by time) Alex Haley, 80% for *Roots*.

13. American uniqueness does not apply here. Note the beginning of "Hermitage" by a contemporary Polish poet:

> *You thought a hermit lived hermetically,*
> *but he's in a hut with a garden*
> *in a pretty little birch wood,*
> *10 minutes from the highway,*
> *along a well-marked path.*
> *You needn't use binoculars from a distance,*
> *you can see him, hear him quite close by,*
> *explaining patiently to a tour-group . . .*
> *why he chose a harsh and lonely life.*

Quoted from Magnus J. Kryński and Robert A. Maguire, "Sounds, Feelings, Thoughts: The Poetry of Wisława Szymborska," *Polish Review* 24, no. 3 (1979): 31.

Index

THIS INDEX is centered on Mark Twain's career, public images, and reputation. A heading such as "Americanism, reputation for" or "bankruptcy" or "irreverence" refers primarily to Twain. His books, essays, sketches, and speeches are integrated with the main alphabetical listing.